GU00566830

QUESTIONS SERIES

40 QUESTIONS ABOUT
Christians and Biblical Law

Thomas R. Schreiner

Benjamin L. Merkle, Series Editor

40 Questions About Christians and Biblical Law
© 2010 by Thomas R. Schreiner

Published by Kregel Publications, a division of Kregel, Inc., 2450 Oak Industrial Dr. NE, Grand Rapids, MI 49505.

This book is a title in the 40 Questions Series edited by Benjamin L. Merkle.

Library of Congress Cataloging-in-Publication Data
Schreiner, Thomas R.
  40 questions about Christians and biblical law / Thomas R. Schreiner.
     p. cm.
  Includes bibliographical references (p. 231).
  1. Law and gospel—Miscellanea. 2. Law (Theology)—Biblical teaching—Miscellanea. I. Title. II. Title: Forty questions about Christians and biblical law.
  BT79.S37 2010
  241'.2—dc22

                                                            2010004080

ISBN 978-0-8254-3891-2

Printed in the United States of America
15 16 17 18 19 20 21 22 23 24 / 7 6 5 4 3

To my doctoral supervisor, Don Hagner,
in gratefulness for his careful scholarship, encouragement,
and love for Christ

Contents

Part 3: The Law in the Gospels and Acts

Part 4: The Law in the General Epistles

Part 5: The Law and Contemporary Issues

Foreword

The trick to a book of this kind is knowing the right questions to ask. Pauline studies these days—indeed New Testament scholarship in general—has become a confusing array of conflicting voices and opinions, and this confusion inevitably filters down to pulpits and churches. Over the course of his career, Dr. Thomas Schreiner has worked to restore a sense of the original order, which has been obscured by modern chaos. When the "New Perspective on Paul" challenged the very underpinnings of the Reformation's reading of the Scriptures, Dr. Schreiner issued one of the earliest and most comprehensive responses in *The Law and Its Fulfillment*. He exposed the false leads and the dead ends. Ultimately, he made the case that Luther and the Reformers had not erred in their understanding of the great apostle.

Schreiner's *The Law and Its Fulfillment* not only responded to the "New Perspective" but also organized Paul's teaching in an amazingly systematic manner. That ability to put the pieces of the puzzle together into a coherent and meaningful whole characterizes all of his subsequent work. Schreiner is typically meticulous in documenting and weighing the range of interpretive options—a model of top-notch biblical study. After his work on Paul and the law, he completed a major commentary on the letter to the Romans, an ambitious theology of Paul the Apostle, and an even more ambitious theology of the New Testament. He is currently completing a short commentary on Paul's letter to the Galatians. In the following pages he returns to his first love, the role of the Mosaic Law in the New Testament.

The elegance and simplicity of Schreiner's prose is deceiving. Books of this kind are rare for good reason. Few scholars possess the ability to explain the complexities of biblical studies in simple, jargon-free terms, and, yet, such an exercise in clarity could well reveal hidden cracks in a scholarly edifice. Specialists these days tend to suffer from myopia as they belabor small sections of the biblical text while overlooking how the pieces fit together into a larger framework.

Those immersed in the scholarly debates will recognize and benefit from an impressive synthesis of diverse biblical materials. Representing the best of evangelical scholarship, Schreiner demonstrates that Scripture remains the best interpreter of Scripture. He always begins with the clear passages before moving to those that are less clear. He ensures that no premise in a chain of reasoning is left unexplained. Questions at the end of each bite-sized chapter give readers, whether pastors and scholars or Bible study groups, a chance to reflect further. In the midst of an endless stream of shallow works that hardly scratch the surface of Scripture's riches, this is a book that will satisfy those who are searching for more.

The book begins with Paul's understanding of the law and then moves on to the controversies over justification and the role of human obedience at the Last Judgment. Schreiner offers a concise defense of a forensic use of the verb "justify" and of righteousness as God's declaration. Dr. Schreiner does not side-step the tough questions. He does not ignore Paul's relation to James or to the Gospel writers. He does not fail to compare Matthew's seeming advocacy of law-observance with Paul's claim of the law's temporary role. He tackles such controversial current issues as Sabbath observance, tithing, and even theonomy. In the end, he demonstrates that the New Testament Scriptures offer a consistent and coherent approach to the Mosaic Law that needs to be reclaimed. This book is an instant classic that deserves a wide readership.

A. Andrew Das
Professor, Religious Studies, Elmhurst College

Preface

I am grateful to Ben Merkle, the editor of the 40 Questions Series, and to Jim Weaver of Kregel Academic for inviting me to contribute. I am also thankful to Steve Barclift for his assistance in editing the manuscript. I have had an interest in the law for a number of years. One of my first books was on Paul's theology of the law,[1] and I have had the privilege since then to write a commentary on Romans[2] and am working on one on Galatians.[3] Hence, I have spent many years considering Paul's theology of the law. Surely, Paul's theology of law is the most crucial in determining one's view of the law canonically, and hence his thought receives more discussion than any other author in this book. Still, it is important to investigate the theme of the law in the Old Testament and in other New Testament authors in order to present the full canon's perspective, and thus this book considers other topics and authors as well.

This book is not a technical and in-depth treatment of the law, and yet I trust it has enough meat and substance to help readers think through and apply the issues in a discerning way. My hope is that it will be helpful to pastors, students, and laypeople who have an interest in biblical theology and the Scriptures. The book is designed in such a way that readers can skip to any question that interests them, so it is not imperative that the book be read in order. Those who read the whole of the book will naturally get a fuller perspective on the theme of the law in the Scriptures. Some of the questions warrant a brief answer, whereas others necessitate a longer response. Hence, readers should not expect that every question is handled in the same detail.

I am very thankful that Justin Taylor took time out of his busy schedule to read the book. His thoughtful questions, comments, and suggestions made the book a better one than it would have been otherwise. Justin has thought deeply on this topic, and his comments were insightful. Of course, I am not suggesting that Justin would put everything in the book the same way I do.

---

1. Thomas R. Schreiner, *The Law and Its Fulfillment: A Pauline Theology of Law* (Grand Rapids: Baker, 1993).
2. Thomas R. Schreiner, *Romans*, BECNT (Grand Rapids: Baker, 1998).
3. It will be published by Zondervan in the Zondervan Exegetical Commentary.

I am also very grateful for The Southern Baptist Theological Seminary for supporting my scholarly endeavors, and particularly to the president, R. Albert Mohler Jr., and to the vice-president and dean, Russell D. Moore, for their encouragement in the scholarly task. What a blessing it is to work under men who believe in the Word of God and in the need to study carefully the whole counsel of God.

Finally, I dedicate this book to my doctoral supervisor, Don Hagner. I am grateful to Don for his scholarly work on the law, his constant encouragement, and his love for Jesus Christ and the gospel.

Introduction

Why write a book about the role of the law in the Bible? A book on the law is important for several reasons. First, one's understanding of the law determines *how one puts the whole Bible together*. How do the new covenant and the old covenant relate? What is the relationship between what is commonly called the law and the gospel? A central issue in forming a whole biblical theology—in proclaiming "the whole counsel of God" (Acts 20:27)—is the place of the law. Is the Mosaic law still normative for believers? How do the various Old Testament covenants, especially the Abrahamic, Mosaic, and the new covenant, relate to one another? Has the Mosaic covenant passed away entirely? Should we make distinctions between the civil, ceremonial, and moral law? These are all questions that Christian theologians have wrestled with throughout history. My hope is that this book will help prime the pump on such issues, even if space is lacking to answer all the questions posed in detail.

Second, even though the purpose of this book is not to study dispensationalism, covenant theology, theonomy, or Lutheranism per se, those who study the role of the law will have a firmer grasp of these *theological systems*. These systems were developed in an attempt to put the whole Bible together, and, as noted above, the law plays a central role in such an enterprise. So, even though this book does not attempt to unpack the various theological systems current today, those who have studied the place of the law, particularly in the New Testament, will have a platform by which to evaluate such theological systems.

Third, the role of the law is closely related to *justification*. Understanding the law, then, is of the utmost importance for one's theology of salvation. What role does the law play in terms of justification? How should we assess the role of human obedience in terms of justification and salvation? The fissures on the role of the law related to salvation and justification run deep, for it is just here that Roman Catholics and Protestants have divided. In the last three decades the relationship of the law to justification has been debated afresh with the rise of the New Perspective on Paul. How should we assess the New Perspective and its teaching on the law and justification?

Fourth, the law relates to *the will of God*. All believers long to do God's will and to please him. What place does the law occupy in terms of Christian obedience and sanctification? Should believers keep the laws written in the Mosaic covenant? Paul speaks of fulfilling the law of Christ, and thus it will be helpful to discern what moral norms apply to believers today. To sum up, the study of the law is intellectually challenging, theologically crucial, and practically relevant. It cannot be dismissed as an academic enterprise that is unrelated to the everyday lives of believers.

Abbreviations

BECNT	Baker Exegetical Commentary on the New Testament
BJRL	*Bulletin of the John Rylands University Library of Manchester*
CBQ	*Catholic Biblical Quarterly*
CD	Cairo Genizah copy of the *Damascus Document*
ExpTim	*Expository Times*
HTR	*Harvard Theological Review*
ICC	International Critical Commentary
JBL	*Journal of Biblical Literature*
JETS	*Journal of the Evangelical Theological Society*
JSNT	*Journal for the Study of the New Testament*
JSNTSup	Journal for the Study of the New Testament: Supplement Series
JTS	*Journal of Theological Studies*
LCC	Library of Christian Classics
LNTS	Library of New Testament Studies
LXX	Septuagint
NIGTC	New International Greek Testament Commentary
NovT	*Novum Testamentum*
NTS	*New Testament Studies*
PBM	Paternoster Biblical Monographs
PNTC	Pillar New Testament Commentary
SBLAB	Society of Biblical Literature Academia Biblica
SBLDS	SBL Dissertation Series
SBLSP	*SBL Seminar Papers*
SNTSMS	Society for New Testament Studies Monograph Series
SR	*Studies in Religion*
TBei	*Theologische Beiträge*
TrinJ	*Trinity Journal*
TSAJ	Texte und Studien zum antiken Judentum
WBC	Word Biblical Commentary
WEC	Wycliffe Exegetical Commentary
WTJ	*Westminster Theological Journal*
WUNT	Wissenschaftliche Untersuchungen zum Neuen Testament
ZNW	*Zeitschrift für die neutestamentliche Wissenschaft*

PART 1

The Law in the
Old Testament

What Does the Word *Law* Mean in the Scriptures?

The word for law in the Old Testament is *torah;* in the New Testament it is *nomos*. It is often said that *torah* in the Old Testament does not refer so much to commands (to the *keeping* of commandments) as it does to *instruction* (to teaching). According to this view, the word *torah* does not focus on admonitions, commands, and requirements. Instead, the word has a more general referent, so that it includes God's *instruction* more generally. Hence, if one follows this view, the word *torah* also includes God's promises to save his people, his threats if they do not obey, and also narrative accounts that we find, for example, in the Pentateuch. But such a wide definition for the word *torah* is almost certainly wrong.

Torah usually refers to what human beings are commanded to do.[1] In some instances, a broader sense (that goes beyond commands and prescriptions) aptly captures the meaning of *torah* (e.g., Job 22:22; Ps. 94:12; Prov. 1:8; 4:2; 13:14; Isa. 2:3; 42:4; 51:4; Mal. 2:6–8), although even in some of these passages the instruction probably consisted of what was required by the law. In the vast majority of instances, however, the word *torah* focuses on doing what is commanded in the law, that is, the commands and requirements that were given to Moses on Mount Sinai. The emphasis on observing the law and carrying out what it demands is evident from the verbs of which *torah* is the direct object (see figure 1a).

---

1. Cf. Stephen Westerholm, "'Torah, *nomos*, and Law: A Question of 'Meaning,'" *SR* 15 (1986): 327–36; Douglas J. Moo, "'Law,' 'Works of the Law,' and Legalism in Paul," *WTJ* (1983): 73–100.

Other terms that are used with the word *torah* and are roughly synonymous with it confirm that the term *torah* focuses on regulations and prescriptions (see figure 1b). All these words convey the idea that Israel must obey what God has required in his law.

We see something quite similar with verbs that describe a wrong response to the law (see figure 1c). In every instance Israel's disobedience to the law, i.e., their failure to keep what the Lord demanded, is featured.

FIGURE 1A: VERBS USED FOR OBEDIENCE TO THE LAW	
Keep	Gen. 26:5; Deut. 17:19; 28:58; 31:12; Josh. 22:5; 1 Kings 2:3; 1 Chron. 22:12; Ps. 119:34, 44; Prov. 28:4; 29:18; Jer. 16:11; Ezek. 44:24
Walk in	Exod. 16:4; 2 Kings 10:31; Ps. 78:10; Jer. 26:4; 32:23; 44:10; Dan. 9:10
Do	Deut. 27:26; 29:29; 31:12; 32:46; Josh. 1:7–8
Break	Ps. 119:126
Obey	Isa. 42:24

FIGURE 1B: WORDS FOR GOD'S COMMANDS	
Commandment(s)	Gen. 26:5; Exod. 16:28; Deut. 30:10; Josh. 22:5; 1 Kings 2:3; 2 Kings 17:34; 2 Chron. 19:10; Neh. 9:13
Statute(s)	Gen. 26:5; Exod. 18:16; Deut. 4:8; 30:10; 1 Kings 2:3; 2 Kings 17:13, 34; 2 Chron. 19:10; 2 Chron. 33:8; Ezra 7:10; Neh. 9:13; Jer. 44:10; Ezek. 43:11
Rule(s)	Lev. 26:46: Deut. 4:8; 33:10; 1 Kings 2:3; 2 Kings 17:34; 2 Chron. 19:10; 33:8; Ezra 7:10; Ps. 89:30
Testimony(ies)	1 Kings 2:3; Jer. 44:23

FIGURE 1C: VERBS USED FOR DISOBEDIENCE TO THE LAW	
Forget	Hos. 4:6; Ps. 119:61, 109, 153
Transgress	Dan 9:11
Abandon	2 Chron 12:1
Forsake	Pss. 89:30; 119:53; Jer. 9:13
Rejects	Isa. 5:24; Jer. 6:19; Amos 2:4
Do violence to	Ezek. 22:26; Zeph. 3:4

Note: The list of verbs in figure 1a is representative, not exhaustive. Nevertheless, the examples demonstrate that in the Scriptures a focus on the prescriptions of the law is pervasive.

Often a particular regulation is introduced especially in Leviticus and sometimes in Numbers, with the words, "this is the law."[2] The law often is associated with a book.[3] In most instances what is written or found in the book are the *regulations* of the law. The emphasis on *doing* what the law commands, on *keeping* it, and on *obeying* what the Lord has prescribed is quite extraordinary. When the word *torah* occurs in the Old Testament, the emphasis is not on instruction in terms of teaching, as if the word *rehearses* God's saving work on behalf of his people. It is quite the contrary. The term *torah* concentrates on what God *requires* his people to do: his commands, statutes, and laws.

The use of the term *law* (*nomos*) in the New Testament is comparable. In some instances the word *law* refers to the Old Testament Scriptures, and the focus is on the Pentateuch: "the Law and the Prophets" (Matt. 5:17; 7:12; 22:40; Luke 16:16; 24:44; John 1:45; Acts 13:15; 24:14; 28:23; Rom. 3:21; cf. Matt. 11:13). In some texts "Law" alone seems to refer broadly to the Old Testament Scriptures (Matt. 22:36; Luke 10:26; John 7:49; 10:34; 12:34; 15:25; 1 Cor. 9:8–9; 14:21, 34; Gal. 4:21), though in some of these texts a particular precept from the Mosaic law may be in view as well (John 7:49; 1 Cor. 9:8–9; 14:34). Nevertheless, in the New Testament, as we saw in the Old Testament, the term *law* most often refers to what is commanded in the Mosaic law. Matthew speaks of every "iota" and "dot" of the law (Matt. 5:18), and it is clear from the next verse that he is referring here to the "commandments" found in the law (Matt. 5:19). Elsewhere Matthew considers particular matters commanded in the law (Matt. 22:36; 23:23). Similarly, Luke often uses the word *law* to refer to what is prescribed in statutes (Luke 2:22, 23, 24, 27, 39; Acts 23:3) or uses the term to refer collectively to what is commanded in the Sinai covenant (Acts 6:13; 7:53; 13:39; 15:5; 21:24; 22:3, 12; 25:8). Similarly, when John does not use the word *law* to refer to the Pentateuch or the Scriptures, he uses it to refer to the Mosaic law (John 7:19, 23, 51; 8:17; 19:7).

Paul regularly thinks of the law in terms of its commands, and this is evident because he speaks of those who sin by violating the law,[4] of the need

---

2. Leviticus 6:9; 7:1, 37; 11:46; 12:7; 13:59; 14:2; 15:32; Numbers 5:29; 6:13; 19:2. Again, the list is representative. The regulation in view in some texts relates to multiple instructions that are given.

3. Deuteronomy 17:18; 28:58, 61; 29:21; 30:10; 31:24, 26; Joshua 1:8; 8:31; 23:6; 24:26; 2 Kings 14:6; 22:8; 2 Chronicles 17:9; 25:4; 34:14–15; Nehemiah 8:1, 3, 8. Or, the law refers to what is written in the Old Testament (Exod. 24:7; Deut. 28:58; 29:21; 30:10; Josh. 1:8; 23:6; 2 Kings 14:6; 1 Chron. 16:40; 2 Chron. 23:18; 25:4; 31:3; 35:26; Ezra 3:2; Neh. 8:14; 10:36; Dan. 9:11, 13).

4. Romans 2:12, 23, 25; 3:20; 4:15; 5:20; 7:2, 3, 5, 7, 8, 9, 12, 14, 16, 22; 8:3, 7. Note how "commandment" is used alternately with "law" in Romans 7, referring specifically to the tenth commandment of the Decalogue (Rom. 7:8, 9, 10, 11, 12, 13).

to do what the law says,[5] and of relying upon and being instructed in the law (Rom. 2:17, 18, 20).[6] When Paul speaks of righteousness (Rom. 3:21; 9:31; 10:4; Gal. 2:21; 3:11; 5:4; Phil. 3:6, 9) or the inheritance (Rom. 4:13–14, 16; Gal. 3:18) not being attained via the law, he has in mind doing what the law commands. Most scholars now agree that "works of law" refers to the deeds required by the law (Rom. 3:20, 28; Gal. 2:16; 3:2, 5; 10),[7] as does the phrase "the law of commandments" (Eph. 2:15). The law is conceived of as a body of commands summarized in the Mosaic covenant, which came at a certain time in history (Rom. 5:13; 7:4, 6; 9:4; 1 Cor. 9:20, 21; 15:56; Gal. 2:19; 3:17, 19, 21), and the phrase "under law" fits here as well (Rom. 6:14, 15; 7:1; Gal. 3:23, 24; 4:4, 5; 5:18). In Hebrews the word *law* always refers to the commands of the Mosaic law and to the Mosaic covenant (Heb. 7:5, 11, 12, 19, 28; 8:4; 9:19, 22; 10:1, 8, 28), with the focus being on the prescriptions for priests and sacrifices that are offered.

Scholars debate intensely whether in some cases Paul uses the word *law* metaphorically to refer to a "principle" or "rule" (see Rom. 3:27; 7:21, 23, 25; 8:2) or whether in every instance the Mosaic law is in view. Deciding this matter is not vital for the purposes of this book, but it seems preferable to think that Paul uses the term metaphorically in these texts.[8] It is hard to conceive of Paul saying that the law in conjunction with the Spirit frees people from sin (Rom. 8:2), since elsewhere Paul emphasizes that those who are "under law" are under sin. In addition, it is most natural to take the noun "law" as a direct object in Romans 7:21 ("So I find it to be a law that when I want to do right, evil lies close at hand") instead of an accusative of general reference ("So I find with reference to the law"). And if "law" is the direct object, the term is clearly metaphorical. Finally, it is quite awkward to say that the phrase "another law" (Rom. 7:23) refers to the Mosaic law. It is more natural to conclude that Paul is playing on the term *law*, using it to refer to another principle or rule in his members. Indeed, understanding what Paul might possibly mean by saying the Mosaic law is in one's members is difficult, but it makes eminent sense to think of another "principle" or "power" in one's members. Hence, it is more likely that Paul uses the term *law* in some texts to refer to a principle or power.

---

5. Romans 2:13–14, 26, 27; 8:4; 10:5; 13:8, 10; 1 Corinthians 9:8; Galatians 3:12, 13; 5:3, 14; 6:13; 1 Timothy 1:7, 8, 9. Here "fulfilling" and "doing" the law are placed together, but the two terms must also be distinguished.

6. Older scholarship distinguished between "law" with the article and "law" without the article. Virtually all agree today that positing distinctions based on the presence or absence of the article is illegitimate. So Thomas R. Schreiner, *The Law and Its Fulfillment: A Pauline Theology of Law* (Grand Rapids: Baker, 1993), 33–34.

7. See the discussion on works of law in question 5.

8. I have changed my mind more than once on this matter. In support of the Mosaic law, see J. D. G. Dunn, *Romans 1–8*, WBC (Dallas: Word, 1988), 392–95. In support of a metaphorical reading, see Douglas J. Moo, *Romans 1–8*, WEC (Chicago: Moody, 1991), 251–53, 487–88, 490–92.

SUMMARY

In both the Old and New Testaments, the word *law* focuses on the commands and regulations of the Mosaic covenant. In most instances the word *law* does not refer to instruction in a general sense but concentrates on what God demands that his people do. In both the Old and New Testaments this is apparent, for verbs like "keep" and "do" are linked with the law.

REFLECTION QUESTIONS

1. Does the word *torah* (law) in the Old Testament focus on instruction in a general sense or on God's commands?

2. What is the relationship in the Old Testament between the law and the Mosaic covenant?

3. What meaning does the word *law* usually have in the New Testament, especially in the Pauline letters?

4. What other meanings does the term *law* have in the New Testament?

5. Do you think Paul ever uses the word *law* to mean "principle" or "rule"?

Was the Mosaic Covenant Legalistic?

In order to answer this question, the word *legalism* must be defined. By legalism I refer to the idea that human beings can earn or merit right standing with God. Clearly, the Mosaic covenant was not legalistic in this sense. The structure of the covenant features the grace of God. The first fourteen chapters of Exodus describe God's redemption of his people from Egyptian bondage. Their redemption is an act of divine grace and cannot be ascribed to the obedience of Israel. The Lord did not choose Israel because of her righteousness, for nothing inherent in Israel commended her as a nation before the Lord. As Deuteronomy 9:4–5 says,

> Do not say in your heart, after the LORD your God has thrust them out before you, "It is because of my righteousness that the LORD has brought me in to possess this land," whereas it is because of the wickedness of these nations that the LORD is driving them out before you. Not because of your righteousness or the uprightness of your heart are you going in to possess their land, but because of the wickedness of these nations the LORD your God is driving them out from before you, and that he may confirm the word that the LORD swore to your fathers, to Abraham, to Isaac, and to Jacob.

Since the Lord did not bring Israel into the land because of her accomplishments but despite them, it is clear that Israel was saved by virtue of God's mercy.

Moses clarifies earlier in Deuteronomy why the Lord chose Israel to be a people for himself in one of the most important texts in the Pentateuch. In Deuteronomy 7:6–8 we read,

For you are a people holy to the LORD your God. The LORD your God has chosen you to be a people for his treasured possession, out of all the peoples who are on the face of the earth. It was not because you were more in number than any other people that the LORD set his love on you and chose you, for you were the fewest of all peoples, but it is because the LORD loves you and is keeping the oath that he swore to your fathers, that the LORD has brought you out with a mighty hand and redeemed you from the house of slavery, from the hand of Pharaoh king of Egypt.

The Lord elected Israel because of his love for her, and the reason given for the Lord's love is his love. In other words, no quality in Israel endeared the nation to the Lord. The Lord set his sovereign love upon Israel because it was his good pleasure to do so.

Observing the Ten Commandments did not constitute the basis upon which Israel would gain life. Israel was rescued by the Lord from Egypt and borne upon eagles' wings (Exod. 19:4). Before the Ten Commandments were given, the Lord declared, "I am the LORD your God, who brought you out of the land of Egypt, out of the house of slavery" (Exod. 20:2). The giving of the law *followed* the salvation of Israel, and hence such obedience signified Israel's grateful *response* to the redemption accomplished by the Lord. There is no basis in the text for the idea that Israel's obedience *established* a relationship with the Lord. The Lord took the initiative in rescuing his people, and they were called upon to respond with faithful obedience.

The gracious character of the Mosaic covenant is supported by the structure of the covenant. Many scholars have argued that the Mosaic covenant represents a suzerain–vassal treaty in which Yahweh is the great suzerain and Israel the vassal.[1] In such treaties the historical prologue, which recounts what the suzerain has done to benefit his vassals, precedes the covenant stipulations and the covenant curses. In the same way, the Lord recounts in the covenant structure what he has done for Israel (historical prologue) in delivering them from Egypt and preserving them from their enemies before he gives them covenant stipulations (the law). The Lord also promises them covenantal blessings if they obey or threatens them with covenantal curses if they disobey. The pattern established in the Mosaic covenant, which is redemption followed by obedience, functions as a type or pattern for New Testament believers. Believers have been redeemed through the work of Christ, and they respond to his saving mercy with grateful obedience. Such grateful obedience, under both the Mosaic covenant and the new covenant established by Jesus Christ, is not legalistic, for there is no idea that such obedience earns or merits salvation under either the old covenant or the new. The obedience

---

1. See, e.g., Meredith G. Kline, *The Structure of Biblical Authority* (Grand Rapids: Eerdmans, 1972).

of believers flows from faith and is a thankful response to God's saving work in Christ.

The common covenant pattern (obedience as a result of salvation) that exists between the Sinai covenant and the new covenant does not lead to the conclusion that the covenants are the same in every respect. The Mosaic covenant was not legalistic, and yet the new covenant and old covenant are not to be leveled out so that no differences are posited between the covenants. We shall pursue this matter further as we explore the theology of the law in the Scriptures. What is emphasized here is that there is no warrant for saying that the Mosaic covenant is legalistic.

SUMMARY

The notion that the Mosaic covenant is legalistic is not borne out by a careful reading of the biblical text. The giving of the law was not the basis upon which the Lord entered into covenant with Israel. The giving of the law followed (and does not precede) God's great redemption of Israel from Egypt. The call to obey the Lord functions as a response to the Lord's saving his people from Egypt.

REFLECTION QUESTIONS

1. How would you define legalism?

2. How does the structure of the Mosaic covenant show that it was not legalistic?

3. If someone preaches the Ten Commandments, are they guilty of legalism?

4. How do we proclaim the importance of obedience without falling into legalism?

5. If the Mosaic covenant is not legalistic, then does it follow that all the covenants are the same?

Does the Old Testament Teach That Salvation Is by Works?

Occasionally, especially in popular circles, one runs across the idea that the Old Testament teaches a different way of salvation, as if salvation were gained through works in the Old Testament but it is by faith in the New Testament. Virtually all scholars agree that there is no warrant for this idea. When Paul wants to support the idea that justification is by faith, he appeals to the life of Abraham (Rom. 4:1–25; Gal. 3:6–9) and David (Rom. 4:6–8), finding in Genesis 15:6 the truth that it was Abraham's faith that was counted to him as righteousness. Abraham was an idolater (Josh. 24:2) and ungodly (Rom. 4:5) before his salvation, and hence he trusted in God to save him. It is quite instructive that both Abraham and David are mentioned in Romans 4. Clearly, salvation was by faith for Abraham, who lived before the law. Some might think that salvation was obtained by another means for David who lived under the law. But Paul makes it abundantly clear that David also was righteous by faith and not by his moral excellence.

Since Paul argues from the Old Testament itself for the truth that salvation is by faith, there is no basis for thinking that salvation can be obtained by any other means in the Old Testament. The reference to David is perhaps particularly important since he lived under the law. The law does not introduce a new era in which salvation is obtained in a different way than it was in the time of Abraham. On the contrary, both Abraham and David were saved in the same way. They trusted that the Lord would save them in spite of their sin.

It also should be noted that both Paul and the author of Hebrews appeal to Habakkuk 2:4 to support the idea that righteousness comes by faith (Rom. 1:17; Gal. 3:11; Heb. 10:38). Habakkuk threatens judgment for Judah, which had blatantly violated God's law. The Lord promised that he would use the Babylonians to inflict his wrath upon his people. Still, in the midst of the judgment that was coming, those who put their faith in the Lord and trusted in him would live (Hab. 2:4). Habakkuk 3 recalls exodus themes as it portrays the judgment and salvation of God, but even in the midst of judgment to come, in which fig trees would not blossom and vines would be barren of fruit, those who trusted in Yahweh would find their joy in him. They would look to the Lord as their strength. To look to the Lord for strength and joy is just another way of saying that one trusts in the Lord. Habakkuk acknowledges that Israel had failed to keep the law (Hab. 1:4), and thus their only hope was a new exodus in which the Lord would save his people. Those who put their trust in the Lord would enjoy his saving work.

I argued in the previous question that the Mosaic covenant was not a legalistic one, and thus it is a complete distortion to understand it as advocating salvation by works rather than by faith. The law was given after the Lord had redeemed his people from Egypt, and hence their obedience was a response of love to the grace of God. Therefore, we have further evidence that the Mosaic covenant itself does not represent a different way of salvation.

Hebrews 11 confirms our understanding of salvation in the Old Testament, emphasizing with its long list of Old Testament saints who received a reward from him that they pleased God because of their faith (v. 6). For example, Abel's sacrifice, rather than Cain's, was acceptable because of his faith (v. 4). Noah also became an heir of righteousness because of his faith in God's promise, which expressed itself in building the ark (v. 7). So too, Abraham's obedience stemmed from his faith (v. 8). In the same way, Moses and the people of Israel exercised faith in leaving Egypt and in offering the Paschal lamb (vv. 23–29), recognizing therein that God saves. The life of Rahab shows that salvation is by faith rather than works, for her life as a prostitute clearly disqualified her to be saved on the basis of her works (v. 31). Indeed, all of those who pleased God in Israel did so by faith (vv. 5–6, 33–38).

SUMMARY

The testimony of Scripture is quite clear on this matter. Salvation in both the Old Testament and the New Testament is by faith. Works are not conceived of as the basis or foundation of one's salvation in either the Old Testament or the New Testament. There is one way of salvation in both Testaments: faith in the God who promises to save his people.

REFLECTION QUESTIONS

1. Does the Old Testament teach salvation by works?

2. What evidence is there in the lives of Abraham and David that salvation has always been by faith?

3. How does the book of Habakkuk as a whole support salvation by faith?

4. What is the role of faith and obedience in Hebrews 11?

5. Does true faith always lead to obedience?

PART 2

The Law in Paul

Questions Related to the New Perspective

What Is the New Perspective on Paul, and How Should It Be Assessed?

The New Perspective on Paul finds its genesis in the landmark 1977 book *Paul and Palestinian Judaism: A Comparison of Patterns of Religion* by E. P. Sanders, who retired from teaching at Duke University in 2005.[1] His book exploded on the scene of New Testament scholarship, and we are still feeling the reverberations today. This is not to say that Sanders was the first to advocate his thesis. Looking back we find similar arguments in two scholars of Judaism, Claude Montefiore (1858–1938) and George Foote Moore (1851–1931).[2] When Sanders wrote, however, the time was ripe for scholars to listen. He wrote about thirty years after the Holocaust, and scholars were still reeling over the murder of six million Jews in "Christian" Germany. Anti-Semitism was not confined to politics; it had been supported in Christian scholarship, which was therefore partially responsible for the slaughter of millions of Jews. Most important, Sanders carefully presented his case from the rabbinic literature, the Apocrypha, the Pseudepigrapha, and the Qumran writings. His book was a tour de force that made the case with a careful exegesis of the relevant Jewish literature. Anyone who doubted Sanders's thesis would need to show that his exegesis was faulty. He could not be refuted by mere assertion.

Sanders argued that the alleged legalism of Judaism was a scholarly myth imposed on the evidence by Christian scholars who read Judaism through jaundiced eyes. Protestants in particular tended to read the polemic against

---

1. E. P. Sanders, *Paul and Palestinian Judaism: A Comparison of Patterns of Religion* (Philadelphia: Fortress, 1977).
2. See George Foote Moore, "Christian Writers on Judaism," *HTR* 14 (1921): 197–254; Claude G. Montefiore, *Judaism and St. Paul* (London: Max Goschen, 1914).

Judaism in the New Testament through the glasses of their conflict with Roman Catholicism in the sixteenth century. They projected the defective view of grace in Roman Catholicism onto Jewish sources. An objective reading of the Second Temple Jewish sources, however, demonstrated that Judaism had a robust doctrine of God's grace.

Sanders argues for a common pattern of religion in Second Temple Judaism, which he labels "covenantal nomism." God entered into covenant with his people by his grace. Israel's observance of the law did not bring them into a covenantal relationship with God. They were inducted into a relationship with him by virtue of the Lord's mercy. The command to keep the law was a *response* to God's grace. Hence, nomism cannot be equated with legalism. Israel did not believe that God weighed one's merits to determine whether they would receive a final reward. Nor did they teach that one earned or merited God's favor in salvation. Israel *stayed in* a gracious relationship with the Lord by observing the law, but they *entered into* an initial relationship with him by his grace.

If Sanders's portrait of Judaism is accurate, how do we account for Paul's critique of the law? Sanders's own solution was that Paul rejected the law for dogmatic reasons. Paul had come to the conviction that Christ was the answer to the human problem; salvation was only through him.[3] But if salvation is only through Christ, how should the law be explained? Paul did not actually see any inherent problem with the law, according to Sanders. The law's inferiority could not be assigned to human inability to keep it or to a legalistic mind-set toward the law. Instead Paul argued from solution to plight. Since Christ represents the answer to the human dilemma (the solution), then the law must be a problem (plight). Still, Paul did not actually perceive any intrinsic defect in the law. Sanders maintains that at times Paul's reasoning on the law is tortuous and verges on the incoherent, but that is explained by his theological presupposition that Christ is the solution to the human plight. So, why doesn't the law save according to Paul? Sanders's answer is that the law cannot save since only Christ saves. So, what is the problem with the law? The law is deficient because it isn't Christ.

Another scholar who concurred with Sanders's reading of Judaism was Heikki Räisänen, who retired from the University of Helsinki in 2006.[4] Räisänen adopted a more radical solution than Sanders. If Sanders's portrait of Second Temple Judaism is correct, then how do we explain Paul? Räisänen argued that the idea that Paul is a coherent and logical thinker is flawed. In other words, Paul's theology of law is shot through with contradictions and is fundamentally incoherent. Scholars have labored to articulate Paul's theology of the law as if it represented a consistent system of thought. They have

---

3. Sanders, *Paul and Palestinian Judaism*, 442–47.
4. Heikki Räisänen, *Paul and the Law* (Philadelphia: Fortress, 1983).

generally failed to realize, according to Räisänen, that Paul operated with two fundamentally contradictory presuppositions. On the one hand, he posited that the Old Testament law was God's authoritative word. On the other hand, he insisted that Gentiles were not required to observe the Old Testament law. Naturally, says Räisänen, Paul could not reconcile these two ideas since they are mutually exclusive.

Many scholars, however, remain unsatisfied with the Paul explained by Räisänen and Sanders. Against Räisänen, they are persuaded that Paul was a coherent thinker. It seems to some that Räisänen read Paul unsympathetically, so that contradictions popped up virtually everywhere. Sanders's interpretation of Paul was more congenial than Räisänen's. Still, as James Dunn observed, the Paul explained by Sanders is rather idiosyncratic and arbitrary.[5] The only problem with Judaism, according to Sanders, was that it was not Christianity. The law was rejected as the solution and identified as a problem since Christ is the only answer for humanity. Dunn rightly responded that the Pauline theology of law had more depth than this. Paul did not reflexively reject the law solely for dogmatic reasons; his rejection of the law had a deeper and more solid foundation.

If the Paul of Sanders and Räisänen should be rejected, how should he be assessed according to Dunn? After all, Dunn accepts that Sanders is right on a fundamental point. Second Temple Judaism was not legalistic, and therefore the standard Protestant reading in which the law does not save because of human inability to keep it or because of legalism must be waved aside. At this juncture, both Dunn and N. T. Wright propose a new reading of Paul ("a New Perspective"!) that has had an enormous influence.[6] When we read Paul in his historical context, we see that Paul's complaint with his Jewish opponents centered on their exclusivism, nationalism, and ethnocentrism. The Jews insisted that Gentiles had to become part of the Jewish people in order to be the people of God; so they emphasized Jewish distinctives and boundary markers, like circumcision, food laws, and the Sabbath. Hence, the Pauline polemic against the law does not bring to the forefront either legalism or human disobedience. Sanders's claim that Second Temple Judaism was not legalistic is therefore vindicated as well in the Pauline writings! What provoked Paul was the insistence that Gentiles submit to circumcision and other badges of Judaism to be included in God's people. Paul's Jewish opponents were not willing to swing the door wide open for the Gentiles, for it was unthinkable to let them become part of God's people without adopting the covenant sign required by the Old Testament. They argued that circumcision was required of Gentiles, and thereby they retained their nationalistic primacy as

5. James D. G. Dunn, "The New Perspective on Paul," *BJRL* 65 (1983): 95–122.
6. See Dunn, *The New Perspective on Paul*; N. T. Wright, *What St. Paul Really Said: Was Paul of Tarsus the Real Founder of Christianity?* (Grand Rapids: Eerdmans, 1997).

Jews. They did not want the church of Jesus Christ to be made up of a variety of ethnic groups and cultures. They wanted to retain their cultural and ethnic superiority as Jews.

What shall we make of the New Perspective on Paul? In a short compass we cannot do justice to all the issues, and here I point readers to longer works that examine the movement in more detail.[7] What must be said here is that Sanders's interpretation of Second Temple Judaism has been examined in some detail since the publication of his book. Some of the evidence in Second Temple Jewish texts supports the pattern of covenantal nomism, which Sanders defended. Nevertheless, the evidence is not nearly as conclusive as Sanders claims.

Friedrich Avemarie has demonstrated that the two themes of election and works stand in an uneasy tension in rabbinic literature, so that one cannot merely say that works are always subordinate to election.[8] Similarly, Mark Elliott maintains that Judaism during the Second Temple period did not typically envision the salvation of all of Israel but only those who kept the *torah*.[9] Along the same lines, Andrew Das maintains that the weighing of merits is quite prominent in rabbinic literature. God's mercy and grace are not forgotten, yet there is considerable emphasis upon human works.[10] Simon Gathercole argues that Sanders's conclusions must be severely qualified since there is significant evidence in Second Temple literature that works played a role in obtaining final salvation.[11]

Furthermore, a careful study of literature during the Second Temple period yields a nuanced conclusion. In some instances Sanders's judgment seems correct regarding covenantal nomism, but in other instances his reading of the evidence is flawed, and he forces his paradigm onto the literature. Sanders admits that *4 Ezra* constitutes an exception to his pattern, but it is apparent that there are more exceptions than this. Consequently, Sanders's claim that Second Temple Judaism did not emphasize the role of works in obtaining salvation is overstated. The Jewish sources do not so neatly support his contention that Second Temple Judaism was a religion of grace. At the very least some segments of Judaism focused on human obedience and had fallen prey to a kind of legalism. All this means, then, that we must not *assume* when

---

7. See especially, Stephen Westerholm, *Perspectives Old and New on Paul: The "Lutheran" Paul and His Critics* (Grand Rapids: Eerdmans, 2004).

8. Friedrich Avemarie, *Tora und Leben: Untersuchungen zur Heilsbedeutung der Tora in der frühen rabbinischen Literatur*, TSAJ 55 (Tübingen: Mohr Siebeck, 1996).

9. Mark A. Elliott, *The Survivors of Israel: A Reconsideration of the Theology of Pre-Christian Judaism* (Grand Rapids: Eerdmans, 2000).

10. A. Andrew Das, *Paul, the Law, and the Covenant* (Peabody, MA: Hendrickson, 2001), 31–43.

11. Simon J. Gathercole, *Where Is Boasting? Early Jewish Soteriology and Paul's Response in Romans 1–5* (Grand Rapids: Eerdmans, 2003).

we come to Paul that it has been established that there is no such thing as legalism or works-righteousness in Second Temple Judaism.

SUMMARY

The foundation of the New Perspective on Paul, allegedly proved by Sanders, is not nearly as secure as some claim.[12] We have significant evidence that Paul rejects the law because of human inability and that some of his opponents had fallen prey to legalism. Even if the New Perspective falls short of providing an adequate explanation of Paul's view of the law, it rightly observes that the inclusion of the Gentiles was a major theme in Pauline theology. What the proponents fail to explain as convincingly is how the Gentile inclusion into the people of God should be integrated with Paul's theology of law. Finally, I have indicated here that scholars have shown that Sanders's reading of the Jewish sources is overly simplistic. A careful reading of the Jewish sources indicates that some Jews emphasized the role of obedience for obtaining eschatological salvation.

REFLECTION QUESTIONS

1. What is covenantal nomism?

2. How did E. P. Sanders explain Paul's rejection of the law?

3. How did James Dunn and N. T. Wright contribute to the debate?

4. How have some recent studies called into question Sanders's reading of Judaism?

5. Do you think the New Perspective on Paul is convincing?

---

12.   I argue in my answers to questions 5–8, 10, 12, 17, 19–20, and 22 that major planks of the New Perspective reading of Paul are flawed.

What Does the Expression "Works of Law" Mean in Paul?

Paul uses the phrase "works of law" (*erga nomou*) eight times in his letters (Rom. 3:20, 28; Gal. 2:16 [3 times]; 3:2, 5, 10). The term does not occur in the Old Testament, though it is found in some Jewish literature that is roughly contemporary with the New Testament. A number of different interpretations of the phrase have been proposed.[1] First, some argue that "law" is a subjective genitive ("the law's works") in the phrase, so that Paul refers to the works produced by the law.[2] According to this reading, the works generated by the law are evil, and Paul thinks along the line of Romans 7, where sin takes the law hostage and produces evil. This interpretation should be rejected as unlikely. Paul definitely argues that human beings are not justified by works of law, but it does not follow from this that the works described are themselves evil. In both Romans 3:20 and Galatians 3:10 Paul explains that works of law do not justify because of human sin, but such an explanation is superfluous if the phrase "works of law" refers to evil works.

Second, others maintain that "works of law" should be defined as legalism.[3] According to this reading, the expression "works of law" focuses on the human desire to obtain favor with God by keeping his law. "Works of law" are flawed, says the legalistic view, because they represent an attempt to bribe God by one's obedience. This interpretation fails to convince as well. I will argue shortly, contrary to the New Perspective, that Paul indicts legalism, even in verses where he refers to works of law. Nevertheless, we must be exceedingly

---

1. For a more detailed survey, see Thomas R. Schreiner, "'Works of Law' in Paul," *NovT* 33 (1991): 217–44.
2. So Paul L. Owen, "The 'Works of the Law' in Romans and Galatians: A New Defense of the Subjective Genitive," *JBL* 126 (2007): 553–77.
3. Daniel P. Fuller, "Paul and 'The Works of the Law,'" *WTJ* 38 (1975): 28–42.

careful to understand precisely what Paul means in referring to works of law. It is one thing to say Paul criticizes legalism; it is quite another to say that the specific phrase "works of law" should be defined as legalism. It is unlikely that Paul intends to say that no one is justified by legalism (Rom. 3:20; cf. Gal. 3:10). I will argue below that a more convincing explanation is available.

Third, those who support the New Perspective on Paul, such as J. D. G. Dunn (retired New Testament scholar at the University of Durham) and N. T. Wright (professor at the University of St. Andrews), maintain that "works of law" focuses on the boundary markers that separate Jews and Gentiles.[4] The boundary markers, or identity badges, of Judaism were circumcision, food laws, and Sabbath. The problem with the Judaism of Paul's day, then, was not legalism but exclusivism. "Works of law" highlights the nationalistic spirit of the Jews by which they excluded Gentiles from the promises of God. According to this interpretation, Paul does not indict the Jews for their failure to obey the law. Their fault was not inability but separatism. For instance, Paul rebuked Peter at Antioch when the latter stopped eating with Gentiles since he feared those of the circumcision (Gal. 2:11–14). What provoked Paul was that Peter was cutting Gentiles off from membership in the people of God. In defending the next view, I will explain why the boundary marker view fails to persuade as well, though the New Perspective rightly sees that exclusivism and separatism troubles Paul. The problem is with what the New Perspective brackets out of Paul's theology.

Fourth is the view that "works of law" refers to the entire law and the actions that are required by the law.[5] This is the most likely reading of Romans 3:20 ("For by works of the law no human being will be justified in his sight, since through the law comes knowledge of sin") and Gal. 3:10 ("For all who rely on works of the law are under a curse; for it is written, 'Cursed be everyone who does not abide by all things written in the Book of the Law, and do them'"). We could gloss "works of the law" as "the deeds required by the law," or "the actions demanded by the law." "Works of law" refers, then, to the entire law. If the term refers to the deeds demanded by the law, then it is clear that "law" cannot be a subjective genitive (works *produced by* the law), for the works demanded by the law are good, not evil. Nor is the focus on boundary markers or identity badges like circumcision, food laws, or Sabbath since "works of law" refers to the entire law. Dunn, it should be noted, agrees that "works of law" includes the whole law, but he insists that there

---

4. For Dunn's latest work on this matter, see James D. G. Dunn, *The New Perspective on Paul* (Grand Rapids: Eerdmans, 2008). See also N. T. Wright, *The New Testament and the People of God* (Minneapolis: Fortress, 1992), 238; idem, *Justification: God's Plan and Paul's Vision* (Downers Grove: InterVarsity, 2009).

5. In support of this view, see Stephen Westerholm, *Israel's Law and the Church's Faith: Paul and His Recent Interpreters* (Grand Rapids: Eerdmans, 1988), 106–21; Schreiner, "'Works of Law' in Paul," 217–44; Douglas J. Moo, "'Law,' 'Works of the Law,' and Legalism in Paul," *WTJ* (1983): 73–100.

is a focus on the boundary markers of the law. A very important distinction must be made here. Often boundary markers (like circumcision or food laws) were the spark that precipitated a controversy over the status of the Mosaic law (e.g., circumcision in Galatians). Still, it would be misleading to say that boundary markers were the focus of the discussion, for the fundamental issue did not center on exclusivism but the role of the Mosaic law and the Mosaic covenant with respect to salvation. In other words, "works of law" does not focus on the identity badges of the law but addresses the role of the law in general.

A number of arguments support the idea that "works of law" refers to the entire law and the deeds commanded by it. First, this is the simplest reading of the phrase. "Works of law" most naturally refers to all the deeds commanded in the law. There is no reason to think that it is limited to or focuses on only part of the law, or that it refers to "evil works," or that it refers to legalism. "Works," after all, should not be defined as legalism, nor does it refer to that which is evil, nor can it be limited to only part of what the law requires. Second, Paul's argument in Galatians and Romans supports this reading, for the place of the law as a whole is addressed, as figure 2 illustrates.

FIGURE 2: REFERENCES TO THE LAW AS A WHOLE	
Dying to the law	Rom. 7:4; Gal. 2:19
Righteousness or inheritance are not via the law	Rom. 3:20–22; 4:13, 14; Gal. 2:21; 3:11, 18; 5:4
Law contrasted with faith	Gal. 3:12
Period of law distinguished from promise to Abraham	Rom. 5:13, 20; Gal. 3:17, 19, 21, 23, 24
Curse of law	Gal. 3:13
Instruction of law	Rom. 2:18, 20
Being "under the law"	Rom. 3:19; 6:14–15; Gal. 4:5, 21; 5:18
Keeping, doing, and obeying the law	Rom. 2:13, 25, 26, 27; 10:5; Gal. 5:3; 6:13; cf. Rom. 8:7
Sinning or transgressing against the law	Rom. 2:12; 4:15; 5:13; 7:7, 8
Relying on the law	Rom. 2:17; cf. 3:27
Holiness, spirituality, and goodness of law	Rom. 7:12, 14, 16
Delight in law	Rom. 7:22

The texts in this figure demonstrate that Paul speaks of the law as a whole and show that the focus is not on what is sometimes called the "ceremonial" law or laws that divide Jews from Gentiles. Indeed, the Galatians are faulted for desiring to be under the law as a whole (Gal. 4:21). No indication is given that only a portion of the law is intended. Hence, the boundary markers may have been the presenting issue, but they raised a larger question. Must Gentiles obey the entire law to be saved?

Does other Jewish literature support this reading of "works of law"? It should be noted first of all that the phrase "works of law" does not occur in the Old Testament, and therefore we do not find such an expression in the LXX (Greek translation of the Old Testament). There are some parallels in Hebrew texts of Second Temple Jewish literature, and these support the thesis argued for here. For instance, in 4QFlor 1:7 there is the Hebrew equivalent "works of law," which is probably a reference to all the works commanded in the law since the context does not limit it precisely. There is a similar phrase "his works in the Torah" (1QS 5:21; 6:18) in the *Rule of the Community*. A careful reading of 1QS V–VII shows that general obedience to the law is described in this passage. Members pledge to "return to the law of Moses according to *all* which he commanded" (1QS 5:8, italics mine). They are "to observe all his statutes which he commanded them to do" (1QS 5:22). The specific sins enumerated focus on humility, gentleness, and avoiding anger (1QS 5:25–26). The laws that are demanded of members of the community focus on moral norms: lying, evil speech, blasphemy, anger, insulting others, revenge, evil words, falling asleep, walking naked, spitting, inappropriate jesting, grumbling (1QS 6:24–7:21). Nothing is said about boundary markers like circumcision, food laws, or Sabbath.

Similarly, the contents of 4QMMT, which speaks of the "works of the Torah," contains numerous regulations about sacrifices and purity regulations, but it is not apparent that these precepts have to do with the exclusion of Gentiles from the covenant. What we find here are purity regulations that relate to the temple in general, so that, for instance, regulations pertaining to the deaf and blind and lepers are included. Language of segregation is used, but it seems to relate to moral matters, for in the context fornication and that which is abominable are specified. Further, the blessings and cursings recorded in Deuteronomy 26–28 are noted, and these focus on moral infractions. Indeed, the forgiveness of David also is mentioned, and this almost certainly has to do with his murder of Uriah and his adultery with Bathsheba. Thus, the evidence we have suggests that in Jewish literature "works of law" also refers to the whole law.

I also will argue in answering question 7 that perfect obedience to the law is required. That such perfect obedience is demanded is particularly clear in Galatians 3:10 and Romans 3:20. If perfect obedience to the law is required, then the claim that works of law has to do especially with boundary markers—the sociological division between Jews and Gentiles—is false. Paul insists that the whole law must be kept to obtain justification; the problem is that all sin and fall short of this demand.

SUMMARY

Different interpretations for "works of law" are proposed today. I have argued both from the Pauline literature and the Second Temple Jewish literature that "works of law" refers to the entire law. The term should not be defined in terms of legalism, nor does it focus on the boundary markers that separate Jews from Gentiles. "Works of law" refers to the entire law.

REFLECTION QUESTIONS

1. What are the interpretations of "works of law" proposed by scholars today?

2. What evidence do New Perspective interpreters set forth to defend their reading of "works of law"?

3. Do you think it is convincing to say that "works of law" should be equated with legalism?

4. How does figure 2 support the view that "works of law" refers to the deeds required by the whole law?

5. What reading of "works of law" is supported by Jewish literature outside the Bible?

Does Paul Condemn Legalism in His Letters?

We have seen earlier that the New Perspective on Paul maintains that the Judaism of Paul's day was not legalistic. A number of scholars who have adopted the New Perspective also have argued that there is no polemic against legalism in Paul's letters. They assert that the Jews are indicted for ethnocentrism, exclusivism, and nationalism, not for legalism or works-righteousness.[1] I am using the terms *legalism* and *works-righteousness* here to denote the idea that our works merit salvation or justification. Under question 4 the cogency of the New Perspective's reading of Judaism was raised. We saw there that there are serious problems with the New Perspective's interpretation of Second Temple Jewish literature. But even if those who support the New Perspective read the Jewish sources correctly, what do we make of Paul's statements about the law? What is most plausible exegetically when we read Paul? The Pauline interpretation must not be determined by outside sources. His statements must be read with integrity in their own right. We must be open to the historical possibility that Paul criticized the Jews of his day for their legalism on the basis of his gospel. The novel and unique does occur in history. Some people arise in a culture who have a very different view of what is happening in their culture. Whatever we make of Jewish sources, it will be argued that decisive evidence exists to show that Paul engaged in a polemic against Jewish legalism.[2]

On eight occasions Paul argues that no one is righteous or receives the Spirit by works of law (Gal. 2:16 [3x]; 3:2, 5, 10; Rom. 3:20, 28). I argued in

---

1. I have noted the contributions of Wright and Dunn previously.
2. Hence, Chris VanLandingham's view that both Paul and Second Temple Judaism espoused a meritorious view of religion should be rejected (*Judgment and Justification in Early Judaism and the Apostle Paul* [Peabody, MA: Hendrickson, 2006]).

question 5 that works of law does not refer to legalism per se but to the deeds or actions required by the law. It is imperative that a careful distinction be understood at this very point. Strictly speaking, in terms of the phrase itself, "works of law" does not refer to legalism. But when we examine the context or the flow of the discourse in which "works of law" occurs, the notion of legalism is present. According to Paul, some Jews apparently believed that they could be righteous before God or receive the gift of the Spirit because they observed the works of the law. Such a stance toward the law is legalism, for it anchors justification in human obedience rather than in faith. In every context in which "works of law" is found, a polarity is established between justification/receiving the Spirit by works of law or by faith (cf. Gal. 2:16; 3:2, 5, 10–12; Rom. 3:20–22, 28). Faith does not trust in what one has accomplished for salvation; it looks outside of itself to Christ and his righteousness for justification. The Spirit is given by virtue of a humble reception of the gospel message, not on the basis of human performance of what the law required. The very desire to carry out the works of law for justification points to an inclination to rest on the accomplishments of the human subject rather than on the grace of God.

Justification by works of law is based on doing, whereas justification by faith rests on what God has done (Gal. 3:12). Galatians 3:18 affirms, "For if the inheritance comes by the law, it no longer comes by promise; but God gave it to Abraham by a promise." Those who trust in God's promise rely upon God's work, whereas those who try to be justified by the law attempt to secure the inheritance on the basis of human achievement. As Romans 4:14 declares, "For if it is the adherents of the law who are to be the heirs, faith is null and the promise is void." Paul clearly teaches here that faith and law are opposed to one another in a certain sense. Faith looks to God's promises and his supernatural work, but law finds blessing through what human beings accomplish. Faith does not focus upon the human being and its accomplishments to secure the eschatological inheritance; it rests entirely upon God's free and certain promise. The final inheritance is guaranteed, for it depends upon God's promise and work, which is received by trusting him. The law represents an entirely different pathway to obtain the inheritance, and it introduces the condition of human obedience, which is insufficient to receive the blessing. As Paul says, "The law brings wrath" (Rom. 4:15). On the other hand, the inheritance "depends on faith, in order that the promise may rest on grace and be guaranteed" (Rom. 4:16). Again, it seems that Paul engages in this polemic because some thought they could gain the inheritance through their obedience, which is an indication of legalism as defined above.

Other texts point to a polemic against Jewish legalism. In Romans 3:27 boasting is excluded on the basis of faith. Such a comment suggests that boasting would be fitting if justification were attainable by works (Rom. 3:28). Paul, of course, utterly rejects the possibility of such boasting since all are sinners (Rom. 3:23). Still, he reminds his readers that boasting is excluded, presumably because some were tempted to boast in what they accomplished. Such boasting is the height of folly. Since all human beings violate God's standards, it is irrational to think human works could secure God's favor.

Paul picks up the theme of boasting when he considers Abraham in Romans 4:2–5. The idea that Paul reflects primarily on boundary markers is mistaken, for he speaks here of "works" (*erga*), not "works of law" (*erga nomou*). Indeed, Paul stresses that Abraham did not live under the law (cf. Rom. 5:12–14; Gal. 3:15–18). According to Paul, Abraham could legitimately boast if he did the necessary works. Nevertheless, Abraham had no grounds for boasting in God's sight, for he was ungodly (Rom. 4:2, 5). He belonged to idolaters when the Lord called him to follow him (Josh. 24:2–3). Abraham was justified, as Genesis 15:6 attests, by believing rather than doing.

Romans 4:4–5 further explicates Romans 4:2–3. Verse 4 is particularly important: "Now to the one who works, his wages are not counted as a gift but as his due." This statement virtually captures the essence of legalism, at least according to my definition. Paul uses the illustration of an employee. If the employee fulfills his contract and does the work required, then he *deserves* wages. He has merited the pay, and hence he does not view his paycheck as a gift of grace. But justification is not attained on that basis: "And to the one who does not work but believes in him who justifies the ungodly, his faith is counted as righteousness" (Rom. 4:5). No one gains justification by working for God, for all are ungodly. Righteousness is obtained by believing instead of doing. Some scholars downplay the content of Romans 4:4, but it is quite prominent in the argument, for Paul takes pains to demonstrate that no one is justified by virtue of what he or she does. Surely Paul excludes works-righteousness here because human beings are prone to trust in their works. Paul was not an academic theologian who discussed matters unrelated to the lives of those he addressed. He contrasts works-righteousness with faith-righteousness so that readers will avoid trusting in their own works (cf. Rom. 4:6–8).

Romans 9:30–10:8 also indicates that Israel struggled with legalism. Again, some think that boundary markers are the main issue here, but this is improbable. Nothing whatsoever is said about boundary markers in this context. One searches in vain for any reference to circumcision, food laws, or Sabbath. Nor is the phrase "works of law" (*erga nomou*) used. Instead, Paul uses the term "works" (*erga*), which refers to human actions performed in a broad and general sense. Israel "pursued a law that would lead to righteousness" (Rom. 9:31) but did not reach the desired goal. Paul asks the vital question in 9:32: Why is it that Israel did not obtain righteousness by means of the law? He replies, "Because they did not pursue it by faith, but as if it were based on works." Israel is criticized for their subjective attitude here. They apparently believed that they could put God in their debt by their works. Such an attitude is the heart of works-righteousness, for even though Israel sinned against God, they apparently believed that they could achieve righteousness before God based on their performance. Hence, they stumbled at the heart of the gospel, which is trusting in Christ for one's end-time inheritance (Rom. 9:33).

The continuation of the argument in Romans 10:1–8 yields the same conclusion. Israel had a zeal for God, but their zeal did not accord with knowledge. They sought "to establish their own" righteousness and therefore "did not submit to God's righteousness" (Rom. 10:3). The establishment of their own righteousness, however, reflects legalism. I already have noted that there is no indication in the context of a dispute regarding boundary markers. Hence, their own righteousness is another way of speaking of works-righteousness. Those who do not find their righteousness in Christ inevitably end up exalting their own righteousness and goodness. Thus, Paul once again contrasts "believing" and "doing" (Rom. 10:4–8). Either we trust in the righteousness that is given to us as a gift or we rely on the righteousness we produce. The latter pursuit is futile, for righteousness by the law is attainable only if one does what the law commands (Rom. 10:5), and all fall short. Therefore, relying on our own righteousness is inherently self-defeating, but sinners in their delusions often think they can merit divine approval.

A polemic against legalism also is supported by Philippians 3:2–11. Here some of the boundary markers do appear in the argument. Paul appeals to his own exploits in comparing himself to the false teachers, arguing that he far surpasses them. Paul's "confidence in the flesh" (Phil. 3:3–4) cannot be limited to exclusivism or nationalism. He was proud of his ethnic heritage and his circumcision. But his boast cannot be restricted to such, for he also was impressed with his devotion to the law. His Pharisaic devotion to the law (Phil. 3:5) demonstrates that he was also proud of what he accomplished, of his own obedience to what the Torah required. So too, his persecution of the church revealed his devotion, albeit misguided, to the law (Phil. 3:6). Indeed, Paul even claims that his obedience to the law was blameless. The New Perspective rightly sees in some texts an interest in the question of boundary markers, but texts like Philippians 3:2–11 do not stop there. Works-righteousness is also clearly evident. And we should not be surprised to discover such, for it is hard to imagine any ethnic group thinking they are superior without also thinking at the same time that they are morally superior.

Two other Pauline texts also evince a focus on works-righteousness. In Ephesians 2:8–9 we find one of Paul's most famous soteriological statements: "For by grace you have been saved through faith. And this is not your own doing; it is the gift of God, not a result of works, so that no one may boast." It is striking, once again, that nothing is said about boundary markers. Indeed, Paul does not refer to "works of law" (*erga nomou*) but to "works" (*erga*). Faith and works are specifically contrasted, and the exclusion of works rules out any boasting. It seems quite evident that a polemic against relying on one's works is reflected here.

Titus 3:5 fits within the same paradigm. Here our works are contrasted with God's mercy, which led to our salvation. Note again that Paul speaks of "works," not "works of law." He leaves no doubt that human performance is in view, speaking of "works done by us in righteousness." Here the words that focus on what human beings accomplish accumulate: "works," "we have done," and "righteousness." Boundary markers are not the issue—human righteousness is. And Paul rejects it as a foundation for a right relationship with God. Most scholars outside evangelicalism reject Ephesians and Titus as post-Pauline, though I would defend Pauline authorship.[3] Even if Ephesians and the Pastorals are post-Pauline, they reflect the view of the earliest Pauline disciples. And what is quite instructive is that Paul's words fit with the interpretations proposed by Martin Luther and John Calvin many centuries later. After all, nothing is said about boundary markers. It looks as if the earliest Pauline disciples (if one adopts such a view) read the other Pauline letters in terms of a polemic against works-righteousness.

SUMMARY

When we interpret major Pauline texts on the law and righteousness, New Perspective interpretations are found to be wanting. Paul critiques Second Temple Judaism for its legalism, and thus he disagrees with the assessment of many modern scholars. Surely Paul's assessment deserves priority, for he writes inspired Scripture and he knew Second Temple Judaism far better than any modern scholar.

REFLECTION QUESTIONS

1. Why does the phrase "works of law" reflect a polemic against legalism in context, even though the phrase itself does not denote legalism?

2. What is the evidence in Romans 4:2–5 that Paul responds to legalism?

3. Is it plausible that Paul would charge his Jewish contemporaries with legalism over against their own assessment of themselves?

4. Do the later Pauline epistles (Ephesians, Titus) support the idea that legalism was a problem his readers faced?

5. How should we preach against legalism today?

---

3. See especially Harold W. Hoehner, *Ephesians: An Exegetical Commentary* (Grand Rapids: Baker, 2002), 202–61.

Is Perfect Obedience to the Law Mandatory for Salvation?

The short answer to this question is "yes." And the way one answers this question is fundamental for one's soteriology, for it speaks both to the truth of God's holiness and the nature of Christ's atonement. The demand for perfect obedience is evident from the earliest pages of the Bible. Adam and Eve were condemned, cursed, and banished from the garden for one sin (Genesis 3). The Lord did not respond by saying that they would have a right relationship with him if they trusted and obeyed him most of the time after their fall into sin. It is clear that the hope for Adam and Eve and all people is the promise that the seed of the woman will crush the head of the serpent (Gen. 3:15). Indeed, God's clothing of Adam and Eve with garments (Gen. 3:21) suggests that their only hope for life in the presence of a holy God is atonement.

It is sometimes claimed that the Mosaic covenant does not demand perfect obedience. Israel was threatened with exile for blatant and sustained disobedience, not for occasionally violating the law. This observation contains elements of truth, but it does not contradict the claim that perfect obedience is mandatory. In one sense, of course, perfect obedience was not required, for the Lord graciously entered into covenant with his people and provided atonement for their sins. Ultimately, however, sinless perfection was demanded, for Israel would not be forgiven of their sins apart from offering sacrifices that atoned for their sin. The very structure of the Mosaic covenant, then, implies that God requires perfection. If significant and substantial obedience were sufficient, then the sacrificial system would be superfluous in the case of those who were remarkably godly. The Old Testament sacrifices would apply particularly to those who sinned egregiously. But the Old Testament gives no such impression. Every Israelite, no matter how godly, must offer sacrifices for his sins. Presumably such sacrifices were needed to atone for *any* faults or sins committed by Israelites. Therefore, the very existence of the sacrificial cult points to the need for perfect obedience.

When we read the New Testament, the same truth is clear. For instance, James enunciates a principle in James 2:10: "For whoever keeps the whole law but fails in one point has become accountable for all of it." The word translated "accountable" (*enochos*) here does not mean "answerable" before the divine Judge as if one could possibly make a convincing defense. Rather, the term means "guilty" before God. That *enochos* means "guilty" is evident in both the LXX (e.g., Exod. 22:2 [LXX]; 34:7; Lev. 20:9; Deut. 19:10; Josh. 2:19) and the New Testament (Matt. 5:21, 22; 26:66; Mark 3:29; 14:64; 1 Cor. 11:27). Hence, James teaches that one transgression renders one guilty before God. If one observes all the rest of the law but violates the law against committing murder, then one is a lawbreaker (James 2:11). Therefore, perfect obedience is necessary, for even one sin renders one a transgressor or sinner before God.

This reading of James 2:10 is confirmed by Galatians 3:10: "For as many as are of the works of the Law are under a curse; for it is written, 'Cursed is everyone who does not abide by all things written in the book of the law, to perform them'" (NASB). "Works of law," as argued above, refers to the actions or deeds commanded by the law. Paul asserts here that those who are of works of law are cursed. The natural question is why a curse lies upon those who are of works of law. The second part of Galatians 3:10 provides a reason, claiming from Deuteronomy 27:26 that those who do not keep everything written in the law are cursed. It is likely that Paul also draws here on Deuteronomy 28:58, where Moses insists that Israel must be "careful to do all the words of this law that are written in this book." If they fail to obey, the Lord will pour out great punishments upon them.

How do we explain Paul's argument here? Sanders dismisses the Old Testament citation, arguing that the key to unlocking Paul's arguments are his own words, not the wording of the Old Testament citation.[1] Such an explanation fails to convince, for throughout Galatians there is ample reason to think that the Old Testament citation contributes to the flow of the argument. Indeed, in three of the citations in Galatians 3:10–13 Paul uses the word *for*, suggesting that a *reason* is given that advances the argument. Another suggestion is put forward by Heinrich Schlier, who states that condemnation comes from *doing* the law.[2] Such a reading, like that of Sanders, bypasses the meaning of the Old Testament citation, for the curse comes upon those *failing* to do the law, not those doing it. James Dunn argues that the curse falls on those who exclude

1. See my fuller examination of Sanders's view: Thomas R. Schreiner, "Paul and Perfect Obedience to the Law: An Evaluation of the View of E. P. Sanders," *WTJ* 47 (1985): 245–78.
2. Heinrich Schlier, *Der Brief an die Galater* (Göttingen: Vandenhoeck & Ruprecht, 1965), 132–33.

Gentiles from Israel's covenantal blessings,[3] but again such a reading does not accord with the argument actually made. Paul does not criticize the Jews for exclusivism or ethnocentrism but failure to keep the law. Nor is it clear that Paul speaks corporately of Israel's sin here, as if he is explaining why Israel corporately went into exile.[4] It is true, of course, that Israel suffered captivity because of their sin, but the argument made does not focus on the fate of Israel. Paul draws from an Old Testament text that zeros in on the sin of individuals (Deut. 27:15–26). Furthermore, Paul individualizes the argument with the introductory words "as many as," which also could legitimately be translated "whoever." Paul does not actually reflect on Israel's past here but makes a universal statement about anyone who attempts to be justified by works of law.[5]

So, what is the argument of the verse if all the interpretations suggested above fail? I would suggest that the argument is a model of clarity:

- *Premise 1*: Those who do not do everything the law commands are cursed (Gal. 3:10b).

- *Premise 2 (implied)*: No one does all that the law commands.

- *Conclusion*: Therefore, those who are of the works of the law are cursed (Gal. 3:10a).

Some object to this interpretation by saying that supplying an implied premise is illegitimate. Such an objection is unconvincing. Paul does not argue like an analytic philosopher. He often leaves implied premises out of his arguments. Indeed, scholars recognize that arguments where one of the premises is absent (an enthymeme) were quite common in the ancient world and in Paul's letters.[6] But why would Paul leave the premise out if it is crucial for his argument? He left it out because the Old Testament itself often teaches that all sin and fall short of what God demands. Consider the following verses:

- "If they sin against you—for there is no one who does not sin . . ." (1 Kings 8:46).

---

3. See his exposition, James D. G. Dunn, "Works of the Law and the Curse of the Law (Galatians 3.10–14)," *NTS* 31 (1985): 523–42.
4. N. T. Wright, *The Climax of the Covenant: Christ and the Law in Pauline Theology* (Minneapolis: Fortress, 1992), 137–56; James M. Scott, "'For as Many as Are of Works of the Law Are Under a Curse' (Galatians 3.10)," in *Paul and the Scriptures of Israel*, ed. Craig A. Evans and James A. Sanders, JSNTSup 83 (Sheffield: JSOT Press, 1993), 187–221.
5. Cf. Seyoon Kim, *Paul and the New Perspective: Second Thoughts on the Origin of Paul's Gospel* (Grand Rapids: Eerdmans, 2002), 138–40.
6. Marc J. Debanné, *Enthymemes in the Letters of Paul*, LNTS 303 (London: T & T Clark, 2006).

- "Who can say, 'I have made my heart pure; I am clean from my sin'?" (Prov. 20:9).

- "Surely there is not a righteous man on earth who does good and never sins" (Eccl. 7:20).

Hence, the notion that all sinned was a common conviction since it was clearly taught by the Old Testament. Paul did not need to spell it out, for it was obvious from the Scriptures themselves that all sinned.

The Pauline argument in Galatians 3:10, then, is elegantly simple. The curse falls upon those who sin, even for the smallest sin. The text emphasizes that one must do "everything" written in the law to avoid the curse. Perfect obedience is necessary to escape the curse, but no one obeys flawlessly; so all are guilty before God. Paul does not merely *threaten* a curse in this verse; he *pronounces* a curse. To read the verse merely as a threat suggests that some might escape what is threatened, but no one (except Christ) completely observes the law, so Paul actually pronounces a curse upon those who rely upon the law.

Two final objections against this proposed interpretation must be considered. Some scholars have claimed that Paul would never argue that the law must be kept perfectly, for sacrifices could be offered under the Mosaic covenant to atone for sin. This objection seems to be plausible initially, but it fails to take into account the historical nature of salvation in Paul's argument. Paul would not accept the notion that Old Testament sacrifices atone for sin now that Christ has come and offered the definitive and final sacrifice. The sacrifices required by the Old Testament point to the sacrifice of Christ and find their fulfillment in his sacrifice (Gal. 3:13; Rom. 3:25–26; 8:3). Hence, those who return to the law now that Christ has come are cut off from the atoning provisions in the law. They would be attempting to live under the Sinai covenant without enjoying the forgiveness offered under that covenant, since the sacrifices were valid only for the time period in which the Mosaic covenant was still in force. In putting themselves under the Mosaic covenant, they would be obligated to keep all the provisions of the covenant perfectly. Any failure, therefore, would bring condemnation.

Another objection to the interpretation offered here is that Paul claims to be blameless in his obedience to the law in Philippians 3:6. But surely Paul does not mean by this that his obedience to the law was perfect. Paul's observance of the law was extraordinary and notable, and yet he must have in mind here as well his offering of sacrifices for the sins he committed. Otherwise, Paul would be claiming, in contradiction to the Old Testament texts noted above (1 Kings 8:46; Prov. 20:9; Eccl. 7:20), to be flawless in his obedience, which is unlikely. Furthermore, Paul, as an unbeliever was unaware of the depth of his sin, as Romans 7:7–25 reveals. The secret sins committed by him (Rom. 2:16) were revealed to him more fully by the gospel. So, as a believer in Christ he understood that his zeal in persecuting the church (cf. Acts 8:1, 3; 9:1–5, 13–14, 21, 26; 22:3–5, 8, 19–20; 26:10–11, 14–15) was not actually an example of his righteousness (Phil. 3:6) but uncovered the depth of sin in his life (1 Cor. 15:9; Eph. 3:8; 1 Tim. 1:15).

A demand for perfect obedience is also probably in view in Galatians 5:3: "I testify again to every man who accepts circumcision that he is obligated to keep the whole law." Paul emphasizes obligation to observe the law here, and certainly he stresses that such an obligation is a burden. But the question that needs to be asked is *why* the law is a burden. "Again" likely hearkens back to Galatians 3:10, suggesting that placing oneself under the law is a burden because no one can sufficiently keep what it commands. One must keep the whole law in order to be justified, but flawless obedience is impossible.

Romans 1:18–3:20 also is in agreement with this interpretation. Paul does not specifically argue that one must obey the law perfectly, but he does emphasize that righteousness cannot come via observance of the law since all people sin. Even the Jews, who were in covenant with God, were not exempt from God's judgment since they did the very things they condemned in Gentiles (Rom. 2:1–2). Their practice of the law did not match their proclamation of the law (Rom. 2:17–24). Circumcision without adherence to the law affords no protection on the Day of Judgment (Rom. 2:25–29). In the Pauline conclusion of the argument, he emphasizes that no one is righteous and that all have violated what God demands. No one can be justified through the works of the law, for the works of the law only reveal the sinfulness of human beings (Rom. 3:19–20). Paul summarizes his argument in the famous declaration that "all have sinned and fall short of the glory of God" (Rom. 3:23). Paul highlights the sinfulness and stubbornness of human beings (Rom. 2:5). When God examines the secrets of our lives, it is evident that we deserve judgment (Rom. 2:16).

SUMMARY

There is significant evidence in both the Old Testament and the New Testament that perfect obedience to the law was necessary for salvation. Paul's fundamental complaint with the Jews of his day was not that they excluded Gentiles. Rather, he indicted them for failing to do God's will, for failing to see the depth of God's demand on their lives. I think we can say with confidence that the same is true today. Many do not rely on Christ's atoning sacrifice for forgiveness and his righteousness because they believe their own obedience is sufficient.

REFLECTION QUESTIONS

1. In what sense does the Mosaic covenant demand perfect obedience?

2. How does the argument of Galatians 3:10 support the idea that perfect obedience is demanded by God for salvation?

3. How does the demand for perfect obedience fit with the offering of sacrifices for atonement under the Mosaic law?

4. Does Paul's statement that he was blameless in keeping the law (Phil. 3:6) contradict the Old Testament idea that all fall short of flawless obedience to God's law?

5. What role should the demand for perfect obedience play in our preaching of the gospel today?

How Should We Understand
the Use of Leviticus 18:5
in the Scriptures?

Leviticus 18:5 is an important verse in the Scriptures, for Paul cites it twice in the midst of two very important arguments regarding justification, namely, in both Galatians 3:12 and Romans 10:5.[1] Galatians 3:12 says, "But the law is not of faith, rather 'The one who does them shall live by them.'" And Romans 10:5 says, "For Moses writes about the righteousness that is based on the law, that the person who does the commandments shall live by them." Both the meaning of the Old Testament verse and its use in Paul has precipitated discussion, and my goal here is to explain briefly the meaning in both the Old Testament and in Paul.

In its Old Testament context the verse reads, "You shall therefore keep my statutes and my rules; if a person does them, he shall live by them: I am the LORD" (Lev. 18:5). We should observe that the verse is addressed to those who belong to the Lord. Israel has been redeemed from Egypt and liberated by God's grace. Therefore, in context the verse should not be construed as legalistic or as offering salvation on the basis of works. Israel's obedience is a response to God's gracious intervention on their behalf. What is the nature of the life promised in Leviticus 18:5? Moses is almost certainly speaking of life in the land, for the laws were given to the Israelites so that they would not follow the practices of the Canaanites and be expelled from the land (cf. Lev. 18:3, 24–28). If we consider the narrative of the remainder of the Old Testament, this interpretation fits nicely. Israel was sent into exile because of her failure to do the Lord's will. They were "vomited" out of the land because of their disobedience (Lev. 18:28).

---

1. Jesus cites the same verse in Luke 10:28.

It is instructive to see where Leviticus 18:5 is cited in the remainder of the Old Testament. Ezekiel picks up the words of Leviticus 18:5 in chapter 20, as he rehearses the history of Israel. He emphasizes the grace of God to the generation delivered from Egypt (Ezek. 20:6–11). Even though they were rebellious and turned to what is detestable, the Lord acted for his name's sake (v. 9) and liberated them from Egypt. He then gave them his "rules, by which, if a person does them, he shall live" (v. 11). We see again that the law was given in a covenantal context, after God had saved his people from Egypt. Nevertheless, Ezekiel immediately turns to the rebellion of Israel. They "rejected my rules, by which, if a person does them, he shall live" (v. 13). In context it is clear that Ezekiel addresses the wilderness generation, and so he has in mind the sin with the golden calf and the many other sins that characterized the wilderness generation. Nevertheless, the Lord did not completely wipe out Israel for his name's sake (vv. 14–17), though he punished the wilderness generation by not allowing them to enter the Land of Promise.

Ezekiel thus far has repeated twice that those who keep his laws will live (Ezek. 20:11, 13), suggesting that Israel was not able to keep God's commands. Such a reading is confirmed as the narrative continues. Ezekiel reiterates a third time the words of Leviticus 18:5. The children of the wilderness generation were disobedient to the law that promised life if kept (Ezek. 20:21). Again, the Lord had mercy in not destroying them altogether, though he threatened exile if their disobedience continued (Ezek. 20:22–24). The reference to exile confirms the interpretation suggested for Leviticus 18:5. Failure to keep the law would result in Israel's expulsion from the land.

Ezekiel concludes his reuse of Leviticus 18:5 with a remarkable statement: "Moreover, I gave them statutes that were not good and rules by which they could not have life" (Ezek. 20:25). Ezekiel does not mean that the content of the law is not good. His point is that the law was not good for Israel since Israel was unable to obey it and to gain life. If Israel had turned from wickedness and pursued goodness, she would find life, as Ezekiel 18 repeatedly emphasizes (Ezek. 18:9, 13, 17, 19, 21, 22, 23, 24, 27, 28, 32).[2] But Israel's consistent unwillingness to do what the Lord commands reveals a problem with her heart that can be remedied only by the grace of God. Israel's only hope is the promise of the indwelling Spirit, which will enable them to keep God's commands (Ezek. 11:19–20; 36:26–27). Ezekiel 20, then, confirms the words of Leviticus 18:5. Since Israel was unable to keep God's law, she was being sent into exile.

Nehemiah rehearses Israel's history in Nehemiah 9, remembering how the creator God chose Abraham and promised to give him the land (vv. 6–8), and how he delivered Israel from Egypt and sustained them in the wilderness (vv. 9–15). He comments that the law given on Sinai contains "right rules

---

2. The father enunciates the same principle to his son in Proverbs. If his son will keep his commands, then he will live (Prov. 4:4; 7:2).

and true laws, good statutes and commandments" (v. 13). Remarkably, Israel rebelled in the wilderness by desiring to return to Egypt and by making a golden calf (vv. 16–18). Still, the Lord showered his mercy on them, for he preserved them in the wilderness (vv. 19–21) and led them graciously into the Promised Land (vv. 22–25). Still, Israel continued to rebel in the land in the days of the judges (vv. 26–28). The Lord handed them over to their enemies when "they cast your law behind their back" (v. 26) and delivered them when they cried out for mercy.

The allusion to Leviticus 18:5 occurs in Nehemiah 9:29, which recalls the repeated warnings to Israel: "You [the Lord] warned them in order to turn them back to your law. Yet they acted presumptuously and did not obey your commandments, but sinned against your rules, which if a person does them, he shall live by them." What Nehemiah emphasizes in citing Leviticus 18:5 is Israel's failure to keep God's law, and hence they were sent into exile (Neh. 9:30). I conclude, then, that Nehemiah's use of Leviticus 18:5 fits with the meaning of the verse as it was originally given in Leviticus.

The references to Leviticus 18:5 in the Old Testament are instructive, for they call attention to Israel's failure to keep the law, even suggesting a moral inability to do what pleases God. The life in view relates to life in the land, and yet there is a suggestion as well that Israel's failure to obey indicates that they do not truly know God. They need the Holy Spirit and the new covenant to do the will of God (Ezek. 36:26–27; Jer. 31:31–34). Israel's constant rebellion and failure to keep the law led to their being sent into exile, as both Ezekiel and Nehemiah attest in citing Leviticus 18:5.

Some Jewish traditions in the period subsequent to the New Testament understood Leviticus 18:5 as promising eternal life to those who keep the law: "And you shall keep my statutes and my judgments, which if a man do he shall live by them an everlasting life" (*Tg. Onq.*) "And you shall keep my statutes, and the order of my judgments, which if a man do he shall live in them, in the life of eternity, and his position shall be with the just" (*Tg. Ps-J.*).[3] In a thorough study of Leviticus 18:5 in the Old Testament and Second Temple Judaism, Preston Sprinkle shows that in some texts the verse is interpreted as requiring obedience for eternal life (cf. CD III, 15–16; 4Q266 11, I–II, 12; *Pss. Sol.* 14:1–5; cf. also 4Q504; Philo, *Prelim. Studies* 86–87).[4] Simon Gathercole also argues that an eschatological reading of Leviticus 18:5 is evident both in the New Testament and in Second Temple Judaism.[5] He rightly remarks,

---

3. Both of these references are reproduced from Richard N. Longenecker, *Galatians*, WBC (Dallas: Word, 1990), 120.

4. See Preston M. Sprinkle, *Law and Life: The Interpretation of Leviticus 18:5 in Early Judaism and Paul*, WUNT 2/241 (Tübingen: Mohr Siebeck, 2008), 1–130.

5. Simon J. Gathercole, "Torah, Life, and Salvation: Leviticus 18:5 in Early Judaism and the New Testament," in *From Prophecy to Testament: The Function of the Old Testament in the New*, ed. Craig A. Evans (Peabody, MA: Hendrickson, 2004), 126–45.

"There is an 'eternalization' of the life that, in its original context in Leviticus, would have been understood in terms of lengthened life and prosperity of one's descendents and the nation as a whole."[6]

The interpretation in Second Temple Judaism is helpful for understanding Paul, for Paul clearly has eternal life in view and not just life in the land. Hence, he understands what is promised in Leviticus 18:5 typologically. As is often the case in the New Testament, the land promises become a type of life to come. In Galatians 3:12 Paul opposes any sort of combination of law and gospel, as if one were saved both by doing the law *and* believing in the gospel. Life is obtained only via the latter, and not by the former, for no one is able to keep what the law demands (Gal. 3:10). We also must interpret what Paul says in terms of redemptive history. Now that Christ has come, forgiveness is granted only through his atoning sacrifice, and hence there is no room for forgiveness via the law. Other scholars have argued that the verse refers to Christ's obedience, but it is doubtful that Christ is in mind here.

Some argue that Paul corrects a misinterpretation of Leviticus 18:5 in both Galatians 3:12 and Romans 10:5, just as the rabbis often responded to a misinterpretation of one verse by citing others.[7] But the misinterpretation view suffers from a major defect. Elsewhere Paul always cites an Old Testament text *positively* to advance his own argument, and we are lacking any clear evidence that he responds to a wrong understanding here. It is most likely, then, that Paul cites the Old Testament to advance his argument.

Paul reads Leviticus 18:5 redemptive-historically.[8] Perfect obedience is demanded from those who place themselves under the law, for the atonement provided by Old Testament sacrifices no longer avails with the coming of Christ. Perfect obedience was not demanded in one sense under the Sinai covenant, for the law provided forgiveness via sacrifices for those who transgressed.[9] In Paul's view, however (see Gal. 3:15–4:7), the Sinai covenant is no longer in force. Hence, those who observe circumcision and the law to obtain justification (Gal. 5:2–4) are turning back the clock in salvation history. The coming of Christ spells the end of the Sinai covenant (Gal. 3:15–4:7). Hence, those who live under the law must keep it perfectly to be saved, for

---

6. Ibid., 140. Gathercole comments on Luke 10 here, but his citation reflects his view in Galatians 3:12 as well. Wakefield fails to see the typological escalation here, and hence limits the word "live" to the Old Testament context (see Andrew H. Wakefield, *Where to Live: The Hermeneutical Significance of Paul's Citations from Scripture in Galatians 3:1–14*, SBLAB 14 [Atlanta: Society of Biblical Literature, 2003], 171, 174–75).

7. I previously defended this view but have changed my mind.

8. See James M. Hamilton Jr., "'The One Who Does Them Shall Live by Them': Leviticus 18:5 in Galatians 3:12," *The Gospel Witness* (August 2005): 10–12. This paragraph, with some changes, comes from my forthcoming commentary on Galatians.

9. Of course, in another sense perfect obedience is always required in every era of redemptive history. Under the Mosaic covenant, the Lord provided a means by which sins could be forgiven.

in returning to the law they are forsaking the atonement provided by Christ (Gal. 2:21; 5:3). Returning to the law is futile, however, for the sacrifices of atonement under the Sinai covenant pointed ahead to the sacrifice of Christ. Therefore animal sacrifices no longer provide forgiveness now that the definitive sacrifice of Christ has been offered (Gal. 3:13).

Some scholars have read the relationship between Romans 10:5 and 10:6–8 as if both describe the life of faith. On this reading, the citation of Leviticus 18:5 in Romans 10:5 *positively* portrays the life of believers.[10] Hence, those who trust in God (Rom. 10:6–8) keep the law (Rom. 10:5). This interpretation should be rejected for the following reasons. First, it is unlikely that Paul would use the same verse (Lev. 18:5) negatively in Galatians 3:12 but positively in Romans 10:5, especially when we consider that the subject is the same in both contexts (righteousness of law versus righteousness of faith). Second, it seems impossible that Paul would speak positively of righteousness *coming from the law* (Rom. 10:5). Righteousness in Paul is invariably by faith, or through Christ, but never from the law. The parallel in Philippians 3 confirms this reading. Paul repudiates his own righteousness "that comes from the law" and rests entirely on the righteousness that is his through faith in Christ. Third, this fits with what we see regularly in Paul's theology, as this book elsewhere documents, where faith in Christ is contrasted with "doing" as the pathway to a right relationship with God. Fourth, the interpretation defended here fits with the context of Romans 9:30–10:4. Israel did not attain righteousness by pursuing it through the law since Israel attempted to establish her righteousness by works (Rom. 9:31–32). They did not know about God's righteousness and attempted "to establish their own" through their obedience to the law (Rom. 10:3–4).

SUMMARY

Leviticus 18:5 in its Old Testament context requires obedience out of gratefulness to the Lord for delivering his people from Egypt. If Israel obeyed, they would remain in the land, but disobedience would lead to exile. Both Ezekiel and Nehemiah cite Leviticus 18:5 to remind Israel that their exile was due to their disobedience. Hence, it was clear from the Old Testament story that Israel was unable to observe the law. Some sectors of Second Temple Judaism picked up Leviticus 18:5 and understood it in terms of eternal life. Paul follows this pattern, using the text typologically and contrasting life via the law to life via faith. Clearly, Paul believes that obtaining life by means of the law is impossible due to human disobedience. Eternal life is obtained only by faith, as believers trust in Christ's atoning sacrifice.

---

10. Daniel P. Fuller, *Gospel and Law: Contrast or Continuum? The Hermeneutics of Dispensationalism and Covenant Theology* (Grand Rapids: Eerdmans, 1980), 67–69, 85–88.

REFLECTION QUESTIONS

1. What is the meaning of Leviticus 18:5 in its historical context?

2. How do Ezekiel and Nehemiah apply Leviticus 18:5 to their readers?

3. How is Leviticus 18:5 used in extrabiblical Jewish literature?

4. Explain Paul's use of Leviticus 18:5 in Galatians 3:12 and Romans 10:5.

5. How should we use Leviticus 18:5 in preaching today?

Questions Related to the Role of the Law in the Christian Life

Does Paul Teach That the Old Testament Law Is Now Abolished?

If by the Old Testament law we mean the laws in the covenant established with Moses, then the answer is "yes," since Paul clearly teaches that Christians are no longer under the law covenant instituted under Moses. For instance, in 2 Corinthians 3:14 the Mosaic covenant is identified as "the old covenant" in contrast with "the new covenant" (2 Cor. 3:6) of which Paul is a minister. The phrase "old covenant" implies that that covenant enacted with Moses is no longer in force and that it has been replaced by the new covenant. The old covenant is clearly identified with the law, for the letters engraved on stone, which are clearly the Ten Commandments, reflect the content of the covenant (2 Cor. 3:6–7). The laws of the covenant are probably particularly in view in the phrases "when they read the old covenant" (2 Cor. 3:14) and "whenever Moses is read" (2 Cor. 3:15). Therefore, it follows that if the Mosaic covenant is no longer in effect because it has been replaced by the "new covenant," then the laws, which belong to that covenant, are no longer binding either. How does this dissolution of the old covenant fit with Paul's citing some of the commands from the Ten Commandments as authoritative? More shall be said on this topic in questions 14–17, but at this juncture it should be noted that the laws are not authoritative as stipulations of the old covenant since that covenant has passed away.

The temporary nature of the old covenant is confirmed elsewhere in 2 Corinthians 3. Moses' ministry is linked with the old covenant in the text. In other words, the ministry of Moses reflects the nature and character of the old covenant. Hence, the fading glory on Moses' face reflects the passing away of the old covenant (2 Cor. 3:7). Scott Hafemann argues that the word *katargoumenēn* in 2 Corinthians 3:7 and 11 (cf. also 3:13) refers to the bringing to an end of the consequences or effects that would have occurred if Moses' face was not covered.[1] The veil on Moses' face, according to Hafemann, represented the mercy of God, for Israel would have been judged and destroyed if it saw the glory of God unmediated since it was a stubborn people. This interpretation once persuaded me, but I now think it is unconvincing. The key to unlocking the passage is the clear contrast between "what remains" (*to menon*) and "what is fading away" (*to katargoumenon*, 2 Cor. 3:11). Paul's ministry and hence the new covenant remains and persists, whereas the Mosaic ministry and covenant passes away. Such a reading is confirmed by the contrast between the old and new covenants. Hafemann distinguishes between Moses' ministry and the old covenant, but Paul links the two together. Thus, the fading glory on Moses' face, which fits very nicely with what Exodus 34:29–35 says about the radiance on Moses' face, is a symbol of the temporary character of the old covenant. Therefore, 2 Corinthians 3:7–18 most naturally teaches that the old covenant has passed away.

The letter to the Galatians supports the interpretation proposed for 2 Corinthians 3. Paul's aim in the letter is to persuade the Galatians to refuse to accept circumcision as the initiation rite into the church of Jesus Christ, even though circumcision was required to belong to the covenant people of Israel (Lev. 12:3). In Galatians 2:15–3:14 Paul emphasizes that circumcision is unnecessary since the Galatians are justified by faith and not works of law. Furthermore, they received the Spirit by faith; hence one becomes a son of Abraham by faith and not by works of law. In this section of the letter, Paul does not specifically address the question of the permanence of the law and circumcision. Clearly, his argument has a salvation-historical character in Galatians 2:16–3:14, but the redemptive-historical nature of his argument is even more evident in Galatians 3:15–4:7. In Galatians 3:15–18 Paul specifically distinguishes the Mosaic covenant from the covenant with Abraham. The latter came 430 years before the former, and thus the provisions and stipulations of the Sinai covenant cannot nullify the promises of the covenant made with Abraham. Now what Paul says here could be interpreted to say that the Mosaic covenant simply supplemented the covenant with Abraham, but verses 17–18 clarify that the two covenants have a different nature. In the Mosaic covenant the inheritance is gained by obeying the law (which, as we have seen, no one is able to do), and in the covenant with Abraham inheritance comes via the promise. The Abrahamic covenant focuses on God's work (and hence the promise is guaranteed), whereas the Mosaic covenant requires obedience to the law (and the inheritance is not realized because of human inability).

---

1. Scott J. Hafemann, *Paul, Moses, and the History of Israel: The Letter/Spirit Contrast and the Argument from Scripture in 2 Corinthians 3*, WUNT 81 (Tübingen: Mohr Siebeck, 1995), 301–13.

In making the argument about the temporal difference between the Abrahamic and Mosaic covenants, Paul claims that they are different kinds of covenants and that the Abrahamic covenant is permanent. The Mosaic covenant and law, then, were added by God for a limited period of time (Gal. 3:19); and now that Christ has come as the promised seed, the law is no longer valid. It was God's intention all along that the law would last only until faith in Christ became a reality (Gal. 3:23). Now that Christ has arrived, the era of the pedagogue ("guardian" in ESV, Gal. 3:24–25) has ended. It seems hard to imagine how Paul could be any clearer in saying that the era of the law has ended. But in case his readers have not grasped what he is saying, he revisits the issue in Galatians 4:1–7. Here he uses the illustration of an heir who is a minor so that the time of his inheritance has not yet arrived. The time of slavery before the promise was fulfilled is identified as the epoch when Israel was "under the law" (vv. 4–5). Now that the "fullness of time" has come (v. 4) and God has sent his Son to liberate those under law, the era of the law has ceased.

The Galatians were tempted to submit to circumcision and to observe the Old Testament law in order to obtain justification. One of Paul's fundamental arguments in the letter is redemptive-historical. Requiring circumcision is folly, for it turns the salvation-historical clock back. Circumcision belonged to the era of Moses, not the era of promise. Now that Christ has come, circumcision and observance of the law are no longer required to belong to God's people.

Interestingly, Romans does not present a sustained argument against the ongoing validity of the law. Some short statements and suggestive comments, however, indicate that it presents the same view as we found in 2 Corinthians 3 and Galatians 3–4. First, Paul says believers are no longer "under law" (Rom. 6:14), and I will argue in answering question 10 that "under law" should be interpreted redemptive-historically, so that it supports the notion that the law is no longer in effect.

Second, Romans 10:4 asserts that Christ is "the end of the law." The word translated "end" here is *telos*, which can be translated as "end" or "goal." Space forbids a long discussion of the term and its meaning in context, but it is probable that both "goal" and "end" are intended in this context. Christ is the goal to which the law points; and when the goal is reached, the law also comes to an end.[2] If this interpretation is correct, then Romans 10:4 also teaches that believers are no longer under the Mosaic law.

Third, Paul's discussion in Romans 5:12–21 suggests that the Mosaic covenant is no longer operative. History, according to this text, is dominated by two figures: Adam and Christ. Adam introduced sin and death into the world, but Christ triumphed over Adam, so that righteousness and life now reign

---

2. For support of this view, see Mark A. Seifrid, "Paul's Approach to the New Testament in Rom 10:6–8," *TrinJ* 6 (1985): 7–8.

through him. Jews in Paul's day believed that the law's role in history was to counter sin, that it was God's agent to reverse the sin and devastation set in motion by Adam. Astonishingly, Paul argues the opposite view in Romans 5:20. The law did not decrease the trespass but increased it. In other words, the law has an interim character in salvation-history. It increased sin until the coming of Christ, who triumphed over sin and death, which Adam brought into the world. The implication, then, is that the law no longer continues since the Christ has come.

Fourth, we see another indication that the law has come to an end from Romans 7:6, where believers are released from the law through the death of Christ. Release from the law intimates that the law is no longer in force.

Fifth, the Pauline discussion on food in Romans 14:1–15:6 suggests that the law is no longer normative. The Old Testament law clearly forbids the eating of certain foods (Lev. 11:1–44; Deut. 14:3–21). Paul, however, identifies the weak as those who have a restricted diet (Rom. 14:2), whereas those who are strong feel free to eat anything. Paul sides theologically with the strong. He clearly speaks about the food laws in the Old Testament when he declares, "I know and am persuaded in the Lord Jesus that nothing is unclean in itself, but it is unclean for anyone who thinks it unclean" (Rom. 14:14). The word *koinos* ("common") is regularly used elsewhere of foods deemed to be unclean in the Old Testament (cf. 1 Macc. 1:47, 62; Acts 10:14; 11:8). It is quite clear that the legitimacy of eating foods forbidden by the Old Testament is the subject of discussion in Romans 14:20: "Do not, for the sake of food, destroy the work of God. Everything is indeed clean, but it is wrong for anyone to make another stumble by what he eats." The term translated "clean" (*katharos*) often refers to what is considered to be pure (e.g., Lev. 10:10; Deut. 14:20; 23:11 LXX). What is remarkable is that Paul declares foods that are forbidden by the Old Testament law and the Mosaic covenant to be clean (cf. also Col. 2:16, 20–22). Such a conclusion indicates that believers are no longer required to obey the stipulations of the Mosaic law, and this in turn suggests that the Mosaic covenant is no longer in force.

Finally, a few other observations confirm that the Mosaic law is no longer in force. Circumcision was mandated in the Mosaic law (Lev. 12:3). Indeed, Moses was nearly killed by the Lord himself because his son was uncircumcised (Exod. 4:24–26). Furthermore, Israel could not enter the Land of Promise without being circumcised (Josh. 5:1–9). But Paul clearly teaches that circumcision is no longer necessary to belong to the people of God (Rom. 4:9–12; 1 Cor. 7:19; Gal. 5:2–4, 6; 6:15). If the initiation rite into the Mosaic covenant is no longer required, then it follows that the covenant itself is no longer operative. In the same way, the Sabbath was a central part of the Mosaic covenant (e.g., Exod. 20:8–11), but Paul identifies the Sabbath along with the food laws as part of the shadows that give way to the substance, who is Christ himself (Col. 2:16–17). Similarly, in Romans Paul is unconcerned if one considers every day to be alike (Rom. 14:5–6). He almost certainly thinks of the Sabbath here, but he reckons it to be a matter of inconsequence. Paul's attitude of indifference relative to the Sabbath indicates that it is no longer normative. A new era has dawned in which the Mosaic covenant has passed away. This reading is confirmed by Ephesians 2:15. Jews and Gentiles in Christ are now one new man, for Christ has "[abolished] the law of commandments expressed in ordinances." In other words, one reason Jews and Gentiles are unified is that the requirements of the Mosaic covenant, which separated Jews from Gentiles, have become passé.

SUMMARY

There is abundant evidence in Paul that the old covenant had an interim character and that it is no longer operative since the coming of Christ. It is imperative that Christians today understand that we do not live any longer under the old covenant but the new covenant that has been inaugurated in Jesus Christ.

REFLECTION QUESTIONS

1. How does 2 Corinthians 3 support the notion that the old covenant is no longer in force?

2. Does Galatians 3 indicate that the Mosaic covenant is temporary? If so, how does it do so?

3. What are some specific indications in Romans that the law has passed away?

4. Does Paul's view on circumcision support the temporary nature of the Mosaic covenant?

5. What is the practical import for Christians today of Paul's teaching on the Mosaic covenant?

What Does the Phrase "Under Law" Mean in Paul?

The phrase "under law" (*hupo nomon*) occurs eleven times in Paul (Rom. 6:14, 15; 1 Cor. 9:20 [4 times]; Gal. 3:23; 4:4–5, 21; 5:18). It is immediately evident that the phrase is particularly important in Galatians since Paul uses it there most often. Some scholars argue that the term refers to the curse of the law or the condemnation that the law brings.[1] But neither of these interpretations works in Galatians 4:21, where Paul asks the Galatians if they want to be "under the law." Certainly they do not desire to be under the curse of the law or the condemnation of the law. Instead, the phrase should be interpreted in terms of redemptive history. The old era of redemptive history refers to the time period when the Mosaic covenant was operative. The Galatians wanted to turn the salvation-historical clock back and put themselves under the law again. But, as we shall see, such a move was fatal, for to be under law is to be under the power of sin.

The law functioned as a pedagogue "until" (*eis*) the coming of Christ (Gal. 3:24). Hence, believers were "under the law" until faith in Christ became a reality. Now that faith in Christ has arrived, believers are "no longer under the pedagogue" (Gal. 3:25, my translation). It should be noted here that "under the pedagogue" is equivalent to being "under the law," and the argument prosecuted here is distinctively redemptive historical, for the temporal difference between the old era and the new is emphasized. Indeed, in Galatians "under law" is matched with the phrases "under the pedagogue" (3:25), "under sin"

---

1. Cf. Wilson and Cranfield for the notion that the term means, respectively, under the curse of the law and the condemnation of the law (Todd A. Wilson, "'Under Law' in Galatians: A Pauline Theological Abbreviation," *JTS* 56 [2005]: 362–92; C. E. B. Cranfield, *A Critical and Exegetical Commentary on the Epistle to the Romans: Introduction and Commentary on Romans I–VIII*, ICC [Edinburgh: T & T Clark, 1975], 320).

(3:22), "under a curse" (3:10), and "under the elements" (4:3). We already have noted that to be under the law refers to the old era of salvation history, to the time period of the law. But those who belong to the previous era are also under a curse (3:10), for they fail to do what the law says. Indeed, those who are "under the law" are also under the power of sin (3:22). Therefore, Paul can say that those who are "under the law" are "enslaved under the elements of the world" (4:3, my translation). Therefore, those who are "under the law" need to be "redeemed" from their slavery so that they can be adopted as the children of God (4:5). Jesus Christ is the exception that proves the rule, for he was the only one who lived under the law and kept the law (4:4–5). Consequently, through his atoning death, he was able to liberate those under the law from the power of sin. The fullness of time—the fulfillment of God's redemptive purposes in Christ—spells the end of the law's reign.

Redemptive-historical and anthropological themes intersect with the expression "under law." On the one hand, the term refers to those who live under the law—the old period of redemptive history, before the fulfillment of the promise made to Abraham. On the other hand, when Israel lived under the law, sin dominated their experience. They were taken into captivity by both Assyria (722 B.C.) and Babylon (586 B.C.) because of their failure to do what God commanded. Those who were under the law, that is, those who lived under the Mosaic covenant, were also under the authority of sin.[2] When we grasp that those who are under law are also under sin, Paul's comment in Galatians 5:18 makes perfect sense. He says that those who "are led by the Spirit . . . are not under the law." This comment appears in the exhortation section of the letter, where Paul enjoins the Galatians to please the Lord by the power of the Holy Spirit. But how does Paul's claim that believers are not under the law fit with the admonition to please the Lord? Could it not be taken as a lax response to sin? Following the example of Paul, I respond, "By no means!" Indeed, the opposite is the case. We have seen that to be "under law" is equivalent to being under the power of sin. Israel's history verifies that those who are under the law are dominated by the power of sin. It follows, then, that the Pauline declaration in Galatians 5:18 fits beautifully with the exhortations in Galatians 5:13–6:10. Paul assures the Galatians that they are not under the law if they yield to the Spirit. In other words, if they are led by the Spirit, they will not be subject to sin, for those who are under the law are also under sin.

Such a reading of Galatians 5:18 fits well with Romans 6:14–15. Paul inquires in Romans 6 whether the grace of the gospel promotes sin, and he argues that it most certainly does not. Paul probably was responding to Jewish opponents here who criticized the Pauline gospel. They claimed that Paul's

---

2. I am not denying that there was a righteous remnant. Paul focuses on what was generally true in Israel's history, not the exceptions.

gospel was clearly false since it taught that the more we sin the more we see God's grace. Such a gospel, they complained, actually encourages sin and provides no basis for living an ethical life. In Romans 6, Paul responded to this objection in a number of ways. But his fundamental response was that those who raise such a criticism fail to understand his gospel, for the grace that is ours in the gospel does not encourage sin but triumphs over it. Hence, those who belong to Christ live a righteous life, for God's grace in Christ has broken the shackles of sin that bound us.

Indeed, Paul turned the tables on his Jewish opponents. He promised in Romans 6:14 that "sin will have no dominion over you." And why is it the case that sin will not rule over believers? Paul's answer on first glance is rather surprising—"since you are not under law but under grace." However, if the line of thought I have traced in the answer to this question has been followed, the Pauline response is actually perfectly sensible. Sin exercises control over those who live under the law, and this truth is confirmed by Israel's history under the Mosaic covenant and the law. Therefore, the power of sin is broken for those who are no longer under the old era of salvation history—for those who live in the new era inaugurated by Christ. It is those who are under the dominion of the law who are enslaved to sin, not those who enjoy the grace of Jesus Christ. Romans 6:14–15 promises liberation from the tyranny and mastery of sin for those who live in the new era of redemptive history.

Does 1 Corinthians 9:20–21 fit with the thesis advanced here? It might seem at first glance that it does not since Paul said that he put himself under the law when ministering to those under the law. Does that mean that Paul lived in the old era of salvation-history and actually lived under the dominion of sin when trying to win those under the law? Clearly not. What Paul says here actually accords with what I have argued above. Paul voluntarily placed himself under the law when he tried to save those under the law, but he immediately adds that he himself as a believer in Christ was not under the law. Strictly speaking, Paul was not under the law as a believer in Jesus Christ. He subjected himself to the law for limited periods of time and in certain situations for evangelistic purposes. Since Paul submitted to the law in order to gain those under the law, it is implied that those under the law are under the dominion of sin and need to be freed from its power.

SUMMARY

Paul's use of the phrase "under law" should be understood in redemptive-historical terms. Those who are under the law are also under the dominion and authority of sin. The history of Israel under the Mosaic covenant confirms the truth that those who lived under the law were subject to sin's mastery. Paul proclaims that believers are no longer under the law. A new era of salvation history has been inaugurated, and hence we have further evidence to confirm what was argued in question 9. The law has been abolished now that Christ has come. Believers are no longer under the law.

REFLECTION QUESTIONS

1. In what terms should we understand Paul's claim that believers are not under the law?

2. What is the relationship between being under the pedagogue and being under the law?

3. How does Israel's history support the idea that to be under law is to be under sin?

4. What does Paul mean when he says that those who are led by the Spirit are not under the law (Gal. 5:18)?

5. Since believers are no longer under the law, are they free to sin?

Are Gentiles Under the Law?

Gentiles are to be distinguished from Jews in that they "do not have the law" (Rom. 2:14). Therefore, Gentiles are said to be "without the law" (Rom. 2:12). When Paul thinks of those who have the law (Jews) and those who do not have the law (Gentiles), he distinguishes between sin and transgression. Gentiles, even though they do not possess the law, still sin. "All who have sinned without the law will also perish without the law" (Rom. 2:12). Transgression can be distinguished from sin, for "where there is no law there is no transgression" (Rom. 4:15). If we adopt this distinction, Gentiles did not transgress the law, for they did not have the written law. But even though they did not transgress a written law, they still sinned, in that they violated the will of God. Similarly, Paul argues that those who lived between the time of Adam and the time of Moses sinned, even if they did not transgress a specifically revealed commandment as Adam did or as the Israelites did under the Mosaic covenant (Rom. 5:14).

But why are Gentiles condemned for sin if they are ignorant of God's law? Even though they did not have a written law from God communicating what was right or wrong, they were familiar with "God's decree that those who practice such things deserve to die" (Rom. 1:32). God's "decree" or "ordinance" (*dikaiōma*) that those who practice evil deserve eternal death is not hidden from them. They know intuitively, presumably because God planted such knowledge in their hearts, that those who practice evil deserve death.

Paul's discussion in Romans 2:14–16 is quite illuminating when we consider whether Gentiles were under the law. We already have noted that Paul says that they were without the law and did not possess the law. On the other hand, Paul declares that they "are a law to themselves" (Rom. 2:14). As such, they occasionally keep the things that are mandated in the written law. Gentiles lack the written law, but the moral norms of the law are written on their hearts (Rom. 2:15). Their consciences either accuse or defend their behavior in accord with the law stamped on their hearts. Paul does not intend to provide a treatise here on natural law, so we should not expect all our questions to be answered. Paul's purposes are rather limited. He wants to show that Gentiles are not bereft of moral norms, for God's requirements are imprinted on their hearts.

Some scholars maintain that Paul refers to Christian Gentiles here, and thus the verses do not speak to the issue of whether unbelieving Gentiles know God's moral requirements.[1] A reference to believing Gentiles in Romans 2:12–16 is possible but unlikely for several reasons. First, the topic sentence of the paragraph refers to those who will perish without possessing the law, not those who will be justified (Rom. 2:12). Second, the obedience described in Romans 2:14 is occasional and sporadic, not a result of the Spirit's work in their hearts. Third, Romans 2:15 emphasizes the accusing role of thoughts, while acknowledging that in some instances ("even," *kai*) the law is kept. But such obedience is viewed as exceptional and unusual; it does not reach to the level where justification is gained (Rom. 2:13). Fourth, the certainty of judgment is emphasized by the concluding thought—the recognition that God will judge "the secrets of men by Christ Jesus" (Rom. 2:16). So, even though unbelieving Gentiles do not have God's written law, God's law—the moral precepts of the law—is imprinted on their hearts. God is righteous in judging them on the last day, for they knew what was morally praiseworthy and failed to carry it out.

It is difficult to discern whether Paul includes Gentiles in Romans 3:19: "Now we know that whatever the law says it speaks to those in the realm of the law" (my translation). Many scholars think that only Jews are intended. Paul has argued earlier in the letter, as noted above, that Gentiles are without the law (2:12–14). So, it seems strange to say now that they are in the realm of the law, for Paul has specifically placed them outside the law's realm. If we adopt this reading, then Paul's argument is as follows. If the Jews who possess so many covenant privileges fail to keep God's law (2:17–29), then surely the Gentiles cannot observe it either. Based on this interpretation, Paul moves from speaking to the Jews in 3:19a to the closing of "every mouth" and the guilt of "the whole world" before God (Rom. 3:19b).

Previously this interpretation seemed persuasive to me, but I now incline to the notion that Gentiles are included in those who are in the realm of the law for the following reasons. Strictly speaking, of course, the Gentiles did not possess the Mosaic law, as Romans 2:12–14 verifies. Still, Paul argues in that very text that the moral norms of the law are etched on their hearts. The catena of sins listed in Romans 3:9–18 focus on the moral infractions

---

1. Simon J. Gathercole, "A Law unto Themselves: The Gentiles in Romans 2.14–15 Revisited," *JSNT* 85 (2002): 27–49; C. E. B. Cranfield, *A Critical and Exegetical Commentary on the Epistle to the Romans: Introduction and Commentary on Romans I–VIII*, ICC (Edinburgh: T & T Clark, 1975), 155–63.

of which all people are guilty, including the Gentiles. Hence, in Paul's concluding statement in Romans 3:19 he may be placing Gentiles in the realm of the law in that they are fully aware of the moral norms stated in the law. Such a reading makes better sense of the following words, which declare that "every mouth" is shut and "the whole world" is guilty before God. Finally, in 3:20 Paul emphasizes that "no human being" (*pasa sarx*) is justified by the works of law, suggesting again that both Jews and Gentiles are in view. On balance, it seems slightly preferable that Paul includes the Gentiles as being in the realm of the law.

When we turn to Galatians, it seems that Paul also places the Gentiles under the law. The two texts that are most important for resolving this question are Galatians 3:23–25 and 4:1–11. Initially, it seems that only Jews are under the law, for Paul argues salvation historically in Galatians 3:23–25, declaring that "we were held captive under the law" (v. 23), that "the law was our guardian until Christ came" (v. 24), and "we are no longer under a guardian" (v. 25). Certainly the Jews must be the focus of Paul's comments here. We have seen already in Romans that Paul distinguishes between the Jews and Gentiles with respect to the law, affirming that Gentiles are not under the law. We see the same sort of distinction in Galatians 2:15, where Jews are distinguished from Gentile sinners. Nevertheless, it also seems that Paul, in a sense, places Gentiles under the law as well. For instance, God sent his Son "to redeem those who were under the law, so that we might receive adoption as sons" (Gal. 4:5). Some commentators have argued that those under the law here refers to Jews only, but it is more likely that the "we" who receive adoption in Galatians 4:5 refers to both Jews and Gentiles. Otherwise Paul would be undercutting one of the central themes of Galatians—that both Jews and Gentiles are adopted as sons. So, there is a sense in which he places the Gentiles under the law here, probably because they lived under the dominion of sin.

This interpretation is confirmed by Galatians 4:8–10. The Galatians are reproached for turning back to the weak elements after their conversion. Does Paul indict them for relapsing into paganism? Not precisely. It seems that the Galatians were beginning to observe "days and months and seasons and years" (4:10). Since the Galatians were tempted to submit to circumcision (5:2–4) and desired to come under the Old Testament law (4:21), it is likely that the observance of days here refers to the Old Testament calendar (cf. Gen. 1:14). Hence, pagan festivals are not in view. What is intriguing is that Paul characterizes observance of the Old Testament law as a return to the Gentiles' former ways. But the Gentiles were not taking up pagan practices again. It seems, then, that Paul lumps together adherence to the Old Testament law with pagan idolatry. Even though the Gentiles were not technically under the law, the life of the Jews under the law and the life of pagans in idolatry coalesce for Paul. In one sense, therefore, the Gentiles can be understood to be under the law.

SUMMARY

Even though Gentiles did not technically live under the Mosaic law, they are still considered to be in the realm of the law, for they have the law written on their hearts and know what God expects of them. Such a view seems to be reflected in Galatians, where the desire of the Gentiles to submit to the law is described as a return to paganism. Such an indictment makes sense if Paul sees the Gentiles in a sense to be under the law.

REFLECTION QUESTIONS

1. Does Romans 2:14–16 refer to Christian Gentiles or to unbelieving Gentiles?

2. How did Gentiles know the moral norms of the law since they lacked the written law?

3. Can unbelievers be saved by keeping the moral norms of the law?

4. How does the first person plural pronoun (i.e., "we") in Galatians place Gentiles under the law?

5. What role should natural law play in Christian theology today?

According to Paul, What Was the Purpose of the Law?

From one perspective the law was intended to give life to Israel. Paul says in Romans 7:10 that "the commandment was intended for life" (my translation). If one kept the law, then the law would be a vehicle for life. If one looks at the law from this restricted perspective, then the law was given to grant life for those who observed it. Nevertheless, what Paul emphasizes repeatedly is that God sovereignly intended the law to reveal transgressions and to bring about death. Are these two perspectives contradictory? Not at all. It is simply a matter of looking at the purpose of the law from two different perspectives. From an immanent perspective, the law was intended to give life; but from a transcendent perspective, it was given to increase sin. The former is not falsified or trivialized by the latter. The promise of life through the law was frustrated by human sin, not by any defect in the law.

The typical Jewish view was that the law was given to bring about life. In Judaism there was the proverb, "The more Torah the more life" (M. Aboth 2:7). This was the standard Jewish view, which is confirmed by a number of texts (Sir. 17:11; 45:5; Bar. 3:9; 4:1; *Pss. Sol.* 14:2; 2 Esd. 14:30; *2 Bar.* 38:2). We have already seen that Romans 7:10 reflects the same perspective, but Paul differs from his Jewish contemporaries in seeing a transcendent purpose to the law that is remarkably different. Jews typically believed that the law was given to counteract the sin Adam introduced into the world. Astonishingly, Paul argues that the law is not a solution but part of the problem: "Now the law came in to increase the trespass" (Rom. 5:20). The law at one level may have been given to bring life (Rom. 7:10), but it actually failed miserably to do so and increased transgressions instead. Such is Paul's argument in Romans 7:7–25. The content of the law is "holy and righteous and good" (Rom. 7:12). Nevertheless, the law has been co-opted by sin, so that sin has increased with the addition of the law. Sin has taken on the character of rebellion, in that commands forbidding particular actions, such as coveting, have actually promoted sin, because the command arouses the desire to do what is prohibited. The cancer that brings death should not be traced to the law but to the human being, who is dominated by the flesh.

If one looks at God's transcendent purpose, then, the law was given to increase sin and reveal sin. Such a conclusion is verified by Romans 2:1–3:20. Even though the Jews enjoyed the privilege of knowing God's law, the privilege brought no saving advantage since Israel transgressed the law. The law did not secure Israel's salvation but revealed her transgression and her hard and unrepentant heart (2:5). The law has disclosed that none is righteous, that all fall short of God's requirements (3:10–12). Indeed, "through the law comes knowledge of sin" (3:20). The law uncovers human sin and discloses to us our inability to please God through our obedience.

When we consider the purpose of the law, Galatians matches what we have found in Romans. Paul remarks in Galatians 3:19 that the law "was added because of transgressions." Scholars have interpreted this brief statement in different ways. Some have said that the law was added to *restrain* transgressions, others that the law was given to *define* transgressions, and still others that the law was added to *increase transgressions*. The first view is almost certainly wrong. Such a perspective would fit with the opponents in Galatia, who believed that the law was necessary to counter the impulse to sin. But Paul argues that it is those who are under the law who are under the power of sin (Gal. 5:18).

It is possible that the idea of defining sin is included in the Pauline meaning here, but there are powerful exegetical arguments supporting the notion that the law was added to increase transgressions. First, Paul declares that the law did not have the power to grant life, and thus righteousness cannot be obtained via the law (Gal. 3:21). The implication here is that the law produces death since it brings only a curse (Gal. 3:10). Second, the verbal words "imprisoned" and "held captive" (Gal. 3:22–23) suggest that the law locked up all under the authority of sin. Paul does not have in mind here the segregation of Jews from Gentiles, which would indicate that the law spared Israel from moral contamination, for we have seen that the issue here is whether the law is a source of life (Gal. 3:21). Instead of granting life, it imprisons human beings. Third, we have seen earlier that "under law" in Paul means that one is under the power and authority of sin (see question 10). The parallel in Galatians 4:3 and 4:5 is particularly instructive, for those who are "under the law" are also "under the elements." But those who are "under the elements" are "enslaved." Hence, the law does not restrain sin or even primarily define sin but enslaves those who are under its authority (cf. Gal. 4:9). Such an interpretation is confirmed by Galatians 4:21–26. The covenant at Sinai and the law led to slavery rather than freedom. The purpose of the law, it seems, is to enclose all under sin and to increase transgression so that all will see that salvation is available only through faith in Christ.

A negative purpose for the law is confirmed by 2 Corinthians 3:7–18. The letter of the law (i.e., the commands of the law) brings death (v. 6). Hence, Moses' ministry and the old covenant are a "ministry of death" (v. 7) and a "ministry of condemnation" (v. 9). They prepare human beings for the righteousness and life that come only through the Spirit and Christ.

If the purpose of the law is to reveal human sin and to increase transgressions, then how do we explain 1 Timothy 1:8–11?

> Now we know that the law is good, if one uses it lawfully, understanding this, that the law is not laid down for the just but for the lawless and disobedient, for the ungodly and sinners, for the unholy and profane, for those who strike their fathers and mothers, for murderers, the sexually immoral, men who practice homosexuality, enslavers, liars, perjurers, and whatever else is contrary to sound doctrine, in accordance with the gospel of the glory of the blessed God with which I have been entrusted.

One could interpret what Paul writes in 1 Timothy in at least two ways. First, Paul may be saying that the law was given to restrain sin and hinder the spread of ungodliness. Such a statement appears to contradict directly what Paul teaches elsewhere, for he often claims, as we have seen in this chapter, that the law advances sin. But if one adopts this interpretation, the contradiction is only apparent. In 1 Timothy Paul may consider the role of the law when it is accompanied by immediate reproof and punishment. If human beings are immediately reproved and punished for their sin, they desist from sinning in order to avoid punishment. The law, then, does not truly dampen sin in human hearts; it merely prevents the sin from being expressed outwardly due to the negative consequences. When Paul writes about the law increasing sin, he considers the law's impotence in conquering sinful inclinations. The desire to sin is not squelched by the law; instead the law fans the desire to sin into a flame. But if there is instant punishment, then human beings fear to translate into action the desires of their hearts.

Another possibility entirely accords with what we have argued about the law's provocation of sin. Paul may be saying that the false teachers in 1 Timothy had no idea of how to use the law, for the law's purpose is to reveal the iniquity of human hearts. If the false teachers truly understood the law, they would have comprehended that the law uncovers the depth of evil in human beings but it plays no role in conquering such evil. It is possible, however, that the false teachers believed that the law was the means God used to dethrone sin. Paul struck back by insisting that the law is not the source of life; it only reveals the cascading evil that flows in human hearts.

SUMMARY

The purpose of the law is to reveal human sin so that it will be clear that there is no hope in human beings. The law puts us to death so that life is sought only in Christ and him crucified.

REFLECTION QUESTIONS

1. What is the difference between the transcendent and immanent purpose of the law?

2. What was the typical Jewish perspective on the law?

3. Does Paul's statement in Romans 7:10 that the law was intended for life contradict his claim elsewhere that the law was given to increase sin (Rom. 5:20)?

4. Why would God give a law that puts us to death?

5. How should we teach and preach the death-dealing character of the law today?

How Do Paul's Negative Comments About the Law Fit with the Positive Statements About the Law in Psalm 19 and Psalm 119?

We saw in answering question 12 that the law increases transgression and puts us to death. It does not bring life but kills. How does this accord with the positive statements about the role of the law in Psalms 19 and 119? Psalm 19:7 says, "The law of the LORD is perfect, reviving the soul." Paul says the law puts to death, but this verse says the law grants life. Similarly, Psalm 119:93 says, "I will never forget your precepts, for by them you have given me life." The psalmist assigns life here to the precepts of the law, whereas Paul sees the law as multiplying transgressions. We find a very similar statement in Psalm 119:25: "My soul clings to the dust; give me life according to your word." It is possible, however, that in this last example that God's word should be understood as his promise, so that the psalmist is not asking the Lord to grant life via the commandment but by means of a word of promise. Other verses in the psalm support such an interpretation: "This is my comfort in my affliction, that your promise gives me life" (Ps. 119:50); and, "Plead my cause and redeem me; give me life according to your promise" (Ps. 119:154). Harder to assess is Psalm 119:156: "Great is your mercy, O LORD; give me life according to your rules." This verse seems closer to Psalm 19:7 and Psalm 119:93, where the law is said to grant life, and the law seems to refer in these instances to God's commands.

Despite initial appearance to the contrary, the psalmist does not contradict what we find in Paul. The writer of Psalm 119 recognizes that the power to keep God's precepts comes from God. Autonomous human beings are unable to please God or keep his law (cf. Rom. 8:7). For instance, we read in Psalm 119:159, "Give me life according to your steadfast love." Life comes from God's steadfast love, that is, from his grace and mercy. Human beings do not merit or gain life by observing the law. Psalm 119:88 is even clearer, "In your steadfast love give me life, that I may keep the testimonies of your mouth." Life comes only from the grace of God, and the *consequence* of such life is the keeping of God's testimonies and precepts. The psalmist does not teach that life is gained by obedience. Life finds its origin in God's gracious work. Surely this sentiment is very Pauline.

In some texts the psalmist emphasizes his obedience. For instance, he says, "My soul keeps your testimonies; I love them exceedingly" (Ps. 119:167; cf. vv. 22, 101, 102, 110, 121, 129). Such comments could be misunderstood, as meaning the psalmist was virtually perfect. On the contrary, he is keenly aware of his failures. The Psalm ends with the words, "I have gone astray like a lost sheep; seek your servant, for I do not forget your commandments" (Ps. 119:176). Apparently, the author is guilty of sin, and yet he does not conceive of himself as forgetting God's commands, even though he has gone astray.

The psalmist's desire does not match his practice. Hence, the psalm is filled with petition in which the author asks God to grant him strength to keep the law. "Let me not wander from your commandments" (Ps. 119:10), he says, and, "I will run in the way of your commandments when you enlarge my heart" (Ps. 119:32; cf. vv. 36, 37). The situation envisioned in Psalm 119 is complex. On the one hand, the psalmist keeps God's rules in contrast to the wicked. On the other hand, he is aware of his moral failings and entreats God to give him the desire to obey him. Any obedience carried out is traced to the grace of God.

But how does the psalmist's claim that "God grants life through his laws and precepts" fit with Paul's declaration that "the law kills"? The best solution recognizes an important distinction between the psalmist and Paul. When Paul says that the law kills and puts to death, he thinks of those in the flesh (Rom. 7:5)—those who are unregenerate (Rom. 8:7). The psalmist is not saying that the law grants life to those who are dead in their sins. The notion that the law actually can grant life to sinners is taught nowhere in the Old Testament or the New Testament. Hence, it seems most likely that the psalmist reflects on the role of the commands in those who already know God. The law can "revive" their affection for God and promote a desire to do his will when the Spirit uses the written word to convict and illumine those who already have new life. The commands of the law remind believers of their moral poverty—of their utter inability to do what God demands—and thus believers are revived through the gospel of Christ, which is the only source of life.

SUMMARY

Paul's negative statements on the law do not contradict Psalm 19 and Psalm 119. Paul emphasizes that the law puts human beings to death and never grants life to those who are unregenerate. Psalms 19 and 119 consider the situation of those who are regenerate. In that case God's commands by the work of his Spirit cast believers onto the grace of God, and God uses the commands in conjunction with his Spirit to strengthen believers so that they rely upon God's grace to please him.

REFLECTION QUESTIONS

1. What role does the law play in Psalms 19 and 119?

2. What evidence is there in Psalm 119 that the psalmist still struggled with sin?

3. Does the psalmist believe that the law can grant life to the unregenerate?

4. How does what the psalmist says positively about the law fit with Paul's negative statements about the law?

5. How should we preach and teach Psalm 19 and 119 now that the new covenant has been inaugurated?

Does Paul Distinguish Between the Moral, Ceremonial, and Civil Law?

A distinction between the moral, ceremonial, and civil law has been quite common in Christian theology.[1] A thorough statement that sets forth the distinctions is found in the Westminster Confession of Faith (19:3–5):

> Besides this law, commonly called moral, God was pleased to give to the people of Israel, as a Church under age, ceremonial laws, containing several typical ordinances, partly of worship, prefiguring Christ, his graces, actions, sufferings, and benefits; and partly holding forth divers instructions of moral duties. All which ceremonial laws are now abrogated under the New Testament.
>
> To them also, as a body politic, he gave sundry judicial laws, which expired together with the state of that people, not obliging any other, now, further than the general equity thereof may require.
>
> The moral law doth forever bind all, as well justified persons as others, to the obedience thereof; and that not only in regard of the matter contained in it, but also in respect of the authority of God the Creator who gave it. Neither doth Christ in the gospel any way dissolve, but much strengthen, this obligation.

The distinction between the moral, ceremonial, and civil law is appealing and attractive. Even though it has some elements of truth, it does

---

1. Longenecker traces the distinction back to Tertullian (A.D. 160–after 222). See Richard N. Longenecker, "Three Ways of Understanding Relations between the Testaments: Historically and Today," in *Tradition and Interpretation in the New Testament: Essays in Honor of E. Earle Ellis for His 60th Birthday*, ed. Gerald F. Hawthorne with Otto Betz (Grand Rapids: Eerdmans, 1987), 24, 31n. 9.

not sufficiently capture Paul's stance toward the law. As stated earlier, Paul argues that the entirety of the law has been set aside now that Christ has come. To say that the "moral" elements of the law continue to be authoritative blunts the truth that the entire Mosaic covenant is no longer in force for believers. Indeed, it is quite difficult to distinguish between what is "moral" and "ceremonial" in the law.[2] For instance, the law forbidding the taking of interest is clearly a moral mandate (Exod. 22:25), but this law was addressed to Israel as an agricultural society in the ancient Near East. As with the rest of the laws in the Mosaic covenant, it is abolished now that Christ has come. This is not to say that this law has nothing to say to the church of Jesus Christ today. As Dorsey says, it still has "a revelatory and pedagogical" function.[3]

Indeed, it could be said that, according to Paul, the law is both abolished and fulfilled in Christ (cf. Rom. 3:31). For instance, *circumcision* is no longer required to belong to the covenant people. Indeed, those who submit to it in order to be saved are cut off from Christ (Rom. 4:9–12; Gal. 2:3–5; 5:2–4; Phil. 3:2–3; Col. 2:11–12). In and of itself, circumcision is a matter of indifference (Gal. 5:6; 6:15; 1 Cor. 7:19). Even though circumcision, as a requirement of the old covenant, has passed away, the significance of circumcision also is fulfilled in Christ. Believers enjoy the circumcision of the heart through Christ's atonement and the work of the Holy Spirit (Phil. 3:3; Col. 2:11–12). Christians are not obligated to observe *Passover* since it an Old Testament festival. Indeed, the observance of days and festivals is a thing of the past (Rom. 14:5–6; Gal. 4:10; Col. 2:16–17). Nonetheless, Passover also points typologically to Christ, so that Christ is now the Passover sacrifice for Christians (1 Cor. 5:7). The same principle is evident in thinking of the *sacrifices* offered under the old covenant. Obviously, such sacrifices are passé with the inauguration of the new covenant under Jesus Christ. Still, such sacrifices find their fulfillment in Christ and therefore function typologically as pointers to Christ's sacrifice (cf. Rom. 3:25–26; 2 Cor. 5:21; Gal. 3:13).

If sacrifices function as a pattern, or model, for Christ's sacrifice, it is to be expected that the *temple* functions similarly. Paul does not explicitly argue that the temple and its sacrifices are passé for believers. Obviously, the temple is part of the old covenant and therefore no longer in force, along with the other prescriptions in the old covenant. Paul's words about how the temple relates to believers point to both its abrogation and its fulfillment. The church of Jesus Christ is now God's temple—the habitation of the living

---

2. See David A. Dorsey, "The Law of Moses and the Christian: A Compromise," *JETS* 34 (1991): 329–30. This article also may be accessed at http://www.etsjets.org/files/JETS-PDFs/34/34-3/34-3-pp321-334_JETS.pdf.
3. Ibid., 325. Dorsey helpfully discusses how the command that forbids the taking of interest applies to believers today (p. 333).

God (cf. 1 Cor. 3:16–17; 2 Cor. 6:16; Eph. 2:21).[4] In addition, since the Holy Spirit indwells believers, their bodies are "a temple of the Holy Spirit" (1 Cor. 6:19). Since the temple in Jerusalem along with the sacrificial cult is part of the old covenant, believers are under no obligation to worship at the temple or to offer sacrifices. The physical temple in Jerusalem seems to be irrelevant to Paul, which is quite astonishing since it was one of the three pillars of Judaism. Still, what the old covenant says about the temple finds its fulfillment in Christ—in Christ and the Spirit indwelling the church and individual believers.

The *food and purity regulations*, which were required under the Mosaic covenant, also have passed away. In Paul's discussion on the status of clean and unclean foods in Romans 14, he clearly teaches that all foods are clean (Rom. 14:14, 20), which stands in radical opposition to what the Old Testament teaches (Lev. 11:1–44; Deut. 14:3–21; cf. also 1 Cor. 8:1–11:1). When Peter ceases to eat with Gentile believers in Antioch, presumably because they were not observing purity regulations, Paul rebukes him sharply (Gal. 2:11–14). We have no indication that he struggled with the idea that Peter might be right. So too, in Colossians 2:16–17, 20–23 Paul utterly rejects the notion that believers must abstain from certain foods. Such regulations are dismissed as shadows that belong to the old covenant, and they are no longer mandatory now that the "substance," Christ, has come. All foods are to be enjoyed as a gift from the Creator (1 Tim. 4:3). And yet Paul also sees a theme of fulfillment in the matter of foods. The cleaning out of leaven, which was required during the Feast of Unleavened Bread (Exod. 12:15–20), symbolizes that believers should not allow evil to infect the church (1 Cor. 5:6–8; Gal. 5:9).

When discussing Passover, I noted that believers are not required to observe the feasts, festivals, and special days of the Old Testament calendar. This includes *the Sabbath*, even though the Sabbath is part of the Ten Commandments (Exod. 20:8–11).[5] Such a judgment surprises some, but it must be recognized that the entirety of the Old Testament law is abrogated in Christ. Paul clearly teaches that Christians are free in regard to the observance of days. No day, in principle, holds pride of place above another (Rom. 14:5). Clearly, the Sabbath is included here; since it was observed weekly, it was *the* day that would naturally come to mind for readers. Colossians 2:16–17 makes this even clearer. The Sabbath belongs to the shadows of the old covenant and is a matter of indifference now that Christ has come. The word for "shadow" (*skia*) is the same term Hebrews uses for Old Testament sacrifices being outmoded (Heb. 10:1; cf. 8:5). Paul does not discuss how the Sabbath is fulfilled for Christians, but in the letter to the Hebrews the Sab-

---

4. Indeed, Jesus is the true temple, according to John (John 2:21), and the church is the temple by virtue of being united to him.
5. For a fuller discussion of the Sabbath, see question 37.

bath finds its fulfillment in the Sabbath rest granted by Jesus Christ (cf. Heb. 3:12–4:13).

Some scholars, especially those who are reconstructionists, declare that the civil law has not been abolished for believers.[6] Clearly, Paul did not believe that the civil law of the Old Testament should be the standard of law for the Roman Empire. The Mosaic covenant had passed away, so the judicial requirements were not binding on governing authorities (see question 39). It should be noted here that the distinction between "moral" and "civil" law is quite fuzzy. Many of the laws and penalties found in the civil code in the Old Testament have a moral nature. Now that Christ has come, however, the status of Israel as a distinct political entity—a kind of church and state combined together—is no longer significant. In Christ, Jews and Gentiles are one (Gal. 3:28). The cross of Jesus Christ has broken down the barrier between Jews and Gentiles, and they are equally members of the people of God (Eph. 2:11–22; 3:4–6). Israel's role as a political and national entity has ended, and now believers from every tribe, tongue, people, and nation belong to the one people of God.

I am not suggesting from the above comments that Old Testament "civil" laws have no relevance to nation states today. Rather, how and whether those laws apply requires careful theological discussion. One cannot simply declare that these laws apply to modern nations simply because they are in scripture. The attempt of Christian reconstructionists to mandate the "civil" laws of the Old Testament is unpersuasive, for they fail to detect sufficiently the differences between the old covenant and the new.

On the one hand, the "civil" laws of the Old Testament are no longer in force, and yet we have a hint that Paul sees such laws as fulfilled in Christ as well. In 1 Corinthians 5, Paul requires the church to expel the man committing incest from the church. The mandate to remove him is expressed in the final words of 1 Corinthians 5:13, "Purge the evil person from among you." Paul here picks up the language of Deuteronomy, where the same language is used to denote the death sentence that the community of Israel must impose upon those who are guilty of blatant sins. Hence, the idolater must be put to death, "so you shall purge the evil from your midst" (Deut. 17:7). A comparison of the Greek clearly shows that Paul draws on Deuteronomy. Indeed, this phrase or one very similar appears on a number of occasions in Deuteronomy (lxx) for those who are to be put to death (cf. Deut. 17:12; 19:19; 21:21; 22:21, 22, 24; 24:7). Nonetheless, a remarkable difference is evident between the Old Testament and the New Testament. In the Old Testament the evil person is put to death, for Israel is both a political entity and a spiritual people. In the New Testament, however, the evil person is not put to death but removed from the church of Jesus Christ. The law is both abolished and fulfilled. It is abolished, for believers are no longer called upon to execute those who commit the sins

---

6. For a fine survey of various views on the law, see Dorsey, "Law of Moses," 321–24.

specified in Deuteronomy, but it does not follow that the command to purge evil from the community has no relevance to the church. It finds its fulfillment in the expulsion of the evil person from the church of Jesus Christ.

We have seen thus far that it is overly simplistic to say that the ceremonial and civil law have passed away, while the moral law still retains validity. Instead, the Mosaic law and covenant are no longer normative for believers. And yet at the same time the law finds its fulfillment in Christ. Further, even though the divisions of ceremonial, civil, and moral have some cogency, they are not clearly articulated in the New Testament, and the distinction between what is moral, civil, or ceremonial is not always clear.

Still, the distinction has some usefulness, for some of the commands of the law are carried directly over to the New Testament by Paul and applied to the lives of believers. It seems appropriate to designate such commands as moral norms. For instance, the injunction to honor fathers and mothers still applies to believers (Eph. 6:2). Paul teaches that love fulfills the law (Rom. 13:8–10), but he clarifies that those who love will not commit adultery, murder, steal, or covet (cf. Rom. 2:21–22; 7:7–8). Those who live according to the Spirit fulfill the requirement of the law (Rom. 8:4). The prohibition against idolatry still stands, though Paul does not cite the Old Testament law in support (1 Cor. 5:10–11; 6:9; 10:7, 14; 2 Cor. 6:16; Gal. 5:20; Eph. 5:5; Col. 3:5). Other commands and prohibitions that reflect the Ten Commandments are found in Paul as figure 3 illustrates.

FIGURE 3: COMMANDS AND PROHIBITIONS THAT REFLECT THE TEN COMMANDMENTS

Honoring and obeying parents	Rom. 1:30; Eph. 6:1–3; Col. 3:20; 1 Tim. 1:9; 2 Tim. 3:2
Murder	Rom. 1:29; 13:9; 1 Tim. 1:9
Adultery	Rom. 2:22; 7:3; 13:9; 1 Cor. 6:9; cf. 1 Tim. 1:10
Stealing	Rom. 1:29–30; 1 Cor. 6:9–10; Eph. 4:28
Lying	Col. 3:9; 1 Tim. 1:10; 4:2; Titus 1:12
Coveting	Rom. 1:29; 7:7–8; Eph. 5:3, 5; Col. 3:5

What do we make of this state of affairs? How can Paul teach that the Mosaic law is abolished and then cite some of its commands as authoritative? It is perhaps instructive to note that in most instances Paul does not argue that the moral norms from the Old Testament are authoritative on the basis of their appearance in the Old Testament, though in some instances he does cite the Old Testament command (e.g., Rom. 13:9; Eph. 6:2–3). We have seen earlier that the law is both abolished and fulfilled. What we typically call the moral norms of the law are fulfilled, at least in some measure, in the lives of believers. Nevertheless, they are not normative merely because they appear in the Mosaic covenant, for that covenant has passed away. It seems that they are normative because they express the character of God. We know that they still express God's will for believers because they are repeated as moral norms in the New Testament. It is not surprising that in the welter of the laws we find in the Old Testament (613 according to the rabbis) that some of those laws express transcendent moral principles. Still, the mistake we make is trying to carve up neatly the law into moral and nonmoral categories. Many of the so-called "ceremonial" laws have a moral dimension that cannot be jettisoned. They are not applicable to believers today because we live in a completely different cultural situation. Dorsey in particular has demonstrated that the cultural and geographic setting for Old Testament Israel is dramatically different from the cultural and geographic background of most Christians today.[7] The fundamental reason the laws of Israel are not binding upon believers is that Christians do not live under the covenant given to Israel.

SUMMARY

The division of the law into moral, ceremonial, and civil categories has some usefulness. Still, neither Paul nor any other New Testament writer explains the role of the law by appealing to such categories.[8] Instead, Paul argues that the law is both abolished and fulfilled in Christ. David Dorsey puts it this way: the entire Mosaic law is abolished, but it continues to be "binding . . . in a revelatory and pedagogical sense."[9] How this abolition and fulfillment work out must be discerned by consulting all that Paul teaches about the law.

REFLECTION QUESTIONS

1. Why have believers throughout history often found it helpful to distinguish between the moral, civil, and ceremonial law?

---

7. Ibid., 325–29.
8. Some might appeal to 1 Corinthians 7:19 to establish distinctions between moral and ceremonial law. What is lacking, however, is a clear hermeneutical distinction between moral and ceremonial law. To put it another way, Paul does not indicate that he used such a principle as a rule for interpreting the Old Testament law. Furthermore, the commandments of God in 1 Corinthians 7:19 should not be limited to the Old Testament moral law in any case. In context, it probably includes the prohibition of divorce and remarriage, which stems from the teaching of Jesus (1 Cor. 7:10–11).
9. Dorsey, "Law of Moses," 325.

2. What is the major problem with splitting the law into the categories of moral, civil, and ceremonial?

3. Why is it more helpful to think in terms of the law being entirely abolished and yet fulfilled in Christ?

4. What does David Dorsey mean when he says that the law is "binding . . . in a revelatory and pedagogical sense"?

5. What is your own view on dividing the law into the moral, ceremonial, and civil categories?

Are Christians Under the Third Use of the Law?

John Calvin argued for the third use of the law, which means God's commands function as a rule for life:

> The third and principal use, which pertains more closely to the proper purpose of the law, finds its place among believers in whose hearts the Spirit of God already lives and reigns. For even though they have the law written and engraved upon their hearts by the finger of God, that is, have been so moved and quickened through the directing of the Spirit that they long to obey God, they still profit by the law in two ways. Here is the best instrument for them to learn more thoroughly each day the nature of the Lord's will to which they aspire, and to confirm them in the understanding of it. . . . For no man has heretofore attained to such wisdom as to enable, from the daily instruction of the law, to make fresh progress toward a purer knowledge of the divine will. Again, because we need not only teaching but also exhortation, the servant of God will also avail himself of the benefit of the law: by frequent meditation upon it to be aroused to obedience, be strengthened in it, and be drawn back from the slippery path of transgression. In this way must the saints press on; for, however eagerly they may in accordance with the Spirit strive toward God's righteousness, the listless flesh always so burdens them that they do not proceed with due readiness. The law is to the flesh like a whip to an idle and balky ass, to arouse it to work. Even for a spiritual man not yet free of the weight of the flesh the law remains a constant sting that will not let him stand still.[1]

---

1. *Institutes* 2.7.12; from *Calvin: Institutes of the Christian Religion*, 2 vols., ed. John T. McNeill, trans. Ford Lewis Battles, LCC (Philadelphia: Westminster, 1960).

Calvin emphasizes the role of the law in living the Christian life, seeing it as a guide that provides moral guidance and instruction. We see the same teaching in the Westminster Confession of Faith (19:6):

> Although true believers be not under the law as a covenant of works, to be thereby justified or condemned; yet is it of great use to them, as well as to others; in that, as a rule of life, informing them of the will of God and their duty, it directs and binds them to walk accordingly; discovering also the sinful pollutions of their nature, hearts, and lives; so as, examining themselves thereby, they may come to further conviction of, humiliation for, and hatred against sin; together with a clearer sight of the need they have of Christ, and the perfection of his obedience. It is likewise of use to the regenerate, to restrain their corruptions, in that it forbids sin, and the threatenings of it serve to show what even their sins deserve, and what afflictions in this life they may expect for them, although freed from the curse thereof threatened in the law. The promises of it, in like manner, show them God's approbation of obedience, and what blessings they may expect upon the performance thereof; although not as due to them by the law as a covenant of works: so as a man's doing good, and refraining from evil, because the law encourageth to the one, and deterreth from the other, is no evidence of his being under the law, and not under grace.

Martin Luther, on the other hand, rejected the notion of a third use of the law, arguing that the entire law was abolished for Christians. Various quotes from Luther illustrate his view of the law:[2]

- "Here the law of Moses has its place. It is no longer binding on us because it was given only to the people of Israel." (p. 164)

- "To be sure, the Gentiles have certain laws in common with the Jews, such as these: there is one God, no one is to do wrong to another, no one is to commit adultery or murder or steal, and others like them. This is written by nature into their hearts." (p. 164)

- "Moses has nothing to do with us. If I were to accept Moses in one commandment, I would have to accept the entire Moses . . . Moses is dead. His rule ended when Christ came. He is of no further service." (p. 165)

---

2. Martin Luther, "How Christians Should Regard Moses," in *Luther's Works*, vol. 35, *Word and Sacrament*, ed. Helmut T. Lehmann (general editor) and E. Theodore Bachman (Philadelphia: Muhlenberg Press, 1960), 161–74.

- "We will regard Moses as a teacher, but we will not regard him as our lawgiver—unless he agrees with both the New Testament and the natural law." (p. 165)

- "Thus I keep the commandments which Moses has given, not because Moses gave commandment, but because they have been implanted in me by nature." (p. 168)

- "Thus we read Moses not because he applies to us, that we must obey him, but because he agrees with natural law." (p. 172)

Strictly speaking, the idea that believers are under the third use of the law is mistaken, for we have seen that the entire law is abolished for believers. Still, the notion is not entirely wrong since Paul's teaching is filled with exhortations that call upon believers to live in a way that pleases God. As we saw in the previous question, some of the commands are from the Old Testament law, and surely they function as a standard for the lives of believers today. Still, derivation from the Old Testament does not make them authoritative. They are God's will for human beings because they represent God's character. Even though the Old Testament law is not literally binding upon believers, we see principles and patterns and moral norms that still apply to us today since the Old Testament is the word of God.

SUMMARY

Calvin and Luther had different positions on the third use of the law. Luther is closer to the truth on this matter than Calvin, for he sees more clearly that the Old Testament law is not normative for believers, and that believers are no longer under the Mosaic covenant. Nonetheless, the difference between Luther and Calvin on this matter should not be exaggerated, since they both believed that there are moral norms for believers, and many of these moral norms are found in the Old Testament. Hence, the Old Testament still has an instructive role for believers today and plays a vital role in Christian ethics.

REFLECTION QUESTIONS

1. What is the third use of the law?

2. What was Calvin's view of the third use of the law?

3. How does Luther's view differ from Calvin's?

4. What are the problems with supporting a third use of the law?

5. In what sense are Calvin and Luther rather close to one another on this matter even though they differ on the question?

QUESTION 16

What Is the "Law of Christ"?

The law of Christ is mentioned only twice in the New Testament. In Galatians 6:2 Paul calls upon the Galatians to "bear one another's burdens, and so fulfill the law of Christ" (*ton nomon tou Christou*). And in 1 Corinthians 9:21 he says that he is "under the law of Christ" (*ennomos Christou*). What Paul means by the law of Christ has provoked extensive discussion.[1] Some argue that the phrase is polemical in Galatians, that is, Paul comes up with the expression in response to opponents, and hence the expression is a play on words. Paul initially may have coined the phrase in reacting to adversaries, though clear evidence is lacking in context to demonstrate the phrase is only polemical. It is legitimate, therefore, to investigate the Pauline meaning of the expression.

Others have suggested that Paul refers to the teaching of Jesus and identifies it as a new law for believers.[2] Instead of the Old Testament Torah, the teachings of Jesus are the new law for believers. Certainly Paul often alludes to the teaching of Jesus, and Jesus' words are authoritative for him. Nevertheless, explicit citations of Jesus' teaching in Paul are rare. Paul regularly alludes to Jesus' words without informing his readers that he appeals to Jesus' teaching. Therefore, it seems unlikely that the law of Christ refers explicitly to Jesus' teaching. If Jesus' teaching were the new Torah for believers, we would expect that Paul would clearly and unambiguously and often indicate to readers that he was citing the words of Jesus. Remarkably, it is infrequent for Paul to use an introductory formula of some kind to signal to his readers that the words came from Jesus (cf. 1 Cor. 7:10–11; 11:23–26; 1 Thess. 4:15).

---

1. See Todd A. Wilson, "The Law of Christ and the Law of Moses: Reflections on a Recent Trend in Interpretation," *Currents in Biblical Research* 5 (2006): 123–44.
2. W. D. Davies, *Paul and Rabbinic Judaism*, 4th ed. (Philadelphia: Fortress, 1980), 142–44; C. H. Dodd, "ENNOMOS CHRISTOU," in *Studia Paulina in honorem J. de Zwaan* (Haarlem: Bohn, 1953), 96–110.

I conclude that the law of Christ does not clearly refer to the tradition of Jesus' teachings.

A rather similar view is that the law of Christ should be identified as the Zion Torah. According to this view, the Mosaic law is abolished while the Zion Torah is established. The Zion Torah hails from Zion (Isa. 2:1–4; Mic. 4:1–4) and is eschatological (Jer. 31:31–34) and universal.[3] This view rightly sees that the Mosaic law is no longer valid, but it is unclear that the Old Testament envisions a different law that comes from Zion.[4]

It seems most promising to identify the law of Christ with the admonition to love one another (Gal. 5:14), for there is a clear link between Galatians 5:14 and 6:2. The Old Testament law "is fulfilled" (*peplērōtai*) in the injunction to love one's neighbor as oneself (Lev. 19:18 in Gal. 5:14). And the law of Christ "is fulfilled" (*anaplērōsete*) when believers fulfill one another's burdens (Gal. 6:2). If we carry the burdens of other believers, we show our love for them. Sacrificial love for fellow believers, then, fulfills the Old Testament law and the law of Christ. Such a reading fits with Romans 13:8–10, where the Old Testament law is capsulized in the admonition to love one another. We also could say that Christ's life, and the sacrifice of his life in his death, exemplifies to the uttermost the law of Christ. That is, Christ's life and death are the paradigm, exemplification, and explanation of love.[5] However, Romans 13:8–10 guards us from oversimplifying the nature of Christ's law, for love is expressed when believers fulfill moral norms. The law of Christ is exemplified by a life of love, but such love is expressed in a life of virtue.

Seeing the law of Christ as the law of love fits well with the Pauline discussion in 1 Corinthians 9. First Corinthians 9 is placed in the midst of Paul's discussion on food offered to idols (1 Cor. 8:1–11:1). The fundamental problem with what we will call "the knowers" (because they were so proud of their knowledge) was their selfishness, for they exalted their right to eat idol food instead of showing love to the weaker believers (1 Cor. 8:1–13). Weaker believers could not shed the idea that idols were a reality, and therefore they were scandalized when others ate food that was offered to idols. Apparently some of the weak tried to be like "the knowers" and ate idol food, even though in their conscience they thought such eating was wrong. By eating, however,

---

3. Harmut Gese, *Essays on Biblical Theology* (Minneapolis: Augsburg, 1981), 80–92; Peter Stuhlmacher, *Reconciliation, Law, and Righteousness* (Philadelphia: Fortress, 1986), 110–33, esp. 114–17.

4. See Martin Kalusche, "'Das Gesetz als Thema biblischer Theologie'? Anmerkungen zu einem Entwurf Peter Stuhlmachers," *ZNW* 77 (1986): 194–205.

5. So Richard B. Hays, "Christology and Ethics in Galatians: The Law of Christ," *CBQ* 49 (1987): 268–90. Hays has modified his view, seeing in addition a reference to the fulfilling of Torah, which fits with what is being argued here. See "The Letter to the Galatians: Introduction, Commentary, and Reflections," *The New Interpreter's Bible*, vol. 11 (Nashville: Abingdon, 2000), 333.

they violated their own sense of right and wrong and began to live on the basis of the convictions of others instead of their own convictions. Those who surrender their own convictions are in danger of destruction, for their behavior is no longer grounded on their own convictions and conscience. Love protects the weakness of others and does not exploit their uncertainty. The knowers should abstain from idol food for the sake of the weak.

Paul appeals to his own example in chapter 9, pointing out that he surrendered his right to be paid as a minister of Christ. Paul deserved to be supported financially since the worker is worthy of his wages, but he desired to remove any obstacle to the gospel, and thus he refused to accept payment. Paul did not live on the basis of his rights. He gave them up for the sake of others, so that more would be converted to Christ. Paul's reference to the law of Christ appears in 1 Corinthians 9:19–23, where Paul emphasizes that he adjusted his behavior so that it accorded with those to whom he ministered. If Paul was with Gentiles, he lived free from the law. If he was with those who observed the law, then he kept the law as well. Paul's flexibility, whereby he adapted himself to his hearers, demonstrated his sacrificial love.

First Corinthians 9:20–21 makes it clear that Paul was no longer under the law. He no longer lived under the authority of the Mosaic covenant, for that covenant had passed away now that Christ had come. Nevertheless, he willingly subjected himself to the law if he ministered to Jews in order to avoid giving offense. In conforming to the law when he was with the weak, he was able to proclaim the gospel to them. When he ministered to Gentiles, however, Paul did not observe the law since he was not obligated to keep it. It is quite likely that Paul thinks particularly of purity laws here, which, if Paul insisted on them, would hinder table fellowship with Gentiles.

It is clear, then, that Paul was free from the Mosaic law. Yet, he adds a qualification, emphasizing that he was still subject to Christ's law. Freedom from the Mosaic law does not mean that Paul was liberated from all moral norms. Freedom from the law does not mean freedom from ought; it is not the pathway to libertinism. Furthermore, the law of Christ to which Paul was subject focuses in this context on the imperative of loving one another. Paul adjusted his lifestyle, whether he was with Jews or Greeks, weak or strong, because of his love for others, so that he could win them to the gospel of Christ.

SUMMARY

I have argued from both Galatians and 1 Corinthians that the law of Christ should be defined as the law of love. We see in 1 Corinthians 9 that Paul's flexibility and sacrifice on behalf of his hearers represents the same kind of sacrificial love that Christ displayed in going to the cross. The life of Christ, then, exemplifies the law of love. It would be a mistake to conclude that there are no moral norms in the law of Christ, for Romans 13:8–10 makes it clear, as do many other texts in Paul, that the life of love cannot be separated from moral norms.

REFLECTION QUESTIONS

1. What is the problem of limiting the law of Christ to the teachings of Jesus?

2. Why is it inadequate to define the law of Christ in terms of the Zion Torah?

3. What are the central texts for understanding the law of Christ?

4. What is the relationship between the law of Christ and the law of love?

5. Should the law of Christ be explained in terms of the paradigm of Jesus' life and his sacrificial death?

Is the Law Fulfilled Through Love?

Two crucial texts in Paul indicate that the answer to this question is yes, but we need to explain carefully what an affirmative answer means. First, Galatians 5:13–14 affirms, "For you were called to freedom, brothers. Only do not use your freedom as an opportunity for the flesh, but through love serve one another. For the whole law is fulfilled in one word: 'You shall love your neighbor as yourself.'" Second, Romans 13:8–10 says, "Owe no one anything, except to love each other, for the one who loves another has fulfilled the law. For the commandments, 'You shall not commit adultery, You shall not murder, You shall not steal, You shall not covet,' and any other commandment, are summed up in this word: 'You shall love your neighbor as yourself.' Love does no wrong to a neighbor; therefore love is the fulfilling of the law."

Obviously, Paul teaches in both of these verses that love fulfills the law. The heart and soul of the Pauline ethic is love (cf. Rom. 12:9). The "knowers" in Corinth may possess knowledge, but they must beware of pride and focus on edifying others in love (1 Cor. 8:1). Some of the Corinthians thought they belonged to the spiritual elite because of the spiritual gifts they exercised, especially if they had the gift of tongues. But Paul reminds them that love, rather than one's spiritual gifting, is the measure of spiritual maturity (1 Cor. 13:1–13). Love is the goal of Paul's instruction (1 Tim. 1:5), and love sums up all the virtues (Col. 3:14).

If particular commands of the law take precedence over love, then Paul would have fallen into casuistry (i.e., resolving specific cases of conduct through overly subtle reasoning). In that case something like a Mishnah would fit the Pauline ethic; specific commands would be needed to explain the right course of action in every situation. But Paul emphasizes that the law points to love rather than vice versa. Believers must discern in every situation what is loving.

Life is much too complex and variegated to codify what one should do in every circumstance. Hence, believers are called upon "to discern what is pleasing to the Lord" (Eph. 5:10) in every situation. Indeed, we are called upon to pray, so that we will gain "spiritual wisdom and understanding," which in turn will help us live in a way that pleases God (Col. 1:9–10). Similarly, Paul prays in Philippians that love will grow but that it will be shaped by "knowledge and all discernment" (Phil. 1:9). The result is that believers will be enabled to "approve what is excellent" (Phil. 1:10). Both of these prayers illustrate the point being articulated here, for the loving thing to do is not always evident. It takes maturity, wisdom, and prayer to assess what is fitting and loving in the concrete details of everyday life. The loving course of action cannot be spelled out in advance through detailed laws. Many situations we face cannot be charted out beforehand, so Paul calls upon believers to reflect on what is the loving way to respond.

If love is the heart and soul of the Pauline ethic, Romans 13:9 warns us against another common error. If it is a serious mistake to turn Paul into a legalistic casuist, it is equally wrong to say that moral norms can be separated from love. Love fulfills the moral norms that reflect the character of God. Hence, no one can credibly claim to follow the pathway of love if he or she commits adultery, murders, steals, covets, etc. Paul speaks principally here, for he clarifies that what he says applies to "any other commandment." Love cannot be exhausted by commandments, but it does not violate them either. Commandments do not capture the whole of love or even the essence of love, but they do encapsulate a particular dimension of love. What Paul says about commandments saves us from sentimentality and deception. Sentimentality defines love in terms of feelings and thus is liable to excuse immorality. For instance, Paul prohibits divorce (1 Cor. 7:10–11), but sentimentality may justify it, and hence contradict what is truly loving. Love is like a river that replenishes the human spirit, but moral norms provide boundaries so that the river is not dispersed abroad but retains its strength and power. Because human beings are sinners, they are prone to deceit and may identify as righteous a course of action that is contrary to love. Moral norms stipulate the nature of love, clarifying what is righteous and what is unrighteous.

SUMMARY

According to Paul, the intention and purpose of the law is fulfilled when we love one another. Moral norms explicate the pathway of love, charting out how love expresses itself. And yet love is not summed up in the keeping of commandments, for one may keep the commandments and still fail to love.[1]

---

1. The New Testament, of course, often *commands* believers to love one another and to love their enemies. The issue I am exploring here is the *content* of love. Other commands help us to see what love looks like in action.

Love is more than keeping the commandments, even if it is not less than keeping them. Love always seeks what is edifying and good for others and does not content itself with calculating whether one has fulfilled the proper rule. In other words, love always seeks what will bring the most glory to God in the life of one's neighbor.

REFLECTION QUESTIONS

1. What is the problem with understanding the law in terms of moral casuistry?

2. Why do we still need moral norms to define love?

3. What is some textual evidence in Paul for the centrality of love?

4. Do you agree that "love is more than keeping commands, even if it is not less than keeping them"?

5. How does the call to love fit with the centrality of the gospel of grace?

Questions Related to Justification

What Is the Old Testament Background for the Righteousness of God?

In most cases the word *righteousness* in the Old Testament refers to conduct and behavior that is pleasing to God. But the aim of this question is to investigate righteousness in the Old Testament insofar as it casts light on the Pauline theology of justification. Hence, the ethical meaning of righteousness in the Old Testament will not be pursued here, except insofar as it relates to justification.

It is common in Old Testament scholarship to say that righteousness has to do with fulfilling the requirements of a covenant relationship instead of conformity to a norm. For instance, Tamar is judged to be more righteous than Judah, even though she offered herself to him as a prostitute, for she was faithful to what was expected in their relationship, whereas Judah was unfaithful in that he held back his sons from Tamar (Gen. 38:26). But this common interpretation is flawed and should be rejected. Righteousness in the Old Testament does have to do with conformity to a norm—to meeting an ethical standard. This is not to say that righteousness has nothing to do with covenant relationships. There is not an either-or here. Righteousness means that one fulfills covenantal obligations *and* that one conforms to a norm. Tamar was "more righteous" than Judah in carrying out the obligations of the covenant, but there is also an implication that she came closer to meeting a moral norm. In the whole sordid affair, she was more righteous than Judah, and so she did not deserve to be executed. But the narrator also suggests that she was less than noble as well. To be "more righteous" should not be equated with being completely righteous.

A very important verse in understanding righteousness in the Old Testament is Leviticus 19:36: "You shall have just balances, just weights, a just ephah, and a just hin" (cf. Deut. 25:15; Ezek. 45:10). In other words, one must conform to a norm in matters of weights and measures. Justice means that people are charged fairly for goods and services rendered. The norms of the covenant are not arbitrary but are codified in the Old Testament law, which enshrines justice and righteousness. Justice must not be perverted, and thus judges are not to be partial to the poor or the rich (Exod. 23:3; Lev. 19:15; Deut. 1:17). As Deuteronomy 16:20 says, "Justice, and only justice, you shall follow, that you may live and inherit the land that the LORD your God is giving you" (cf. Amos 5:24). God himself is the norm of behavior, for "the Almighty" does not "pervert the right" (Job 8:3).

Another common notion is that God's righteousness both in the Old Testament and in Paul concerns only salvation and not judgment. Even though my focus is on the Old Testament, I will show briefly from the Old Testament and from Paul that this interpretation is mistaken. The psalmist declares that the Lord "judges the world with righteousness" (Ps. 9:8). This righteous judgment does mean deliverance for David (Ps. 9:4), but David's enemies will perish and be destroyed forever (Ps. 9:5–6). The Lord will avenge the blood of his own (Ps. 9:12) and will repay them for their sins (Ps. 9:15–16), so that they end up in Sheol (Ps. 9:17). Clearly, God's righteousness is not limited to salvation in this context. Similarly, Rehoboam and his princes confessed that the Lord was "righteous" in judging Israel (2 Chron. 12:6), by bringing Shishak, king of Egypt, against Judah (2 Chron. 12:1–5). There is no doubt here that God's righteousness consists in the judgment imposed upon Israel.

Nehemiah rehearses the history of Israel in Nehemiah 9, recounting the kindness of the Lord and the rebellion of Israel. Israel finally ended up being exiled because of her sin. Nevertheless, the Lord did not abandon his people despite their wickedness. How does Nehemiah explain the judgments that have come upon Israel? "Yet you have been righteous in all that has come upon us, for you have dealt faithfully and we have acted wickedly" (v. 33). Nehemiah 9 directly ties God's righteousness to the judgments that had been meted out to rebellious Israel, demonstrating that God's righteousness cannot be restricted to his saving righteousness.

Likewise, the author of Lamentations reflects on Israel's exile: "The LORD is in the right, for I have rebelled against his word" (Lam. 1:18). In what sense is the Lord in the right? It is unnecessary to rehearse the content of Lamentations 1 here, for it is evident that the Lord is righteous in judging Israel.

Finally, Daniel 9:14 testifies to the same theme: "Therefore the LORD has kept ready the calamity and has brought it upon us, for the LORD our God is righteous in all the works that he has done, and we have not obeyed his voice." Daniel says something quite similar to Lamentations. The calamity that has come upon Israel in her exile demonstrates God's righteousness in judging her. No one doubts that righteousness in the Old Testament often refers to God's saving righteousness, but it is abundantly clear from the texts cited that it also denotes in some instances his judging righteousness.

It is often said as well that in Paul righteousness is restricted to God's salvation, but again such an assertion is overstated. For instance, Romans 2:5 declares, "But because of your hard and impenitent heart you are storing up wrath for yourself on the day of wrath when God's righteous judgment [*dikaiokrisias*] will be revealed." God's eschatological wrath reflects his "righteous judgment," which is certainly not salvific. Indeed, the phrase "the righteousness of God" in Romans 3:5 probably refers to God's judgment of the wicked. Further, 2 Thessalonians 1:5 speaks of God's "righteous judgment." In context this judgment manifests itself in God's repayment of the wicked with vengeance on the day Jesus returns, so that they "suffer the punishment of eternal destruction" (2 Thess. 1:9). The root word for righteousness (*dik**) occurs several times in this text. Paul speaks of God's "righteous judgment" (*tēs dikaias kriseōs*, 2 Thess. 1:5), of God's "justice" (*dikaion*) in punishing the wicked (2 Thess. 1:6), of God's "vengeance" (*ekdikēsin*) on those who do not know God or obey the gospel (2 Thess. 1:8), and of the final "punishment" (*dikēn*) of "eternal destruction" for the wicked (2 Thess. 1:9).

The connection forged between these words certifies that Paul uses the language of righteousness for God's retributive punishment of the wicked. It is likely that the notion of God's judging righteousness is present in Romans 3:25–26 as well. God's holiness and justice are satisfied in Jesus' atoning sacrifice. To conclude, we have seen a number of examples in Paul and in the Old Testament in which God's righteousness includes the idea that he judges the wicked. The idea that God's righteousness is only salvific is a scholarly myth that needs to be exploded.

It is also instructive to note that righteousness in the Old Testament is often *forensic*. For instance, Deuteronomy 25:1 presupposes that judges will "acquit the innocent and condemn the guilty" (my translation). Clearly, the judges do not make a person righteous or guilty but declare whether the person under trial is innocent or guilty. God himself says that he "will not acquit the wicked" (Exod. 23:7), which means that he will not declare the wicked to be in the right. Similarly, Proverbs 17:15 declares, "He who justifies the wicked and he who condemns the righteous are both alike an abomination to the LORD." How such a declaration fits with the Pauline teaching on justification will be considered in the next question. What is evident here is that judges do not *make* someone righteous or wicked. They render a forensic declaration based on the reality that is before them. Unrighteous judges "acquit the guilty for a bribe" (Isa. 5:23; cf. 2 Sam. 15:4). God's righteousness as a judge is explained in Solomon's prayer as "condemning the guilty by bringing his conduct on his own head and vindicating the righteous by rewarding him according to his righteousness" (1 Kings 8:32).

The forensic character of righteousness comes to the forefront in Job, for Job longed to establish his innocence before the divine Judge. Eliphaz doubted Job's innocence and queried, "Can mortal man be in the right before

God?" (Job 4:17). Job asked the same question from a different framework, "But how can a man be in the right before God?" (9:2). Job insisted upon his innocence, "Though I am in the right, I cannot answer him; I must appeal for mercy to my accuser" (9:15). He even questioned God's justice: "Though I am in the right, my own mouth would condemn me; though I am blameless, he would prove me perverse" (9:20). Even if Job was innocent, the righteousness that should be declared to all is not acknowledged by others since he suffers humiliation: "If I am guilty, woe to me! If I am in the right, I cannot lift up my head, for I am filled with disgrace and look on my affliction" (10:15).

Zophar was convinced that Job was guilty: "Should a multitude of words go unanswered, and a man full of talk be judged right?" (Job 11:2; cf. 15:4; 22:3; 25:4; 33:12; 35:7) Job, on the other hand, was persuaded that he would be vindicated: "I know that I shall be in the right" (13:18; cf. 33:32).[1] Elihu was furious with Job for exalting himself over God: "He burned with anger at Job because he justified himself rather than God" (32:2). Elihu captured the essence of Job's protest: "For Job has said, 'I am in the right'" (34:5). Finally, God reproached Job: "Will you condemn me that you may be in the right?" (40:8). The book of Job testifies to the forensic character of righteousness, especially in the verbal form.

Three texts in Isaiah have a forensic character. "All the nations gather together, and the peoples assemble. Who among them can declare this, and show us the former things? Let them bring their witnesses to prove them right, and let them hear and say, It is true" (Isa. 43:9). The legal nature of the dispute is evident here. So too, in Isaiah 43:26 the Lord calls for a lawsuit, knowing that he will prevail: "Put me in remembrance; let us argue together; set forth your case, that you may be proved right." Perhaps most significantly, Isaiah speaks of the work of the Servant of the Lord: "Out of the anguish of his soul he shall see and be satisfied; by his knowledge shall the righteous one, my servant, make many to be accounted righteous, and he shall bear their iniquities" (Isa. 53:11). The forensic use of the verb elsewhere confirms that the verb should be interpreted similarly. Here we have the antecedent of the Pauline teaching on justification, for those who are full of iniquity are counted righteous through the work of the Servant. Similarly, Isaiah 45:25 says, "In the Lord all the offspring of Israel shall be justified and shall glory." Again, the verbal form should be construed forensically, which fits beautifully with the notion that salvation is entirely the work of the Lord.

The noun *righteousness* often refers in the Old Testament to God's saving righteousness. Abraham "believed the Lord, and he counted to him as righteousness" (Gen. 15:6). The righteousness was granted to Abraham as a gift, for he did not receive it by working for God but by believing in his promise. The righteousness given to Abraham does not constitute evidence of his transformation. It is a gift granted by God as a result of his faith. The gift-character of

---

1. The verbal form is used here (אֶצְדָּק) and it could be translated, "I shall be justified."

righteousness is clear from Deuteronomy 9:4–6, where the Lord impressed on Israel that their possession of the land cannot be ascribed to their own goodness.

> Do not say in your heart, after the LORD your God has thrust them out before you, "It is because of my righteousness that the LORD has brought me in to possess this land," whereas it is because of the wickedness of these nations that the LORD is driving them out before you. Not because of your righteousness or the uprightness of your heart are you going in to possess their land, but because of the wickedness of these nations the LORD your God is driving them out from before you, and that he may confirm the word that the LORD swore to your fathers, to Abraham, to Isaac, and to Jacob. Know, therefore, that the LORD your God is not giving you this good land to possess because of your righteousness, for you are a stubborn people.

These verses do not explicitly say that Israel's righteousness was an alien righteousness, but such an idea is implied. Israel received the land as a gift from the Lord.

The plural of the noun *righteousness* also is used to speak of God's righteous acts or his saving acts in the Old Testament. The ESV renders the plural noun in various ways, and hence the term under consideration is put in italics below. We read in Judges 5:11, "To the sound of musicians at the watering places, there they repeat *the righteous triumphs* of the LORD, *the righteous triumphs* of his villagers in Israel." The "righteous triumphs" of the Lord here refer to the salvation he brought in the victory of Barak and Deborah over Sisera. In Samuel's concluding speech as Israel's judge, he rehearsed the Lord's goodness to Israel, recounting the deliverance he accomplished from the Exodus onward: "Now therefore stand still that I may plead with you before the LORD concerning all *the righteous deeds* of the LORD that he performed for you and for your fathers" (1 Sam. 12:7). Again, "the righteous deeds" refer to God's saving acts for Israel.

When Daniel prayed for Israel in exile, confessing their sins, he asked the Lord to show mercy: "O Lord, according to all *your righteous acts*, let your anger and your wrath turn away from your city Jerusalem, your holy hill, because for our sins, and for the iniquities of our fathers, Jerusalem and your people have become a byword among all who are around us" (Dan. 9:16). When Daniel appealed to the Lord's "righteous acts," he asked the Lord to save Israel, despite their sin. Similarly, Micah called upon Israel to repent, reminding them of what the Lord did for them in the past: "O my people, remember what Balak king of Moab devised, and what Balaam the son of Beor answered him, and what happened from Shittim to Gilgal, that you may know *the saving acts* of the LORD" (Mic. 6:5). The translation "saving acts" is fitting, for even though Balak wanted Balaam to curse Israel, the Lord ordained that Israel be blessed and saved. God's "righteous acts" designate his grace, which he poured out in saving Israel.

The singular noun *righteousness* also is used often to refer to God's salvation of his people. For instance, Psalm 31:1 says, "In your righteousness deliver me!" God's righteousness here does not lead to judgment but to deliverance and salvation. When David pleaded with the Lord to forgive him of his sins with Bathsheba and Uriah, he said, "Deliver me from bloodguiltiness, O God, O God of my salvation, and my tongue will sing aloud of your righteousness" (Ps. 51:14). God's forgiveness and salvation here lead David to praise God for his saving righteousness.

Psalm 143 uses words for righteousness in an intriguing way. David entreated the Lord, "Enter not into judgment with your servant, for no one living is righteous before you" (v. 2). The Day of Judgment is feared since no one has lived in a way that pleases God. At the same time, David used "righteousness" in reference to God's salvation. "Hear my prayer, O Lord; give ear to my pleas for mercy! In your faithfulness answer me, in your righteousness!"(v. 1). How can God answer in his righteousness if David was unrighteous (v. 2)? Verse 11 helps in finding an answer: "For your name's sake, O Lord, preserve my life! In your righteousness bring my soul out of trouble!" (v. 11). God's righteousness here saves because it delivered David from trouble. The righteousness of God also stands in parallelism with his name, indicating that God exercises his saving righteousness to display the honor and glory of his name.

Often the word *righteousness* is parallel with terms like *steadfast love, faithfulness*, and salvation. This is apparent in a number of texts:

- "Steadfast love and faithfulness meet; righteousness and peace kiss each other. Faithfulness springs up from the ground, and righteousness looks down from the sky." (Ps. 85:10–11)

- "The Lord has made known his salvation; he has revealed his righteousness in the sight of the nations." (Ps. 98:2)

- "Shower, O heavens, from above, and let the clouds rain down righteousness; let the earth open, that salvation and righteousness may bear fruit; let the earth cause them both to sprout; I the Lord have created it." (Isa. 45:8)

- "I bring near my righteousness; it is not far off, and my salvation will not delay; I will put salvation in Zion, for Israel my glory." (Isa. 46:13)

- "My righteousness draws near, my salvation has gone out, and my arms will judge the peoples; the coastlands hope for me, and for my arm they wait. Lift up your eyes to the heavens, and look at the earth beneath; for the heavens vanish like smoke, the earth will wear out like a garment, and they who dwell in it will die in like manner; but my salvation will be forever, and my righteousness will never be dismayed. Listen to me, you who know righteousness, the people in whose heart is my law; fear not the reproach of man, nor be dismayed at their revilings. For the moth will eat them up like a garment, and the worm will eat them like wool; but my righteousness will be forever, and my salvation to all generations." (Isa. 51:5–8)

- "For Zion's sake I will not keep silent, and for Jerusalem's sake I will not be quiet, until her righteousness goes forth as brightness, and her salvation as a burning torch. The nations shall see your righteousness, and all the kings your glory, and you shall be called by a new name that the mouth of the LORD will give." (Isa. 62:1–2)

It is apparent from these texts that in these instances God's righteousness has to do with his saving righteousness by which he delivers his people from sin and evil.

Scholars debate whether God's righteousness, especially when it stands in parallelism with his salvation, faithfulness, and steadfast love, should be described as covenantal faithfulness. Many scholars answer this question in the affirmative, and we can see why this is so, given the parallel terms that are used. Mark Seifrid, however, has questioned this judgment, arguing that righteousness harkens back to creation but not to covenant since terms for righteousness are rarely paired with the word *covenant*.[2] Perhaps such a criticism relies too heavily on a word-study approach since the parallel terms are covenantal. On the other hand, the warrant for defining righteousness as "covenantal faithfulness" is questionable. Some scholars make the mistake of assigning the same definition to all the terms used upon seeing the parallelism. It is illegitimate to say that steadfast love means righteousness, and righteousness means faithfulness, and faithfulness means salvation. Even if words overlap in meaning, the terms still have different nuances, and they should not be indiscriminately lumped together. It is more precise to say that God's saving righteousness *fulfills* his covenant instead of saying that we should *define* it as his covenantal faithfulness. The idea that God conforms to a norm should not be washed out of the term *righteousness*. The norm, we should be quick to say, is not a law above God. Rather, the norm is God himself. Moral norms are a description of his character and being.

But how can God be righteous—how can he conform to a norm in saving sinful people? The Old Testament consistently ascribes God's saving righteousness to God himself. As Isaiah 59:16–17 says, the Lord "saw that there

---

2. See Mark A. Seifrid, "Righteousness Language in the Hebrew Scriptures and Early Judaism," in *Justification and Variegated Nomism*, vol. 1, *The Complexities of Second Temple Judaism*, ed. D. A. Carson, Peter O'Brien, and Mark A. Seifrid (Grand Rapids: Baker, 2001), 423–42.

was no man, and wondered that there was no one to intercede; then his own arm brought him salvation, and his righteousness upheld him. He put on righteousness as a breastplate, and a helmet of salvation on his head; he put on garments of vengeance for clothing, and wrapped himself in zeal as a cloak." Salvation and righteousness are his gracious works. Hence, Jeremiah declares that the salvation of Israel and Judah is God's gracious gift, which is signified in the words, "The LORD is our righteousness" (Jer. 23:6; 33:16). But how can the Lord be righteous in forgiving those who have done evil? How do human beings escape his judging righteousness and experience his saving righteousness? Isaiah 53:11 points to the answer, which is developed more fully in the New Testament: the Servant of the Lord will bear the iniquities of many, so that they will be declared righteous before God.

SUMMARY

God's righteousness in the Old Testament especially focuses on his saving righteousness by which he delivers his people because of his steadfast love. The saving righteousness of God *fulfills* his covenant with Israel, but God's saving righteousness should not *be equated* with covenant faithfulness. Righteousness in the Old Testament is often forensic, addressing whether the defendant is innocent or guilty before the divine judge. Finally, God's righteousness in the Old Testament cannot be limited to his saving righteousness but also refers to his judging righteousness.

REFLECTION QUESTIONS

1. Why is it unconvincing to say that righteousness in the Old Testament has to do only with covenant relationship instead of conformity to a norm?

2. Does righteousness in the Old Testament refer only to salvation, or does it also include the idea of judgment?

3. What evidence is there for a forensic understanding of righteousness in the Old Testament?

4. When the Old Testament uses the Hebrew noun *righteousness* in the plural, what is its meaning?

5. Is it fitting to describe righteousness in terms of covenant faithfulness?

What Does the Word
Justify Mean in Paul?

Here we are asking what the verbal form *justify* (*dikaioō*) means in Pauline usage. It will be argued that the term is forensic, so that it means "declare righteous" rather than "make righteous." In the history of interpretation Augustine argued that the term meant "make righteous," and this reading ultimately was defended by Roman Catholicism.[1] The Reformers understood the term to be forensic and therefore argued that a declaration of righteousness was intended. Recently a number of scholars, both Protestant and Roman Catholic, have argued that God's righteousness is effective and transformative, and hence the Augustinian view that righteousness means "make righteous" has been revived among Protestant interpreters. We should always be open to more light dawning upon us from the Word of God, but it seems to me that the forensic interpretation of the verbal form is more convincing.

The forensic character of the verb *justify* is evident in Romans 8:33: "Who shall bring any charge against God's elect? It is God who justifies." The legal setting of the text is clear, for the issue is whether anyone will bring a charge of condemnation against believers on the Day of Judgment. God is represented as a judge, and charges are brought against believers. But God dismisses the charges, for he already has declared that believers are justified before him. Clearly, "justifies" here means that God has declared believers to be in the right. The legal dimension of "justify" is also apparent in 1 Corinthians 4:4 as well where Paul claims: "For I am not aware of anything against myself, but I am not thereby acquitted [ESV rendering of the verb *justify*]. It is the Lord who judges me." Paul considers the day when he will stand before the Lord as

---

1. Perhaps Augustine's dependence upon Latin instead of Greek contributed to his definition of righteousness.

the final Judge. Paul's own subjective feelings about his standing will not be decisive. What matters is the pronouncement of the Lord, and it is the Lord who "acquits" or condemns on the last day. This text does not suggest that the Lord makes Paul righteous on the last day. Instead, what Paul teaches here is that the Lord declares who is righteous, that is, he announces to the world whether Paul stands in the right before him at the final judgment.

First Timothy 3:16, which says that Jesus was "vindicated by the Spirit," should be interpreted similarly. Certainly Paul is not saying that Jesus "was made righteous" by the Spirit. Rather, the verb means that he was shown to be in the right, declared to be in the right by the Spirit. The reference here is to the resurrection of Christ, which vindicated the self-claims of Jesus.

Romans 2:13 should be interpreted forensically as well: "For it is not the hearers of the law who are righteous before God, but the doers of the law who will be justified." It would not make sense to say that those who do the law will be made righteous, for they are already righteous inasmuch as they fulfill the law. Rather, the verse means that God will declare that those who keep the law are righteous. Similarly, even though every human being is a liar, God remains true, so "that you may be justified in your words" (Rom. 3:4). "Justified" here cannot mean "make righteous." God is proved to be right or vindicated in his words—which is certainly a forensic judgment.

Paul particularly emphasizes that believers are not justified by works of law (Rom. 3:20, 28; Gal. 2:16), or by works (Rom. 4:2), or by the law (Gal. 3:11; 5:4). In each of these instances the verb "justify" is best rendered "declared righteous." A legal setting is presupposed as in the texts cited above. The question is whether the divine Judge will pronounce a favorable verdict on those who appeal to their observance of the law or their obedient works. The answer is a vigorous no since all fail to do the required works or to keep the law. Hence, a divine declaration of unrighteousness is announced.

Conversely, Paul often teaches that God justifies those who believe (Rom. 3:26, 28, 30; 5:1; Gal. 2:16; 3:8, 24) by the blood of Christ (Rom. 5:9; cf. Gal. 2:17) and by his grace (Rom. 3:24; Titus 3:7). The emphasis on justification by faith suggests that a divine declaration is in view instead of a transformation. Justification is received by human beings when they believe. Indeed, God "justifies the ungodly" (Rom. 4:5) on the basis of what Christ has accomplished by his death. In conclusion, the emphasis upon the reception of justification by the ungodly supports a divine declaration, the notion that justification is a forensic reality.

The remaining uses probably should be interpreted in light of the evidence presented above. In 1 Corinthians 6:11 we read, "But you were washed, you were sanctified, you were justified in the name of the Lord Jesus Christ and by the Spirit of our God." The verbs translated "washed," "sanctified," and "justified" are parallel. Furthermore, all three verbs refer to conversion: washing to the cleansing of sins at baptism, sanctification to the definitive sanctification that occurs when believers are saved, and justification to the verdict announced when one believes.[2] It is unlikely that justification here refers to being made righteous. Instead, every verb focuses on the forgiveness of sins and the new position of believers. Upon conversion they are cleansed of their sins, they are placed in the realm of the holy, and they are pronounced to be righteous. Paul is not emphasizing here that they are actually made holy or made righteous (of course the transformation in the lives of believers is expressed elsewhere), only that they have a new relationship with God.

Paul reflects on God's work of salvation from the beginning to the end in Romans 8:29–30. In verse 30 he remarks, "Those whom he called he also justified, and those whom he justified he also glorified." The use of the word translated "justified" in this context does not cast much light upon its meaning. The meaning of the term elsewhere suggests a divine declaration of a new status. This seems to be confirmed by the near reference in Romans 8:33, which, as noted above, clearly supports a forensic reading.

If there is any instance in which the word *justify* may have a transformative reference in Paul, it is found in Romans 6:7: "For one who has died has been set free from sin." The ESV may support a transformative reading since it is translated as "set free" instead of "justify." It may be the case that in this instance Paul uses the term to denote transformation, since it is commonly accepted that words derive a particular nuance from their context. Romans 6 features the transforming grace of God, and hence the word *justify* may focus on God making us righteous in this instance. Such a judgment would not necessarily change the fact that Paul ordinarily uses the term forensically. On the other hand, it is more likely that the word has a forensic meaning in this context as well since such a rendering fits with the use of the term in every other instance in Paul. In that case, the forensic declaration functions as the basis of the transformation that is ours in everyday life.

I have argued that Paul typically uses the word *justify* forensically to denote one's status before God. One other question, however, must be addressed. It is often said today that God's forensic verdict is an effective one. Therefore, it is argued that justification cannot be limited to a legal verdict. God's verdict introduces a new reality, and therefore believers are truly righteous as a result of God's verdict, and any idea of a legal fiction is avoided. This argument must be assessed carefully.

First, I agree that the forensic verdict of righteousness is an effective one. Believers are truly righteous before God, for God's verdict constitutes reality. Second, an effective verdict, however, does not necessarily lead to the conclusion that righteousness means transformation. Believers really do stand in

---

2. In defense of the notion that sanctification is definitive, see David Peterson, *Possessed by God: A New Testament Theology of Sanctification and Holiness* (Grand Rapids: Eerdmans, 1995).

the right before God, but it does not logically follow that the *word righteousness* should be defined as "make righteous." The continuing presence of sin in believers also makes it difficult to see how *justify* should be defined as "make righteous." Further, a transformative view easily could lead one to the idea that justification is a process, but there is no basis in Paul for seeing justification as a process.

SUMMARY

The evidence supporting a declarative or forensic meaning for the verb *justify* in Paul is significant. The Augustinian view that *justify* means to make righteous is not supported by the use of the verb in the Pauline writings.

REFLECTION QUESTIONS

1. What was Augustine's understanding of the verb *justify*?

2. How did the Reformers define the verb *justify*?

3. What Pauline evidence supports a forensic interpretation of the verb *justify*?

4. What is the relationship between justification and the transformed lives believers should live?

5. What is meant by saying that the divine verdict in justification is effective?

What Does Paul Mean by "the Righteousness of God"?

What I am trying to answer here is what Paul means by the phrase *righteousness of God* (*dikaiosynē theou*) and by the term *righteousness* when he uses these expressions to refer to God's saving righteousness. Paul often uses the noun *righteousness* to denote ethical righteousness—the kind of behavior that pleases God (e.g., Rom. 6:13, 16, 18, 19, 20; 2 Cor. 6:7, 14; 9:9; 11:15; Eph. 4:24; 5:9; 6:14; Phil. 1:11; 3:6; 1 Tim. 6:11; 2 Tim. 2:22; 3:16; 4:8; Titus 3:5). Everyone agrees that Paul often uses the word *righteousness* to denote a life that is pleasing to God. But the intention here is to understand what God's righteousness means when Paul uses it in theologically weighty passages—in texts where he speaks of God's gift of righteousness.[1]

Some scholars have maintained that God's righteousness refers to his transforming righteousness.[2] This view is supported by five arguments. First, God's righteousness is said to be "revealed" (Rom. 1:17) and "manifested" (Rom. 3:21). Hence, it is argued that God's righteousness is an effective work of God that cannot be limited to a mere declaration, for it includes the entire creation and not just the individual. What God declares becomes a reality since he is redeemer and creator.

Second, the parallelism between God's "power" (Rom. 1:16), his "righteousness" (Rom. 1:17), and his "wrath" (Rom. 1:18) is also set forward to

---

1. The view that God's righteousness refers to his covenant faithfulness is treated in question 18.
2. Adolf Schlatter, *The Theology of the Apostles: The Development of New Testament Theology*, trans. Andreas J. Köstenberger (Grand Rapids: Baker, 1999), 234–36; Ernst Käsemann, "The Righteousness of God," in *New Testament Questions of Today*, trans. W. J. Montague (Philadelphia: Fortress, 1982), 168–82. My discussion here stems, with some changes, from Thomas R. Schreiner, *New Testament Theology: Magnifying God in Christ* (Grand Rapids: Baker, 2008), 351–62.

defend a transformative view. All of these are understood as genitives of source, indicating God's activity unleashed in the world. His righteousness is not merely a static pronouncement but represents the unleashing of his power in an active way. In the same way God's wrath is effective, judging people for their sin of failing to worship and praise God (Rom. 1:18–32).

Third, God's righteousness in the Old Testament is often parallel to his salvation, truth, and mercy (see question 18). This background demonstrates that God's righteousness is his saving action on behalf of his people and should not be limited to a forensic declaration. God's gift and God's power cannot be separated from one another.

Fourth, in Romans 3:24 God's righteousness is "through the redemption that is in Christ Jesus." Redemption signifies the freedom and liberation from sin through Jesus Christ, finding its precedent in God's liberation of his people from Egypt. If righteousness becomes ours through the liberation from sin effected by Jesus Christ, then righteousness must include the idea of freedom from sin. Righteousness, then, includes the notion of God's transforming power.

Fifth, Paul speaks of grace reigning through righteousness (Rom. 5:21), of the service of righteousness (Rom. 6:18–19; 2 Cor. 3:9), and of submitting to God's righteousness (Rom. 10:3). Therefore, justification cannot be limited to legal categories. God transforms those whom he declares to be in the right. The same point is argued from 2 Corinthians 3:8–9. Those who benefit from the "ministry of righteousness" also enjoy the "ministry of the Spirit." The effective work of the Spirit is part and parcel of the righteousness of God.

Despite some valid insights in the notion that righteousness is transformative, the case for such a view is overstated, and righteousness in Paul should be understood as forensic only.[3] First, it has been noted in the previous question that the verbal form in Paul should be understood in terms of God's declaration.

Second, Paul often says that human beings are righteous by faith (e.g., Rom. 1:17; 3:22, 26; 4:3, 5, 9, 13; 9:30; 10:4; Gal. 2:16; 3:6, 11; 5:5; Phil. 3:9). In such contexts Paul contrasts righteousness by faith with righteousness by works. Ordinarily, people are declared to be righteous in human courts on the basis of their good behavior. That is, if they did what is good, they are declared to be in the right; but if they did what is evil, they are condemned. Paul, however, maintains that it is not those who work but those who believe who are righteous before God (Rom. 4:4–5). Indeed, no one can be righteous by works

---

3. So C. E. B. Cranfield, *A Critical and Exegetical Commentary on the Epistle to the Romans: Introduction and Commentary on Romans I–VIII*, ICC (Edinburgh: T & T Clark, 1975), 95–99; Moo, *Romans 1–8*, 65–70, 75–86; Stephen Westerholm, *Perspectives Old and New on Paul: The "Lutheran" Paul and His Critics* (Grand Rapids: Eerdmans, 2004), 261–96.

before God, for all have fallen short of what he requires (Rom. 3:23). Righteousness by faith, then, must refer to the *gift* of righteousness given to human beings by God. Human beings are not justified on the basis of doing but on the basis of believing. God declares the *ungodly* to be righteous (Rom. 4:5). Nor does Paul view faith as a "work" that merits the declaration of righteousness. Faith saves because it looks entirely to what God has done for believers in Christ. It rests on Christ's death for the forgiveness of sins and his resurrection for the sake of their justification (Rom. 3:21–26; 4:25). The righteousness given to believers, then, is alien since it is not based on anything they have done but only on God's work in Christ. This suggests that righteousness as a gift is granted to those who believe.

Third, that righteousness is a forensic declaration also is supported by the link between righteousness and forgiveness. We already have seen the connection between righteousness and forgiveness in Romans 4:25 and Romans 8:33. Paul slides easily from justification to forgiveness in Romans 4:1–8. David's forgiveness of sins is nothing less than his justification—his being in the right before God (Rom. 4:6–8). The idea is not that David was transformed by God, even though Paul stresses the transforming power of God's grace in other contexts. The text calls attention to David's sin and his forgiveness by God, confirming the extraordinary nature of God's grace, for he forgives sinners and declares them to be in the right.

Fourth, the idea that righteousness is counted (*logizomai*) to believers indicates that righteousness is not native to believers, that it is granted to them by God (Rom. 4:3–6, 8–11, 22–24; 9:8; Gal. 3:6). This argument is strengthened when we add that righteousness is counted to those who believe—not to those who work. God does not "count" sins against those who have put their faith in Christ (2 Cor. 5:19). This is a strange reckoning or counting, indeed, when those who have done evil are considered to be righteous since God "justifies the ungodly" (Rom. 4:5). However, this fits with the notion that believers have received "the free gift of righteousness" (Rom. 5:17).

Fifth, should "the righteousness of God" also be understood as forensic (esp. Rom. 1:17; 3:21, 22; 10:3; 2 Cor. 5:21)? Some scholars have maintained that Romans 3:5, where righteousness is parallel to God's "faithfulness" and truth, supports the interpretation of covenantal faithfulness. Such an interpretation is scarcely clear in Romans 3:1–8, for it seems that God's righteousness here refers to his *judgment* of sinners.[4] Romans 3:4, citing Psalm 51:4 (LXX), refers to God's victory when he judges sinners. The righteousness of God is used in a context that speaks of his wrath inflicted on the wicked (Rom. 3:5) and his judgment of the world on the Last Day (Rom. 3:6). Rather than referring to God's covenant faithfulness, this text refers to God's judging the wicked because they have lived in an evil manner. Romans

---

4. Rightly, Rudolf Bultmann, "Δικαιοσύνη Θεου," *JBL* 83 (1964): 13.

3:5, then, does not bear on the discussion at all, for it does not refer to God's *saving righteousness* but to his *judging righteousness*. And the question before us here is what is meant by the saving righteousness of God. Based on these reasons, it is best to understand "the righteousness of God" as a forensic declaration.

That the "righteousness of God" refers to a divine gift is clear from Philippians 3:9, where Paul speaks of "the righteousness from God" (*tēn ek theou dikaiosynēn*). The righteousness is not Paul's own, deriving from his observance of the law. It is a righteousness *from* God himself, obtained by faith in Jesus Christ. Philippians 3:9, then, provides an important clue as to how we should interpret God's righteousness in Romans 1:17 and 3:21–22. It refers to God's saving righteousness, given as a gift to those who believe. The lack of the preposition "from" (*ek*) in the texts in Romans is not decisive, for in every instance the same subject is treated: the saving righteousness of God that is given to those who believe. It is unlikely that Paul would use a different definition of the word for righteousness in texts that are so similar in content—in texts that contrast righteousness by faith with righteousness by observing the law. We have seen that some argue that righteousness is transformative in Romans 1:17 since it is parallel to God's power and wrath. It is correct to say that each of the genitives should be identified as a genitive of source. God's anger and power and righteousness all come from him. It does not follow, however, from the collocation of terms that the words all refer to a divine activity—if by that one concludes that God's righteousness must be a transforming one. "Power," "wrath," and "righteousness" (Rom. 1:16–18) do not all have the same meaning. The phrase "righteousness of God" makes perfect sense if it designates the gift of God's righteousness.

A powerful argument supporting the idea that God's righteousness in Romans and Philippians has the same meaning are the numerous parallels between Romans 10:1–6 and Philippians 3:2–9 (see figure 4). First, there is a reference to God's righteousness. Second is the contrast between righteousness by law and righteousness by faith. Third is the parallel between Israel's quest to establish its own righteousness and Paul's quest to establish his righteousness by his observance of the law. Fourth, in particular we should note Paul's emphasis on "not having a righteousness of my own that comes from the law" (Phil. 3:9), and Israel's attempt to establish its own righteousness (Rom 10:3)—a "righteousness that is based on the law" (Rom 10:5).

The point I am making is that the parallel contexts indicate that righteousness in Romans 10 cannot have a different definition from what we see in Philippians 3. In the latter, righteousness is clearly a gift given to sinners—a declaration that those who have failed to keep the law but have trusted in Jesus Christ stand in the right before God. The same gift character of righteousness, therefore, is in view in Romans 10.

FIGURE 4: PARALLELS IN TWO PAULINE PASSAGES	
Romans 10:3–6	Philippians 3:9
"the righteousness of God" (v. 3)	"the righteousness from God"
"righteousness . . . based on the law" vs. "righteousness based on faith" (vv. 5–6)	"righteousness . . . from the law" or "under the law" vs. "righteousness . . . through faith" or "depends on faith"
Israel sought to establish her own righteousness by observing the law (v. 3)	Paul sought to establish his own righteousness by observing the law
Israel attempted to establish her own righteousness based on the law (vv. 3, 5)	Paul did not have a righteousness of his own that comes from the law

Furthermore, if such is the meaning in Romans 10, it is highly unlikely that Paul means anything different in Romans 1:17 and 3:21–22. Indeed, Romans 3:21–22 unpacks Romans 1:17, clarifying further how God pronounces as righteous those who deserve God's wrath because of their sin. When he speaks of God's righteousness in declaring sinners to be in the right before him by faith in Christ, he has in mind the gift of righteousness—God's declaration of not guilty. Paul would confuse the readers if in some instances he used the expression "righteousness of God" to refer to a gift of a righteous status from God and in others of a divine activity that transforms believers, particularly since the phrase invariably occurs in contexts that contrast righteousness by faith with righteousness by observing the law. If a different definition were intended, this would need to be signified by further clarifying statements. But such clarifying statements are lacking, confirming that the same definition of righteousness is found in all these theologically weighty passages.

That Paul refers to the gift of righteousness is also clear from 2 Corinthians 5:21. God made Christ to be sin, even though he was without sin, so that believers would "become the righteousness of God." The meaning of God's righteousness is explicated by verse 19, which refers to forgiveness of sins. This verse also explains how God could grant the gift of righteousness to those who are sinners. The extraordinary gift of righteousness is secured through Christ's death on the cross. God "made him to be sin" so that those who are wicked could become righteous. An interchange between Christ and sinners is posited here. Christ was not actually transformed into a sinner. He was reckoned or counted as a sinner, so that believers would be reckoned or counted as righteous. When we observe that Jesus did not actually become a sinner and that the language of substitution is used, it seems quite likely that the righteous status of believers is in view.

Romans 3:21–26 is a key text that is remarkably parallel to 2 Corinthians 5:21. This paragraph functions as the hinge for the letter to the Romans and is one of the most important (if not the most important) sections in the letter. The placement of the text in the letter should be noted. Paul has finished arguing that all without exception sin and deserve judgment (Rom. 1:18–3:20). He summarizes this truth in Romans 3:23: "For all have sinned and fall short of the glory of God." God demands perfect obedience, and all fall short of his standard. How then will people become right with God? Paul argues in verses 21–22 that a right relation with God is not obtained by keeping the law but through faith in Jesus Christ. All people who trust in Christ are justified by God because of the redemption accomplished by Christ Jesus (v. 24).

Verses 25–26 are of particular importance for our subject. God set forth Christ as a propitiatory sacrifice by virtue of Jesus' bloody death. "Propitiation" and "blood" point back to the Old Testament cultus and sacrificial system. Discussion has centered on the meaning of the term hilastērion and whether it should be rendered "expiation" (wiping away or forgiveness of sins) or "propitiation" (the satisfaction of God's wrath).[5] I would argue that those who defend the notion of propitiation are more convincing, for the term includes the sense of the averting of God's wrath—the appeasement or satisfaction of his righteousness. This fits nicely with Romans 1:18, where the wrath of God against sin is announced, and Romans 2:5, where the final judgment is described as the day of God's wrath. The line of argument in Romans 1:18–3:20 provokes the reader to ask how God's wrath can be averted. The answer in Romans 3:25 is that God's wrath has been satisfied or appeased in the death of Christ.

The words following "propitiation" substantiate this interpretation. Paul explains that Christ was set forth as a "propitiation," or "mercy seat," to demonstrate God's righteousness. The context reveals that by "righteousness" Paul refers to God's holiness or justice, for Paul immediately refers to the sins God passed over in previous eras. The passing over of sins refers to the sins committed previously in history, which did not receive the full punishment deserved. God's failure to punish such sins calls into question his justice. How can he wink at sin and tolerate it and still maintain his righteousness and holiness? Paul's solution is that God looked ahead to the cross of Christ, where his wrath would be appeased and justice would be satisfied. Christ as the substitute would absorb the full payment for sin.

---

5. In support of expiation and the notion that judgment is merely the natural result of sin, not the expression of God's personal wrath, see C. H. Dodd, *The Bible and the Greeks* (London: Hodder & Stoughton, 1935), 82–95. Supporting a reference to propitiation are Leon Morris, *The Apostolic Preaching of the Cross*, 3rd ed. (Grand Rapids: Eerdmans, 1965), 144–213; Roger R. Nicole, "C. H. Dodd and the Doctrine of Propitiation," *WTJ* 17 (1955): 117–57.

The interpretation suggested above is confirmed by verse 26: "It was to show his righteousness at the present time, so that he might be just and the justifier of the one who has faith in Jesus."[6] Christ's death as a propitiation, Paul repeats, demonstrates God's holiness and justice at the present juncture of salvation history. Thereby God is both "just and the justifier" of those who put their faith in Christ. God's justice is satisfied because Christ bore the full payment for sin. But God is also the justifier because on the basis of the cross of Christ sinners receive forgiveness through faith in Jesus. In the cross of Christ, the justice and mercy of God meet. God's holiness is satisfied by Christ's bearing the penalty of sin, and God's saving activity is realized in the lives of those who trust in Christ. Some object that retribution cannot be in view, for the focus is on personal relationships rather than retribution. But personal relationships and retribution are not at odds with one another. God's justice is not an attribute that can be separated from his person.

Some of the arguments supporting transformative righteousness have been answered, but we need to pause to comment on a few that have not been examined thus far. First, the revelation of God's saving righteousness in history does not establish a transformative righteousness. God's righteousness in Christ is certainly an eschatological work of God. Such a statement, however, does not necessarily establish that righteousness should be defined in terms of transformation. God's declaration about sinners is an end-time verdict that has been announced before the end has arrived. The verdict is effective in the sense that every verdict announced by God constitutes reality.

Second, the argument from redemption fails to establish the transformation view as well. Justification belongs to believers through redemption (Rom 3:24). In some instances in Paul, however, redemption is defined primarily in terms of forgiveness of sins (Eph.1:7; Col. 1:14). The forgiveness of sins is communicated as well in Colossians 2:13–14. Paul pictures it as the erasure of debts that had accrued against believers. The definitive nature of forgiveness is portrayed in the nailing of sins to the cross, indicating that Christ has definitively and finally put away sin. The fundamental bondage of human beings can be attributed to guilt that stains us through sin. Hence, the reference to redemption does not clearly indicate that righteousness is transformative.[7]

Third, the collocation of the "ministry of righteousness" and the "ministry of the Spirit" in 2 Corinthians 3:8–9 does not clearly establish a transformative view. Paul never imagined that one could be righteous in God's sight without then being transformed by the Spirit. And yet it still should be said that it does not follow that the transforming power of the Spirit and righteousness

---

6. For further support of the interpretation offered here and interaction with the literature, see Thomas R. Schreiner, *Romans*, BECNT (Grand Rapids: Baker, 1998), 176–99.
7. So John Piper, *Counted Righteous in Christ: Should We Abandon the Imputation of Christ's Righteousness?* (Wheaton: Crossway, 2002), 73–75.

are precisely the same.[8] Too many of those who defend the transformative view argue for identity of meaning from parallelism of terms. Such an approach is flawed, for it collapses the meaning of words so that they become virtually indistinguishable.

SUMMARY

It is often claimed today that God's righteousness in Paul refers to his transforming righteousness, but a careful analysis of the evidence indicates that God's righteousness in Paul is forensic. When Paul speaks of the "righteousness of God" and "righteousness," he refers to our right-standing with God, the fact that we are now in a new and right relationship with him. The word does not mean that God's people are internally transformed by his grace. Certainly such transformation is part of Paul's theology as well, but the point being made here is that God's gracious work in changing sinners is not communicated by the phrase "righteousness of God."

REFLECTION QUESTIONS

1. What are the best arguments for a transformative understanding of the righteousness of God?

2. How do the parallels between Philippians 3 and Romans 10 support the notion that "righteousness of God" refers to a gift from God?

3. What do we learn from 2 Corinthians 5:21 about God's righteousness?

4. How does Romans 3:21–26 develop the theme of God's righteousness, and why is the paragraph crucial for Pauline theology? Does the relationship between righteousness and redemption in Romans 3:24 support a forensic understanding of righteousness?

5. What are the practical implications of accepting a forensic rather than a transformative understanding of righteousness? Why is it important to say that God's righteousness is a gift given to us?

---

8. Cf. Murray J. Harris, *The Second Epistle to the Corinthians: A Commentary on the Greek Text*, NIGTC (Grand Rapids: Eerdmans, 2005), 287–88.

Does the Pauline Teaching on Justification Contradict Jesus' Message?

Obviously I cannot treat all of Jesus' teaching in such a short space, but it can be shown that the Pauline teaching on justification accords with the teaching of Jesus. It should be noted at the outset that Jesus did not typically use the terminology of justification as Paul did. Still, the same concepts of the grace of God and the centrality of faith are present. And it is not as if the language of justification is completely absent from Jesus' teaching.

The parable of the Pharisee and the tax collector clearly functions as an antecedent for Paul's theology of justification (Luke 18:9–14). The Pharisee was convinced that God was pleased with him because of his devotion to the law, which went beyond what was expected. He expected to be justified because of his moral excellence, which elevated the Pharisee far above the tax collector. The tax collector, however, was deeply conscious of his sins and pled with God to have mercy on him as a sinner. And it was the tax collector who "went down to his house justified" (Luke 18:14) rather than the Pharisee. Those who "trusted in themselves that they were righteous" (Luke 18:9) are condemned. Those who exalt themselves are humbled (Luke 18:14). The only pathway to justification is to follow the example of the tax collector in saying, "God, be merciful to me, a sinner" (Luke 18:13). It is hard to imagine a closer parallel to the Pauline teaching on justification.

A concrete illustration of the radical grace of God was Jesus' table fellowship with tax collectors and sinners (e.g., Matt. 9:10–13). Table fellowship with such signified Jesus' acceptance of them despite their sin. The good news of God's grace is evident in Jesus' claim that it is the sick who need a physician. He came to call upon sinners to repent. Thus, Jesus offered forgiveness to those who had failed dramatically, promising them a relationship with God if they would repent of their sins. The account of the prodigal son resonates with the same themes (Luke 15:11–32). The son rebelled against the father by squandering his father's wealth and by living a dissolute life. Still, when he repented of his sin and returned to his father, the father was waiting for him and even ran to greet him out of compassion, offering him full and free forgiveness. Clearly, the son in the parable stands for the tax collectors and sinners who do not merit the Father's grace and forgiveness (Luke 15:1–2), and yet God forgives them of all their sins.

When Jesus said that the kingdom belongs to the "poor in spirit" (Matt. 5:3), we see another parallel with the Pauline teaching on grace. According to Matthew, those who recognize their spiritual poverty receive the kingdom. Those "who hunger and thirst for righteousness" will "be satisfied" (Matt. 5:6). But if they long for righteousness, they recognize that they lack it and stand in need of the righteousness of another.

Along the same lines, in the Synoptic Gospels faith is fundamental for entrance into the kingdom. The centurion stands out above those in Israel because of his faith (Matt. 8:10), and this faith cannot be limited to the realm of healing, for Jesus speaks immediately of Gentiles who will participate in the eschatological banquet (Matt. 8:11–12). Interestingly, the synoptics often use the phrase "your faith has saved you" (Matt. 9:22; Mark 5:34; 10:52; Luke 7:50; 8:48; 17:19; 18:42, my translation).[1] In every case, except for Luke 7:50, Jesus makes this declaration to someone whom he has healed. It would be a mistake, though, to restrict his words to physical healing, for physical healing functions as an emblem of spiritual healing in the synoptics. For example, the healing of the blind man leads him to follow Jesus in discipleship (Mark 10:52), showing that more than physical sight is involved. Similarly, even though Jesus healed ten men of leprosy, only the Samaritan returned to give thanks (Luke 17:11–19). And only the Samaritan heard the words, "Your faith has saved you" (Luke 17:19, my translation). The thanksgiving of the Samaritan indicates that more than physical healing occurred. We see indications, then, that faith is central to one's relationship with God in the synoptics, just as it is in the Pauline literature.

In the gospel of John faith plays a central role as well. John uses the verb for "believe" ninety-eight times, showing how prominent believing is in John's gospel. Jesus identifies the fundamental work that God calls upon human beings to do in John 6:29: "This is the work of God, that you believe in him whom he has sent." This statement, to speak anachronistically, is remarkably Pauline. John underscores that the fundamental work of human beings is to believe in the Son of God. It is the one who believes that Jesus is the Christ and the Son of God who enjoys eternal life (John 20:31). Those who stubbornly

---

1. The ESV, unfortunately, translates all of these texts (except for Luke 7:50), as "your faith has made you well."

refuse to believe in Jesus will die in their sins (John 8:24). Spiritual hunger and thirst are satisfied only through belief in Jesus (John 6:35). Only those who receive Jesus are the children of God (John 1:11–12). God calls upon all people to come to Jesus to receive life (John 5:40).

SUMMARY

Obviously much more could be said about the teaching of Jesus, but there is enough evidence here to conclude that the Pauline gospel of justification by faith is not novel. Jesus himself emphasized that life comes from putting one's faith in him, that human beings are spiritually impoverished, and that life comes from believing in Jesus rather than working for God. Hence, it is not too bold to conclude that Paul derived his message of justification from the historical Jesus.

REFLECTION QUESTIONS

1. How does the parable of the Pharisee and tax collector (Luke 18:9–14) fit with Paul's theology of justification?

2. What does Jesus' table fellowship with tax collectors and sinners signify?

3. What phrase does Jesus often use when healing the sick?

4. What theme is prominent in the gospel of John?

5. Why is it important that Paul and Jesus agree on justification?

Should "Faith of Christ" (*pistis Christou*) Be Translated "Faithfulness of Christ" or "Faith in Christ"?

The human response of faith is fundamental, according to the Pauline gospel. Human beings are "justified by faith" (Rom. 5:1), which means that people stand in the right before God through faith.[1] When Paul gives thanks and praise for God's work in the lives of his converts, he often mentions their faith (Rom. 1:8; Eph. 1:15–16; Col. 1:3–4; 1 Thess. 1:2–3; 2 Thess. 1:3; 2 Tim. 1:3–5; Philem. 4–5). Paul preached so that the Corinthians would put their faith in God's power rather than the artistry with which he presented his message (1 Cor. 2:5; cf. Col. 2:12). Faith for Paul is not a vague and slippery entity but is always directed to what God has done in Christ. Hence, faith trusts in the atonement achieved through Christ on the cross. Human beings are to put their faith in God, who sent Jesus as the crucified and risen one (Rom. 4:24–25).

Paul emphasizes that human beings are justified by faith (Rom. 1:17; Gal. 3:11), seeing in Habakkuk 2:4 a grounds for this claim. A right relation with God is obtained "through faith in Jesus Christ for all who believe" (Rom. 3:22; cf. 3:25, 26). In Galatians 2:16 Paul places "works of the law" in opposition to faith in Jesus Christ, stating three times that justification does not come through works of law but only through faith in Jesus Christ. Similarly, the Spirit is received through faith rather than through the works of the law

---

1. Much of the material here is taken from Thomas R. Schreiner, *New Testament Theology: Magnifying God in Christ* (Grand Rapids: Baker, 2008), 573–76, with significant additions and revisions.

(Gal. 3:2, 5). We see in Romans 3:28 "that a person is justified by faith apart from works prescribed by the law" (NRSV). In Philippians 3:9 righteousness based on law is contrasted with righteousness that comes through faith in Christ.

Many scholars, however, read the above texts in a remarkably different way, claiming that the verses refer to "the faithfulness *of* Christ" rather than "faith *in* Christ."[2] The construction consists of a head noun followed by the genitive (*pistis Christou*),[3] so that both "faithfulness of Christ" and "faith in Christ" are grammatically possible. A number of arguments are presented in support of "faithfulness of Christ."

1. In Romans 3:3 *tēn pistin tou theou* clearly refers to "the faithfulness of God," not "faith *in* God."

2. In Romans 4:12 *pisteōs . . . Abraam* means "the faith of Abraham," not "faith *in* Abraham."

3. It is argued that the genitive in such constructions is most naturally understood as subjective and that it is awkward to understand them as objective genitives.

4. If one takes the genitive as objective, faith in Christ is superfluous since in the key texts (e.g., Rom. 3:22; Gal. 2:16; Phil. 3:9) Paul already mentions the need to trust in Christ. In such tightly packed texts in which the argument is dense, it is most satisfying to discern a distinct nuance in the genitival construction.

5. The "faithfulness of Jesus" is another way of referring to Jesus' obedience, which achieved salvation (Rom. 5:19; Phil. 2:8).

6. The coming of "faith" refers to redemptive history (Gal. 3:23, 25), designating the faithfulness of Christ at the time of fulfillment of God's promise to save. "Faith" always has been a reality, but in Galatians 3:23–25 Paul thinks of an objective event in history: the faithfulness of Jesus Christ to his divine commission. Hence, Paul does not

---

2. E.g., Luke T. Johnson, "Rom 3:21–26 and the Faith of Jesus," *CBQ* 44 (1982): 77–90; Sam Williams, "Again *Pistis Christou*," *JBL* 49 (1987): 431–47; Richard B. Hays, *The Faith of Jesus Christ: An Investigation of the Narrative Substructure of Galatians 3:1–4:11*, 2nd ed., SBLDS 56 (Chico: Scholars, 2001); Ian G. Wallis, *The Faith of Jesus Christ in Early Christian Traditions*, SNTSMS 84 (Cambridge: Cambridge University Press, 1995).

3. The genitive after πίστις varies from Ἰησοῦ Χριστοῦ (Rom 3:22; Gal. 2:16; 3:22), to Χριστοῦ (Gal. 2:16; Phil. 3:9), to Ἰησοῦ (Rom 3:26). For the sake of simplicity, we shall restrict it to πίστις Χριστοῦ.

reflect upon the subjective human response but on Christ's faithful obedience.

7. The focus in Paul's theology is the work of God in Christ, not the human response of faith. The "faithfulness of Christ" features the grace of God in salvation, showing that salvation is a divine gift.

Despite some strong arguments supporting a subjective genitive, there are still good reasons to prefer an objective genitive, so that Paul refers to "faith *in* Christ."[4]

1. The genitive object with "faith" is clear in Mark 11:22 ("Have faith in God") and James 2:1 ("My brothers, show no partiality as you hold the faith in our Lord Jesus Christ, the Lord of glory"). Even though some scholars understand these texts as subjective, such a view is intolerably awkward and contextually unlikely. Hence, we have in analogous texts clear examples of an objective genitive.

2. A genitive object with other verbal nouns shows that an objective genitive with the noun *faith* is quite normal grammatically—for example, "knowledge of Christ Jesus" (Phil. 3:8, my translation). Just as Christ in the genitive functions as the object of knowledge, so too he can function as the object of faith.

3. Hence those who claim that the genitive *must* be subjective fail to convince. Grammar cannot settle the question of whether the genitives are objective or subjective. It must be determined by context.

4. It is possible that in a theologically dense text that the genitive construction should be understood as subjective. But it is more likely that the simplest interpretation of the text should be preferred, so that the reading which adds the least to text should be adopted. Hence, the texts which use the verb "believe" in a verbal construction and the noun faith with the genitive are not superfluous but emphatic, stressing the importance of faith to be right with God. Furthermore, such an interpretive judgment does not preclude the notion that there are different nuances

---

4. See e.g., Otfried Hofius, *Paulusstudien I*, WUNT 51 (Tübingen: Mohr Siebeck, 1989), 154–56; James D. G. Dunn, "Once More Πίστις Χριστοῦ," in *SBL Seminar Papers*, ed. E. H. Lovering Jr. (Atlanta: Scholars, 1991), 730–44; Barry Matlock, "Detheologizing the Πίστις Χριστοῦ Debate: Cautionary Remarks from a Lexical Semantic Perspective," *NovT* 42 (2000): 1–23; Moisés Silva, "Faith Versus Works of Law in Galatians," in *Justification and Variegated Nomism*, vol. 2, *The Paradoxes of Paul*, ed. D. A. Carson, Peter O'Brien, and Mark A. Seifrid (Grand Rapids: Baker, 2004), 217–48.

in the verses. For example, Galatians 3:22 says in the participial phrase that the promise is for "those who believe," but the genitive noun reveals that the promise is for those who exercise "faith in Jesus Christ." In both instances, faith is emphasized, but the genitive specifies that faith has Jesus Christ as its object.

5. Paul often contrasts works and human faith in his theology (e.g., Rom. 3:20–22, 27–28; 9:30–32.; 10:5–8; Gal. 3:2, 5, 10–12; Eph. 2:8–9; Phil. 3:9). Hence, seeing a polarity between works of law and faith in Christ—both *human activities*—fits with what we would expect from Pauline theology.

6. On the other hand, nowhere else does Paul use the word *faith* to describe Jesus' obedience. Those who defend the subjective genitive view often find a parallel to the obedience of Christ in Romans 5:19 and Philippians 2:8. But the alleged parallel is not truly established, for in those texts Paul refers to Jesus' *obedience*, not his faithfulness. So there is no evidence outside disputed passages where Paul clearly describes Jesus' obedience in terms of his faithfulness.

7. The salvation historical argument fails to persuade as well. Certainly, Galatians 3:23 and 25 refer to the coming of faith at a certain time in redemptive history. But such an observation hardly excludes the reading "faith in Christ," for faith in Christ becomes a reality when he arrives and fulfills God's saving promises. We should not pit redemptive history against anthropology. When God fulfills his promises, a new anthropological reality also commences, so that now those who are saved put their faith in Jesus Christ.

8. Nor is the emphasis on faith in Christ Pelagian, as if it somehow detracts from God's work in salvation. A human response of faith does not undercut the truth that God saves, nor does it cancel out the grace of God. Paul makes it very clear that salvation is by grace but also includes the idea that human beings believe (Eph. 2:8–9). Their faith, after all, is a gift of God.

What is the significance of the reading "faith in Christ?"[5] Some of those who defend the subjective genitive reading "faithfulness of Christ" maintain

---

5. A few scholars have argued for a genitive of source. See, e.g., Mark A. Seifrid, *Christ, Our Righteousness: Paul's Theology of Justification* (Downers Grove: InterVarsity, 2000), 139–46; Francis Watson, *Paul and the Hermeneutics of Faith* (London: T & T Clark, 2004), 74–76 [including the objective genitive as well]. Such a reading is possible, but it is a less

that the importance of faith in Christ is not denied since the need for faith in Christ is taught in other texts. The point may be granted, but it needs to be qualified, for the *emphasis* on believing *in Christ* for justification is lost, for only in Galatians 2:16 among the texts where *pistis Christou* occurs does Paul use a verbal form that expresses the need for faith *in Christ*. Indeed, the number of texts in which Paul speaks of the need to trust in Christ decreases quite dramatically. If *pistis Christou* reflects an objective genitive, as is argued here, Paul highlights the importance of faith in Christ for justification. We should linger on this point for a moment. Paul often calls attention to the importance of faith, but this expression goes beyond saying that people need to believe. Now that Jesus Christ has come and accomplished atonement, human beings need to put their faith *in him* as the crucified and risen Lord to be saved. The Christological focus of faith is stressed.

The polarity between faith in Christ and works of law also clarifies that human beings become right with God by believing instead of by doing. I argued earlier that works of law refers to all that the law demands, so that "works of the law" functions as a subset of works in general (see question 5). Paul insists in a number of texts that righteousness is not obtained by works or works of law but through faith. He develops this theme at some length in Romans 3:19–4:25; 9:30–10:13; Galatians 2:16–3:14; and Philippians 3:2–9. These texts teach that no one can be righteous by works of law or any other works since all fall short of what God demands. People can be righteous by works only if they have done *all* that God requires (Gal. 3:10; Rom. 3:9–20), and no one has obeyed to that extent. Even Abraham and David are classified among the ungodly because of their sins (Rom. 4:5–8). The only hope for right standing with God, then, is trusting what God has done in Christ rather than depending on one's attainments. Human boasting is ruled out since human beings rest on what Christ has done to save them (Rom. 3:27–28; 4:1–3). Faith calls attention to the power of God, who justifies the ungodly (Rom. 4:5). A new reality is called into existence by the death and resurrection of Christ, so that a new relation with God is established through faith in Christ (Rom. 4:17–25).

SUMMARY

Scholars today debate whether the genitive *pistis Christou* should be defined as "the faithfulness of Christ" or "faith in Christ." I have argued here that the translation "faith in Christ" is more convincing. Such a conclusion is impor-

---

likely reading and has not won many adherents. See the recent discussion of the matter in Silva, "Faith Versus Works of Law in Galatians," 218–20, 227–36.

tant, for it underscores the *importance* of believing in Christ as the crucified and risen Lord for our justification.

REFLECTION QUESTIONS

1. What are some of the best arguments in your judgment for the translation "faithfulness of Christ"?

2. Does grammar alone resolve whether the phrase should be translated "faithfulness of Christ" or "faith in Christ"?

3. What are the most persuasive arguments supporting "faith in Christ"?

4. What role does the contrast between "doing" and "believing" in Paul's thought play in the debate?

5. Does the debate make any difference? Why?

Does Justification by Faith Alone Lead to Moral Laxity?

A common concern throughout history is that justification by faith alone opens the door to moral laxity. Actually, the first person to ask this question was the Apostle Paul himself. We read in Romans 5:20–21, "Now the law came in to increase the trespass, but where sin increased, grace abounded all the more, so that, as sin reigned in death, grace also might reign through righteousness leading to eternal life through Jesus Christ our Lord." Sin's dominion was extended through the law, but grace is more powerful than sin and death. Hence, the power and beauty of grace are featured the more sin increases, for God's grace shines against the backdrop of sin and death. But if the wonder of grace is clarified and augmented by its victory over sin and death, then one might think that the best thing in the world would be to sin even more, for then grace is displayed and God is glorified. Therefore, Paul poses the following question in Romans 6:1, "What shall we say then? Are we to continue in sin that grace may abound?" Paul himself asks whether God's righteousness and his free grace lead to libertinism. His answer is an emphatic "By no means" (Rom. 6:2).

Paul explains his answer in the remainder of Romans 6. The substance of his response is that believers are united with Christ in both his death and resurrection. When Christ died, he triumphed over sin and death. Sin and death no longer rule over him, though he subjected himself to them during his earthly life.[1] But Jesus' victory over sin and death is not restricted to himself. All believers share in his triumph because they are in Christ. Hence, the tyranny and dominion of sin has been dethroned in the lives of Christians. They are no longer enslaved to the power of sin, for now resurrection life is

---

1. This does not mean, of course, that Jesus himself sinned, but that for our sake and for our salvation he took sin upon himself and died on our behalf.

theirs. The old person—the person we were in Adam—has now been rendered ineffective, so sin no longer reigns over believers. It does not follow from this that believers are now perfected. As long as they are in their earthly bodies, they struggle with sin. Believers are not yet perfect; they still await the day of resurrection when they will be completely transformed (Phil. 3:12–16). Nevertheless, those who belong to Christ are not what they once were. Even though they still sin, they are no longer enslaved to sin. The dominion of sin has been broken, even if sin has not yet been eradicated. Believers have been handed over to a new master (cf. Rom. 6:17) and have been liberated from what previously subjugated them.

We can answer the question whether justification leads to moral laxity another way. Justification is not the only dimension to the salvation accomplished in Christ in Pauline theology. Believers also are united with Christ in his death and resurrection. Justification is crucial and fundamental to Paul's theology, but it is not all there is to say about Paul's teaching. Even if justification itself should not be defined as the transformation of believers, it does not follow from this that believers are not transformed. Such a conclusion veers close to saying that justification is the whole of Pauline theology. We must remember that Paul's theology is multifaceted; it includes themes like union with Christ, reconciliation, redemption, salvation, and sanctification. It is possible to diminish the centrality of justification, but it is also possible to exaggerate its importance so that other aspects of Pauline soteriology are shoved into the background.

All of this is not to say that there is no connection between justification and ethics. The very heart of worship is praise to God. Unbelievers dishonor God because they do not glorify him or give him thanks (Rom. 1:21). But those who are right with God by faith, based on what God has done for them in Christ, are filled with praise and thanksgiving for the indescribable gift given to them. Countless songs and hymns have been written throughout Christian history celebrating the gift of forgiveness. If the failure to give thanks to God is the root of all sin, praising him is also the wellspring for a life that pleases him. The joy of forgiveness leads believers to give their lives entirely to God for the mercy bestowed upon them (Rom. 12:1–2). Surely the mercies in view in Romans 12:1 include the gift of justification. Those who are thankful for being rescued from death yield their lives to God in gratefulness for what he has accomplished for them in Christ. It is misleading, then, to suggest that justification has no relationship to the new life in Christ.

SUMMARY

Does justification encourage libertinism and a life of moral laxity? By no means. Believers also are united with Christ in his death and resurrection.

The Holy Spirit works in them so that they are empowered to please God. It is imperative to avoid reductionism, as if justification were the only part of Pauline theology. At the same time, justification itself is not severed from the ethical life. Those who are graciously forgiven by the Lord are filled with praise and gratitude. In response, they long to give their lives wholly to the Lord (Rom. 12:1–2).

REFLECTION QUESTIONS

1. How does Paul in Romans 6 respond to the charge that righteousness by faith opens the door for moral license?

2. When Paul says in Romans 6 that believers have died to sin, what does he mean practically?

3. Is there a danger that some will make justification the whole of Paul's theology?

4. What role does union with Christ play in the new life believers enjoy in Christ?

5. Is it correct to say that justification is disconnected from ethics?

Does Paul Teach That Christians Are Judged by Their Good Works on the Last Day?

I have argued thus far that Paul teaches that believers are justified by faith alone and that works do not contribute to or form the basis for their justification. But there are other texts in Paul that teach that believers are judged by good works and that these works are necessary for salvation and justification. Does this contradict what Paul teaches elsewhere about justification? I will argue here that there is no contradiction.[1]

We must begin, though, by showing that good works in Paul are necessary for salvation. The whole of Romans 2 plays an important role in discerning the Pauline view. He says in verse 6 that God "will render to each one according to his works." Those who do evil will experience God's "wrath and fury" on the Last Day (v. 8). Conversely, God will grant "eternal life" to "those who by patience in well-doing seek for glory and honor and immortality" (v. 7). Similarly, in verse 13 Paul declares that "the doers of the law will be justified." Some scholars argue that both of these statements are hypothetical.[2] That is, if human beings did what the law said, then they would be justified by works, but we know from all of Romans 1:18–3:20 that no one actually keeps the law, and therefore, no one is justified by doing the law.

The hypothetical interpretation can be defended from the context of Romans 2:12–16. Verse 12 teaches that both Gentiles without the law and Jews under the law will be judged on the Last Day. The hypothetical interpretation is attractive, for it explains how Paul can assert that no one is justified by

---

1. For a fuller response to this question, see Thomas R. Schreiner, *The Law and Its Fulfillment: A Pauline Theology of Law* (Grand Rapids: Baker, 1993), 179–204.
2. Douglas J. Moo, *Romans 1–8*, WEC (Chicago: Moody, 1991), 139–41.

works of the law while saying at the same time that those who do what the law commands will be justified. According to this reading, the assertion that those who keep the law will be justified is not denied. But there is a proviso or condition in the argument. They will be justified *if* they do what the law says, but since no one does everything required by the law, no one is actually justified by means of the law.

We see, then, that the hypothetical interpretation of Romans 2 is plausible. Still, when we survey the whole of Romans 2, it seems that Paul teaches that one must do good works in order to be justified on the Last Day. I argued previously that Romans 2:12–16 does not describe *Christian* Gentiles. Instead, it speaks of an occasional obedience of the law by Gentiles, but their obedience is not saving (see question 11). Romans 2:6–10, on the other hand, does not give any indication of a hypothetical state of affairs. A simple reading suggests that those who do good works will receive eternal life. Those who support the hypothetical interpretation argue, however, that the flow of the argument as a whole (Rom. 1:18–3:20) indicates that no one does the works demanded by Romans 2:6–10. It is difficult to see how Romans 2:6–10 alone can resolve the question, since both interpretations introduce strong evidence in support of their reading.

A decisive text for understanding Romans 2 is the final paragraph (Rom. 2:25–29). I would argue that Paul is clear in teaching that good works are necessary to obtain eternal life. Furthermore, he makes it plain that he is not speaking hypothetically. The Jews, Paul claims, receive benefit from the covenant sign of circumcision if they keep the law. If they transgress the law, however, their "circumcision becomes uncircumcision" (v. 25). Membership in the covenant depends upon their obedience. Conversely, a Gentile who is uncircumcised will be counted in God's sight as circumcised, that is, as a covenant member, if he keeps the law (vv. 26–27). Is the language of Gentiles keeping the law hypothetical? The conjunction "for" connects verses 28–29 to verses 26–27, showing that Paul gives the reason why Gentiles who keep the law should be counted as members of the covenant. Indeed, the logical connection between the verses makes it difficult to believe that only hypothetical obedience is described. True Jewishness and true circumcision are ascribed to the heart, not to ancestry or to the physical act of being circumcised. Paul adds that such a heart change is due to the work of the Spirit, not to the letter of the law. The reference to the Spirit in contrast to the letter supports the claim that there is a reference to real obedience, for the Spirit is the gift of the new covenant inaugurated by Christ.

On two other occasions the Spirit-letter contrast appears in Paul (Rom. 7:6; 2 Cor. 3:6), and in both instances the Spirit's work represents the coming of the new era in Christ. So, it seems that the obedience that qualifies one to be truly circumcised and truly a Jew is the Holy Spirit's work. So then, the reference to the Spirit suggests that the obedience in view is not hypothetical but genuine. Paul may be provoking the Jews to jealousy (Rom. 10:19; 11:14) by reminding them of Gentile obedience. If genuine obedience is in view here, and the obedience is such that it renders Gentiles as covenant members, it seems that Paul picks up Romans 2:6–10, where works are said to be necessary for eternal life. But if works are necessary for eternal life and justification, do we have a contradiction with the claim that no one can be justified by works of law since all have disobeyed? I would argue that there is not a contradiction even in this case, for the good works are the result of the Spirit's work and do not function as the *basis* or *foundation* of one's relationship with God. They are evidence and fruit of the Spirit's work in one's life.

So far I have discussed a text that is controversial in Pauline studies, but there are many other texts that emphasize that good works are necessary to receive eternal life. After rehearsing the works of the flesh, Paul declares, "I warn you, as I warned you before, that those who do such things will not inherit the kingdom of God" (Gal. 5:21). No one who regularly practices the works of the flesh will belong to the eschatological kingdom. The teaching of 1 Corinthians 6:9–10 is similar: "Or do you not know that the unrighteous will not inherit the kingdom of God? Do not be deceived: neither the sexually immoral, nor idolaters, nor adulterers, nor men who practice homosexuality, nor thieves, nor the greedy, nor drunkards, nor revilers, nor swindlers will inherit the kingdom of God." Paul certainly does not mean that anyone who commits such sins is excluded from the kingdom, for he immediately adds, "and such were some of you" (1 Cor. 6:11). His point is that no one can enter the kingdom who continues to practice such sins. Such threats do not cancel out the Pauline teaching on justification. In fact, Paul appeals to the Corinthians' justification in this very context (1 Cor. 6:11). The good works demanded, then, are best understood as the fruit or evidence of justification, not as the ground of our righteousness.

We are not surprised to read, then, in Ephesians 5:5, "For you may be sure of this, that everyone who is sexually immoral or impure, or who is covetous (that is, an idolater), has no inheritance in the kingdom of Christ and God." As if to underline the gravity of the warning and to avoid the idea that he engages in hyperbole, Paul adds, "Let no one deceive you with empty words, for because of these things the wrath of God comes upon the sons of disobedience" (Eph. 5:6; cf. Col. 3:5–6). A similar theme is sounded in Galatians 6:8: "For the one who sows to his own flesh will from the flesh reap corruption, but the one who sows to the Spirit will from the Spirit reap eternal life." The contrast between "corruption" and "eternal life" clarifies that one's eternal destiny is at stake. And eternal life will be obtained only if one sows to the Spirit. If one surrenders to the flesh, final corruption will be the end result. Paul addresses Christians in declaring that "the wages of sin is death" (Rom. 6:23). Death here cannot be restricted to physical death but includes the idea of eternal separation from God.

SUMMARY

The emphasis on good works is seriously misunderstood if such works are conceived of as the basis of justification. Such a view would contradict the assertion that no one is justified by works of law. Believers are justified by grace alone through faith alone, but faith always produces good works, and such good works are necessary for eternal life.[3] They function as the necessary evidence that one has new life in Christ.

REFLECTION QUESTIONS

1. Are good works necessary for justification?

2. What evidence is there in Romans 2 (especially vv. 25–29) that Paul speaks of Christian obedience?

3. Are good works the evidence for or the basis of justification?

4. Is the main problem for Christians today legalism or antinomianism? Or, are both equally dangerous?

5. What role does the Spirit play in the good works that Christians do?

---

3. Calvin also believed good works were necessary for eternal life (*Institutes*, 3.17.15).

Do James and Paul Contradict One Another on Justification by Works?

I will argue that James and Paul do not actually contradict one another on the role of works in justification,[1] despite the claims of some scholars.[2] The arguments supporting a contradiction are as follows: (1) James specifically denies that justification is by faith alone (James 2:24), whereas Paul clearly implies that believers are justified by faith alone (Rom. 3:28). (2) Paul claims Abraham was justified by faith, but James asserts that he was justified by works in sacrificing Isaac (Rom. 4:1–8; Gal. 3:6–9; James 2:21). (3) Paul appeals to Genesis 15:6 to support Abraham being justified by faith apart from works (Rom 4:3; Gal. 3:6), but James cites the same verse from Genesis to substantiate justification by works (James 2:23). The arguments that favor a contradiction between Paul and James are striking, but I will argue that James is responding to a *distortion* of Pauline teaching in which an antinomian lifestyle was defended from a twisting of the Pauline teaching on justification.

Other solutions have been suggested to reconcile the discrepancy between Paul and James. One possibility is that James and Paul mean something different by the word *works* (*erga*). Historically, Roman Catholic interpreters have suggested that Paul excludes *ceremonial works* as playing a role in justification. According to this interpretation, James refers here to *moral works*. Therefore, no contradiction is involved, for Paul, according to the Roman Catholic view, also believed that good works contribute to justification. The Reformers, of course, strenuously disagreed with the Roman Catholic

---

1. The answer given here stems from Thomas R. Schreiner, *New Testament Theology: Magnifying God in Christ* (Grand Rapids: Baker, 2008), 599–605, with some revisions.
2. Representative of this view is Martin Hengel, "Der Jakobusbrief als antipaulinische Polemik," in *Tradition and Interpretation in the New Testament: Essays in Honor of E. Earle Ellis for his 60th Birthday*, ed. Gerald F. Hawthorne and Otto Betz (Grand Rapids: Eerdmans, 1987), 248–65.

interpretation, maintaining that works in Paul could not be limited to ceremonies like circumcision or the observance of days.

Interestingly, as we have seen, the New Perspective on Paul typically identifies the works that Paul rules out for justification as those that erect barriers between Jews and Gentiles, so that the focus is on circumcision, food laws, and Sabbath. Those who endorse the New Perspective are coming from a different place than Roman Catholic scholarship of the sixteenth century, and yet the interpretations share a fascinating convergence at this particular point. The New Perspective solution fails, as we argued earlier, for it is not evident that Paul restricts "works of the law" or "works" to ceremonial works or to those laws that divide Jews from Gentiles. In the same way, it is not evident, contrary to the Roman Catholic view, that Paul and James use the term *works* in a different sense. Rainbow, however, may be correct in saying that Paul rules out works done before conversion, while James focuses on postconversion works.[3] This is not to suggest, however, that postconversion works are perfect or that in themselves they warrant justification before God, since James freely acknowledges that even as believers we all sin in many ways (James 3:2).

It is likely, however, that Paul and James use the term *justify* (*dikaioō*) with a different nuance.[4] Paul uses the word *dikaioō* to refer to a righteousness given to the ungodly, teaching that it is the ungodly who are declared to be righteous by virtue of the righteousness of Christ. James, on other hand, uses the verb *dikaioō* to refer to God's declaration that those who do good works are in the right before him. Hence, the common view that *dikaioō* in James means "proved to be righteous" or "shown to be righteous" is unpersuasive.[5] The term means "declare righteous" in both Paul and James, but in Paul it refers to divine declaration that those who trust in Christ are righteous even though they are ungodly, while in James it refers to the divine declaration that those who do good works are justified.

Often the view of the Reformers is understood to say that human beings are *shown* to be righteous (cf. Matt. 11:19; par. Luke 7:35) before other people by their works, but they are not *declared* to be righteous before God by their works.[6] This solution is attractive, and it resolves satisfactorily the alleged

---

3. Paul A. Rainbow, *The Way of Salvation: The Role of Christian Obedience in Justification* (Waynesboro, GA: Paternoster, 2005), 216–17.

4. Jeremias argues that δικαιόω in Paul is normally synthetic, in that God adds something to the ungodly that they do not enjoy, viz., righteousness. In James, on the other hand, δικαιόω is analytic, so that God at the Last Judgment recognizes the righteousness that now exists (Joachim Jeremias, "Paul and James," *ExpTim* 66 [1955]: 368–71).

5. Davids advocates the view disputed here. See Peter H. Davids, *The Epistle of James*, NIGTC (Grand Rapids: Eerdmans, 1982), 51, 127. In support of what I am defending, see Douglas J. Moo, *The Letter of James*, PNTC (Grand Rapids: Eerdmans, 2000), 134–35.

6. R. C. Sproul, *Faith Alone: The Evangelical Doctrine of Justification* (Grand Rapids: Baker, 1995), 166. See also the quote from Calvin to this effect in Sproul, *Faith Alone*, 167. I

contradiction between Paul and James. Nevertheless, it is doubtful that such a view handles the evidence satisfactorily. As argued previously, it is correct to say that Paul uses the term *dikaioō* to mean "declared righteous." What is less convincing is the claim that James uses the term to mean "proved righteous" or "shown to be righteous." The term *dikaioō* may have this meaning in Luke 7:35, but such a definition would be unusual. Further, in a context that discusses faith, works, and justification, we need good contextual evidence to assign a *different* meaning to the word *justify*. Assigning the word *justify* the meaning "declare righteous" fits with its typical meaning, and it makes good sense in the context of James.

It seems that both James and Paul use the word *justify* soteriologically, but Paul uses the word in an unusual sense in that he thinks of God declaring those who are unrighteous to be righteous. James, on the other hand, emphasizes that God declares those who are righteous to be righteous, though, I will argue shortly that it still does not follow that James and Paul ultimately contradict one another. The soteriological context in James is evident since he asks if a faith without works can "save" (*sōzō*, James 2:14). "Save" almost certainly refers to deliverance from God's wrath on the day the Lord returns (cf. James 5:7–9), which is the same meaning that it often has in Paul. Both *save* and *justify*, then, relate to one's standing before God. James appeals to Genesis 22 to support the need for works (James 2:21), and there is no suggestion in that chapter that the sacrifice of Isaac was commanded so that *people* would commend Abraham. In Genesis, God asserts that he now knows that Abraham fears God because of his willingness to sacrifice his son (Gen. 22:12), and he confirms the blessing given to Abraham because of the latter's *obedience* (Gen. 22:18). To see a reference to righteousness in the eyes of human beings does not account well for the argument in James 2:14–26 or the flow of the narrative in Genesis 22.[7]

If James uses *dikaioō* to refer to a declaration of righteousness by virtue of works, whereas Paul uses the term *dikaioō* to refer to the gift of righteousness granted to the ungodly, then do James and Paul contradict one another? Another solution proposed is that James differs from Paul because he uses the term to refer to eschatological justification—the pronouncement that will be

---

would maintain that even though Calvin and Sproul are off-kilter on this particular point, their reading of James substantially matches what is argued for here.

7. An even more unlikely solution is proposed by Radmacher. He argues that James does not refer to a faith that saves from God's eschatological wrath, nor does justification refer to standing in the right before God (Earl D. Radmacher, "First Response to 'Faith According to the Apostle James' by John F. MacArthur Jr.," *JETS* 33 [1990]: 35–41). Instead, James refers to a faith that gives one a happy and fruitful life on earth, and hence the faith that has works as its fruit is entirely unnecessary for salvation on the Last Day. The problem with Radmacher's view is that he has to posit definitions for σώζω and δικαιόω that do not fit with the remainder of the New Testament, nor does it square with the rest of James.

made on the Last Day.[8] Such a reading gets us closer to resolving the differences between Paul and James, but it still does not quite succeed. The term *justify* is eschatological in Paul, in that it refers to the final judgment, which has been announced ahead of time. Paul, of course, emphasizes that believers are *now* justified by faith (Rom. 5:1). The final verdict already belongs to believers who are in Christ Jesus (Rom. 8:1). It is important to add at this point that James likely uses the word *save* to refer to eschatological deliverance (James 1:21; 2:14; 4:12; 5:20). Paul often uses the verb *save* to refer to end-time deliverance as well (cf. Rom. 5:9). Evidence is lacking, however, that James and Paul use the word *justify* (*dikaioō*) differently in terms of eschatology. We can agree that *justify* is eschatological in that it represents God's verdict pronounced on the Judgment Day. James, however, emphasizes that this verdict *already* has been pronounced in history, just as Paul does.

The most natural way to read James 2:21 is to conclude that Abraham was "justified by works *when* he offered his son Isaac on the altar" (my italics). One could argue that the participle should be translated as causal, but even so the aorist passive "he was justified" (*edikaiōthē*) seems to point to a justification that belonged to Abraham *in history*. In the same way, Rahab was declared to be righteous by works "when she received the messengers and sent them out by another way" (James 2:25). In addition, Abraham's being reckoned as righteous seems to be connected to the offering of Isaac (James 2:21–23), and not reserved for the Day of Judgment alone. James appears to use the word *justify* within the same time frame as Paul, referring to the final verdict of God that already has been announced in advance.

I have argued that James and Paul use the term *dikaioō* with a different nuance (though not a different definition): James refers to the declaration of righteousness pronounced by virtue of the works performed, whereas Paul refers to the verdict by God that the ungodly who trust in Christ are righteous. Still, it does not follow that James and Paul ultimately contradict one another. We must recognize that they address different situations and circumstances, and those situations must be taken into account in understanding the stance of Paul and James relative to justification. Indeed, we are on the way to resolving the tension between James and Paul in seeing how they both use the term *faith* (*pistis*). When James says faith alone does not justify, faith here refers to mere intellectual assent. For instance, demons affirm monotheism, but such "faith" is not wholehearted and glad-hearted assent that leads demons to embrace Jesus Christ as Lord and Savior. Instead, the faith of demons is theologically orthodox but leads demons to shudder in fear of judgment (James 2:19).

---

8. So Rainbow, *The Way of Salvation*, 217. Moo argues that the time of justification is not resolved entirely by James, though verses 21, 24, 25 relate only to the Last Judgment (*The Letter of James*, 134–35, 138–39, 141–42).

According to James, the faith that saves embraces Jesus Christ as Savior and Lord, placing one's life entirely in his hands. James criticizes a "faith" that notionally concurs with the gospel but does not grip the whole person. In other words, James does not disagree with Paul's contention that faith alone justifies, but he defines carefully the kind of faith that justifies. The faith that truly justifies can never be separated from works. Works will inevitably follow as the fruit of such faith. Faith that merely accepts doctrines intellectually but does not lead to a transformed life is "dead" (James 2:17, 26) and "useless" (James 2:20). Such faith does not "profit" (*ophelos*, James 2:14, 16 RSV) in the sense that it does not spare one from judgment on the Last Day. Those who have dead and barren faith will not escape judgment. True faith is demonstrated by works (James 2:18). James does not deny that faith alone saves, but it is faith that produces (*sunergeō*) works and is completed (*teleioō*) by works (James 2:22). The faith that saves is living, active, and dynamic. It must produce works, just as compassion for the poor inevitably means that one cares practically for their physical needs (James 2:15–16).

SUMMARY

James and Paul do not actually contradict each other on the role of faith and works in justification. James affirms with Paul that faith is the root and works are the fruit.[9] James addresses a different situation from Paul, for the latter denies that works can function as the basis of a right relation with God. A right relation with God is obtained by faith alone. Paul responds to those who tried to establish a right relation with God on the basis of works. Paul argues that God declares those to be in the right who lack any righteousness, if they put their faith in Christ for salvation. James counters those who think that a right relation with God is genuine if there is faith without any subsequent works. James looks at God's pronouncement of righteousness from another angle, not as the *fundamental basis of one's relation to God but as the result of faith*. James responds to antinomianism, whereas Paul reacts to legalism.[10]

The above comments, of course, need qualification. As argued earlier, in some contexts Paul also emphasizes that good works are the fruit of faith[11]

---

9. For this observation, see also Laato, who argues that James differs from Judaism in rejecting the native ability of the human will and emphasizes instead God's work (Timo Laato, "Justification according to James: A Comparison with Paul," *TrinJ* 18 [1997]: 43–84). He remarks, "Good works subsequently brought into effect the living nature of faith" (p. 69). And he notes that faith "*only subsequently* (but nevertheless inevitably) will yield fruit" (p. 70, italics his).

10. Jeremias rightly observes that James fights on a different "field of battle" ("Paul and James," 370).

11. So also Laato, "Justification according to James," 72.

and are necessary for justification (e.g., Rom. 2:13; 4:17–22).[12] The purpose of James as a whole, as is evident from our entire discussion, is to emphasize that good works are necessary for salvation. His letter apparently responds to a situation where moral laxity was accepted. Nevertheless, James should not be interpreted to teach that believers can gain salvation on the basis of good works. Righteous deeds are the fruit of faith.[13]

James recognizes that all believers sin in numerous ways (James 3:2), and that even one sin makes one a lawbreaker (2:10–11). Humans lack the capacity, as sinners, to do the works required to merit justification. They are saved by the grace of God, for in his goodness and generosity he granted believers new life (1:18). Even faith is a gift of God, for God chose some to "be rich in faith and heirs of the kingdom" (2:5). What James emphasizes is that such faith must always manifest itself in good works if it is genuine faith. But such good works are a far cry from perfection, as James 3:2 clarifies. Kierkegaard captures memorably the intention of James: "It is like a child's giving his parents a present, purchased, however, with what the child has received from his parents; all the pretentiousness that otherwise is associated with giving a present disappears since the child received from the parents the gift that he gives to the parents."[14]

It seems, then, that Paul and James do not contradict one another, even though they address different circumstances. Both affirm the priority of faith in justification, and both also affirm that good works are the fruit of faith but not the basis of justification. What James teaches, then, fits with Paul and what we have seen elsewhere in the New Testament.

REFLECTION QUESTIONS

1. How do Roman Catholic scholars typically explain the meaning of the term *works* in Paul and James?

2. Do Paul and James employ a different meaning for the word *justify*?

3. What did I suggest that the word *faith* means in Paul and James?

4. How did the situations addressed by Paul and James help explain their emphases regarding justification?

5. What is the relationship between good works and faith?

---

12. On the role of Romans 4:17–22, see ibid., 76.
13. Laato rightly speaks of "the priority of faith" (ibid.,71).
14. Quoted from Richard J. Bauckham, *James: Wisdom of James: Disciple of Jesus the Sage* (New York: Routledge, 1999), 164.

PART 3

The Law in the Gospels and Acts

What Is the Role of the Law
in the Gospel of Mark?

The law plays a more prominent role in both Matthew and Luke than in Mark, and yet what we learn from Mark is not insignificant. Mark does not work out clearly and definitively a theology of the law, for his purpose was to proclaim the good news of Jesus Christ as the Son of God (Mark 1:1). Hence, the law appears in the story insofar as it relates to Christ and is not pursued for its own sake. When we think of the story of Mark as a whole, however, important implications for his theology of law emerge. The kingdom of God has arrived in the preaching and ministry of Jesus (1:14–15). God's saving promises are becoming a reality in Christ, and the fulfillment of God's promises certainly has important implications for Mark's theology of the law. The law does not occupy the same place and play the same role now that the kingdom promises are being fulfilled in Jesus.

The newness that accompanies Jesus' coming is pervasive in Mark. In the Transfiguration, both Moses and Elijah appear and speak with Jesus (Mark 9:2–8). It is likely that they represent the Law and the Prophets, and yet they clearly take a secondary place to Jesus, suggesting that the Law and Prophets point to him. Jesus is God's "beloved Son," and all should "listen to him" (Mark 9:7). The latter words pick up Deuteronomy 18:15, "The LORD your God will raise up for you a prophet like me from among you, from your brothers—it is to him you shall listen," indicating that Jesus is the final prophet and the fulfillment of what Moses prophesied. Jesus' centrality is communicated in the concluding words of the account: "they no longer saw anyone with them but Jesus only" (Mark 9:8). The Old Testament law, then, must be interpreted in light of the coming of Jesus Christ.

The account of the rich ruler points in the same direction (Mark 10:17–31). When the man asked how he could enjoy eternal life, Jesus pointed him to the commands in the law (vv. 17–18). The rich man claimed that he had kept such rules, but Jesus said that he would truly inherit life only if he gave up all his possessions and followed Jesus in discipleship (Mark 10:20–22). On the one hand, Jesus said nothing here to relativize the commands of the law. They represent the will of God for the rich man. On the other hand, the law rightly interpreted leads to Christ, for if the rich man truly loved God he would follow Jesus in discipleship and surrender all his possessions. We have another indication here that the law must be interpreted in light of the coming of Jesus Christ and that the law points to him.

The story of the rich ruler naturally leads us to Mark 12:28–34, where a scribe asked Jesus to indicate which commandment is the most important. Jesus pointed him to the Shema and to the injunction that one must love the Lord with all of one's being (Deut. 6:4–5). Furthermore, Jesus cited Leviticus 19:18 and the call to love one's neighbor as oneself. He argued that these two commands are supreme in the Torah and that all other commands are related to these. The scribe recognized the truth of Jesus' answer, and commended him, commenting that loving God with all that one has and loving one's neighbor "is much more than all whole burnt offerings and sacrifices" (Mark 12:33). Jesus recognized the wisdom of the man's response and said he was not far from the kingdom.

How should we interpret the account? Jesus did not say that the man was *in* the kingdom but that he was not far from the kingdom. If we put this story alongside the story of the rich ruler and the whole of Mark's gospel, which proclaims Jesus as the Christ and the Son of God (Mark 1:1), the reason the man is not part of the kingdom is clear. If one truly loves God and his neighbor, then he will confess Jesus as the Son of God and follow him in discipleship. The scribe is not in the kingdom because he does not understand yet that the law, rightly interpreted, points to Jesus Christ. Such a reading fits with the text that immediately follows Mark 12:28–34. Those who truly love the Lord will see that Jesus has been enthroned at God's right hand as Lord (vv. 35–37). Those who are actually in the kingdom recognize that Jesus shares the same identity as God and that the oneness of God is not compromised by the exaltation of Jesus.

The law no longer occupies the same status now that Christ has come. In the Old Testament anyone who touched a leper became unclean. Lepers were to reside outside the camp so that they would not infect others with their uncleanness (Lev. 13:46). Jesus' healing of the leper, then, in Mark 1:40–45 is quite striking. Indeed, Jesus cleansed him by touching him (v. 41). Jesus could have cleansed him with a pronouncement, as he did on many other occasions. In fact, Jesus could have taken precautions to avoid touching the leper in order to avoid contact with the unclean, so that he himself would not be ritually defiled, for in the Old Testament one who touches what is unclean becomes unclean. But the new order inaugurated by Jesus is evident here, for when Jesus touched the unclean leper, Jesus was not defiled by uncleanness.

Instead, the leper became clean. In Jesus the power of the holy was such that his holiness consumed and destroyed the uncleanness of the leper. The story suggests that Jesus is greater than the Old Testament law, that the law points to him and is fulfilled in him.

We see something similar in Mark 5:24–43, where Jesus healed the woman who had a hemorrhage of blood for twelve years and raised a twelve-year-old girl from the dead. Mark emphasizes that the woman touched Jesus, calling attention to it four times (vv. 27, 28, 30, 31). The Old Testament clearly teaches that a woman who has a discharge of blood is unclean so that anything or anyone who touches her becomes unclean (Lev. 15:25–27). So it is quite striking that she touched Jesus. But again the power of the holy overwhelms and conquers and irradiates her uncleanness. Instead of Jesus becoming unclean, his touch made her clean. The old rules do not apply in the same way in the case of Jesus. The Old Testament also teaches that one who touches the dead is rendered unclean (cf. Lev. 21:1, 11; 22:4; Num. 5:2). But again, when Jesus approached Jairus's dead daughter, he took her by the hand (Mark 5:41). Instead of contracting uncleanness from a corpse, Jesus cleansed her and granted her new life by raising her from the dead. These accounts suggest that the law is no longer central with the coming of the Christ. Jesus' healings and his raising of the dead show that the new age has arrived in his ministry.

Further support for this thesis is found in Mark 2:18–22. A controversy ensued over fasting and why Jesus' disciples did not fast. Jesus retorted that fasting does not fit with a wedding and the coming of the bridegroom. Jesus likely alluded here to the messianic feast prophesied in Isaiah 25:6. The fulfillment of God's promises does not call for fasting but feasting. The unexpected nature of the fulfillment also is suggested here, for Jesus forecasted a day when he would be removed from his disciples—the day when he would be nailed to a cross. Still, the emphasis is on the newness that has commenced with the coming of Jesus. Hence, the text concludes with the contrast between the old and the new. The newness that has come with Jesus cannot be simply patched onto the old (Mark 2:21), and "new wine" cannot be placed "into old wineskins" (Mark 2:22). The new wine must be put into new wineskins. The fulfillment brought about through Jesus does not simply represent a patching up of the old. A new era has commenced. A new order has arrived. Jesus does not merely represent a restoration or patching up of the Torah, but his coming means that the Torah must be interpreted in light of him.

The Sabbath accounts in Mark (2:23–3:6) should be explained along similar lines. Mark does not teach that Jesus somehow violated Sabbath regulations. In fact, Jesus emphasized that what he did was lawful (2:24–26; 3:3–5). Still, the accounts must be interpreted Christologically as well. Jesus is the new David who has sovereign authority over the Sabbath (2:25). He "is lord even of the Sabbath" (2:28). Again we find the truth that the Sabbath must be interpreted in light of his coming since Jesus is the Lord of the Sabbath. The Sabbath does not take precedence over the Son of Man; the Son of Man takes precedence over the Sabbath.

The newness that has come in Christ is quite apparent in Mark 7:1–23. Jesus scolded the Pharisees for exalting their oral tradition over God's commands and especially emphasized the need to honor one's father and mother (v. 10). But the text takes an interesting twist, for Jesus declared that what enters a person cannot defile him but only what comes out of him (v. 15), arguing that it is the evil that comes out of the hearts of human beings that renders them unclean (vv. 20–23). Jesus underscored the idea that food cannot defile anyone since it passes through one's system and is eliminated (vv. 18–19). The original hearers may not have grasped clearly what Jesus intended, but we have a Markan comment on Jesus' meaning that conveys the significance of Jesus' words. Indeed, this comment was probably mediated to Mark through Peter, for the early tradition that Mark wrote his gospel under Petrine influence is pervasive and should be accepted. We probably see here Peter's reflection on Jesus' words as a result of his experience with Cornelius (Acts 10:1–11:18). What Peter came to understand was that with the coming of Jesus all foods are clean. Hence, the Markan comment here, "Thus he declared all foods clean" (Mark 7:19). Certainly the Mosaic covenant and its laws no longer maintain the same status since the food laws are no longer mandatory. The new wineskins brought about by the Christ replace the old wineskins.

SUMMARY

Is the Markan Jesus inconsistent in citing the command to honor one's parents as authoritative and in criticizing the Pharisees for exalting the oral law over God's commands, when he himself relativizes the authority of the law? We must recognize that Mark does not attempt to work out for the reader a theology of the law. Since this was not Mark's purpose, it is impossible to provide a full-scale theology of the law. If we view Mark's statements on the law from a certain perspective, however, it fits nicely with what we saw in the more extensive Pauline treatment. The Mosaic law is no longer binding since a new era inaugurated by Christ has arrived. At the same time, it does not follow that the commands of the law have no application for believers. When the law is interpreted in light of Christ's coming, for instance, the command to honor one's parents remains, for this is part of Christ's law for believers. On the other hand, the food laws no longer have any function or role in the lives of God's people. Now that Christ has come, the purity laws are fulfilled in him, signified by his healing of the leper, his touching of the woman with the flow of blood, and his healing touch of Jairus's daughter. The new wineskins have arrived in Christ, and thus the old wineskins of the law must be interpreted in light of his coming. Mark does not give us a full picture, but the picture he gives fits with the larger scene found in the remainder of the New Testament.

REFLECTION QUESTIONS

1. According to Mark, what is the fundamental reality for the interpretation of the law?

2. What stands out as unique in Jesus' encounter with the rich ruler?

3. What is distinctive in Jesus' teaching on the Sabbath?

4. How would you explain Jesus' complex teaching on the law in Mark 7:1–23?

5. Is the Markan theology of the law a full exposition of the subject?

How Should We Understand Matthew's View of the Law?

Scholars often have pointed out that Matthew's conception of the law emphasizes continuity between the Old Testament and the New Testament. In Matthew 5:17–20 the abiding validity of the law is underscored. Jesus did not come "to abolish the Law or the Prophets" but "to fulfill them" (v. 17). Indeed, not even an iota or dot "will pass from the Law until all is accomplished" (v. 18). Those who minimize even the least of the commandments will be least in the kingdom (v. 19). Those who maintain that Matthew preserved a conservative view of the Old Testament law argue that Jesus did not violate the Sabbath but upheld it (12:1–14). Matthew excludes Mark's explicit statement that all foods are clean (Mark 7:19; cf. Matt. 15:1–20). The antitheses (Matt. 5:21–48) can be understood, as we shall see in the next question, as preserving the true intention of the law. Sacrifice in the temple (Matt. 5:24) and tithing (Matt. 23:23) are commended, and disciples are exhorted to pray that their exit from Jerusalem will not take place on the Sabbath (Matt. 24:20), which could be understood as a validation of the Sabbath by Matthew. Jesus even endorses everything the scribes teach (Matt. 23:2–3), though he criticizes their hypocrisy.

The notion that Matthew emphasizes only continuity in his view of the law should be rejected. The theme of fulfillment is prominent in the gospel (Matt. 1:22; 2:15, 17, 23; 4:14; 8:17; 12:17; 13:35; 21:4; 27:9; cf. also 3:15; 26:54, 56), but the fulfillment centers on Jesus Christ and thus should be understood in terms of the newness that is realized in Christ. Jesus fulfills the law, but the law also points to him. Jesus' life, ministry, teaching, death, and resurrection explicate the true meaning of the law. Matthew features both continuity and discontinuity relative to the law; so it is misleading to see only continuity. For instance, Matthew justifies Jesus' actions on the Sabbath with legal arguments (12:5, 11–12), and yet there is another dimension to the accounts.

Jesus is the greater David (vv. 3–4), greater than the temple (v. 6), and "lord of the Sabbath" (v. 8). Jesus does not abolish the Sabbath in Matthew, but he emphasizes that the Sabbath points to him and finds its fulfillment in him, so that the Sabbath must be interpreted Christologically. It follows, therefore, that the Sabbath must be interpreted in a new way with the coming of Jesus and the kingdom.

Even though Matthew does not explicitly include the Markan comment that all foods are clean (Mark 7:19), it does not follow that Matthew 15:1–20 emphasizes only continuity relative to the law. Jesus severely criticized those who exalted their tradition over the word of God (vv. 1–9). Here laws that reflect moral norms, such as honoring parents, are cited. And in verse 11 Jesus declared that food does not render one unclean. The word used for "defile" confirms that food laws in the Old Testament are under consideration (cf. Lev. 11:1–44; Deut. 14:3–21), and Jesus specifically said that food does not make one unclean. We clearly have an instance, then, in which the newness introduced by Jesus leads to the abolition of laws found in the Old Testament. Theologically, what we find here fits with what is called the law of Christ in Paul. The law is fulfilled in Christ and must be interpreted in light of Christ's coming. Hence, the focus is no longer on the law but on Christ himself.

The temporary character of the law is particularly clear in Matthew 17:24–27. The temple tax was required of all Jews (Exod. 30:13–16). When Peter was challenged about whether Jesus paid the temple tax, Peter answered in the affirmative (Matt. 17:24–25). When Peter encountered Jesus, however, the latter responded in a most astonishing way. Jesus declared that "the sons are free" from the temple tax (v. 26), indicating that the Old Testament law regarding the temple tax was no longer in force. Jesus paid the tax to avoid giving offence (v. 27), but he clearly did not think such payment was required. The newness inaugurated by Jesus led to a change in the status of the law. It must now be interpreted in light of Jesus' coming. He is greater than the temple (Matt. 12:5–6); therefore the temple must be understood in light of Jesus rather than vice versa.

Furthermore, Jesus envisioned the destruction of the temple (Matt. 24), and thus a new day was on the horizon where the temple would no longer play a central role among the people of God. The reference to sacrifice in the temple (Matt. 5:24), then, should not be construed as a permanent endorsement of sacrifices, since the temple would be destroyed in a generation. Jesus simply used an illustration that spoke to his contemporaries since he ministered in the period in which the Mosaic law was still in force. The references to tithing (23:23) and the difficulty of traveling on the Sabbath (24:20) also reflect life under the old covenant and do not represent a ratification of these laws for Jesus' new assembly (16:18). It is clear, then, that Matthew does not envision a flat-line continuity between the Mosaic law and the good news of the kingdom inaugurated by Jesus.

SUMMARY

It is better to describe Matthew's view of the law in terms of continuity and discontinuity. We saw above that the command to honor parents remains in force. Further, the entire law is summed up the injunctions to love God and one's neighbor (Matt. 22:34–40; cf. Deut. 6:4–9; Lev. 19:18). The new wine of the kingdom proclaimed by Jesus must be placed into new wineskins (Matt. 9:14–17). The wise scribe in the kingdom is like the householder who rightly relates the old to the new (Matt. 13:52) insofar as it relates to the kingdom of God. Hence, Jesus does not endorse everything the scribes and Pharisees say. Their teaching is to be followed only if it accords with God's will as it is proclaimed by Jesus.

REFLECTION QUESTIONS

1. What features in Matthew's presentation of the law point toward continuity with the Old Testament?

2. What one word best characterizes Matthew's perspective on the law?

3. How does Matthew 17:24–27 contribute to our understanding of Matthew's teaching on the law?

4. What role does redemptive history play in explaining the law in Matthew?

5. How should we preach Christ when considering the passages on the law in Matthew?

How Should We Understand the Antitheses in Matthew 5:21–48?

Many scholars argue that Matthew sets aside the validity and authority of the Old Testament law in these verses. Certainly he sees some discontinuity, for the law, as was argued in the previous question, is fulfilled in Jesus Christ. Jesus is the new and better Moses, for he regularly contrasts what was said under Moses ("you have heard that it was said," Matt. 5:21, 27, 33, 38, 43; "it was also said," 5:31) with the authority of his words ("But I say to you," 5:22, 28, 32, 34, 39, 44). Nevertheless, I will argue that in these particular verses Jesus corrected misinterpretations of the Mosaic law, explaining as the sovereign and final interpreter of the law how it relates to the hearers of his day. In other words, Jesus explicated the true meaning of the law and corrected erroneous interpretations.

For instance, the Pharisees likely interpreted the prohibition against murder (Exod. 20:13) as fulfilled if they did not literally murder anyone. But Jesus astonished them (and us!) by saying that one violates the commandment if one is angry with his brother (Matt. 5:21–22). Jesus interpreted the commandment at a deeper and more radical level, uncovering the sin lurking in the heart of human beings (cf. Prov. 14:29; 22:24; 29:22). Similarly, the Jewish interpreters of Jesus' day apparently believed that they had carried out the prohibition against adultery (Exod. 20:14) if they refrained from the physical act. Jesus cut to the root of the matter, reminding them of what they already should have known from the Old Testament (Job 31:1; Prov. 6:23–25). Adultery stems from lust in the heart, and such lust also violates the seventh commandment (Matt. 5:27–28).

Many—perhaps most—interpreters think that Jesus set aside the Mosaic command regarding divorce in Matthew 5:31–32. Such an interpretation is certainly possible and would accord with what I argued in the previous question regarding Matthew's view of the law as a whole. Nevertheless, it seems that in this segment of Matthew's gospel (5:21–48) Jesus corrected misinterpretations of the Old Testament by his Jewish contemporaries. When we read Deuteronomy 24:1–4 carefully, it is evident that Moses did not endorse or commend divorce but permitted it. Some Jewish interpreters of Jesus' day distorted the Old Testament teaching. Indeed, the school of Hillel permitted divorce for the most trivial reasons, justifying it if a wife ruined a meal or if one found someone prettier (*m. Gittin* 9:10). Jesus defended his reading of the Old Testament canonically, pointing to the creation account (Matt. 19:3–12). God's intention from the beginning was that one man be married to one woman. Some Jewish interpreters exploited the permission found in Moses as if it commended divorce and remarriage; thus Jesus penetrated to the core issue, arguing that such divorces lead to adultery and violation of the seventh commandment.

Space is lacking here to discuss the matter of divorce thoroughly. I follow the traditional Protestant view, which argues that divorce is permissible (but never ideal), where there is sexual infidelity.[1] Hence, Jesus did not actually contravene the Old Testament permission for divorce, for he also granted permission to divorce for sexual immorality. Nevertheless, he emphasized the permanence of marriage and corrected distortions that open up the floodgates to divorce. Divorce exists because of the hardness of the human heart (Matt. 19:8). Ultimately, Jesus corrected a misreading of the Old Testament that was popular in his day and explained God's intention for marriage from the Old Testament as a whole.

If Jesus' words on divorce seem to contravene the Old Testament law according to many interpreters, his words on oaths, on first glance, certainly seem to lead to such a conclusion (Matt. 5:33–37). The Old Testament clearly permitted oaths but underlined the seriousness of them (e.g., Num. 30; Josh. 9:20). Jesus, however, banned all oaths, saying, "Do not take an oath at all" (Matt. 5:34), forbidding oaths by heaven, earth, Jerusalem, or by one's head (vv. 34–36). He concluded, "Let what you say be simply 'Yes' or 'No'; anything more than this comes from evil" (v. 37). What strengthens this interpretation even more is a comment from James, and James's view almost certainly stems from Jesus tradition: "But above all, my brothers, do not swear, either by heaven or by earth or by any other oath, but let your 'yes' be yes and your 'no' be no, so that you may not fall under condemnation" (James 5:12). Certainly if Jesus forbade the taking of all oaths, which seems to be confirmed by James, then he overturned part of the Old Testament law.

Despite the impressive evidence in support of the above interpretation, it is more likely that Jesus corrected a misinterpretation of the Old Testament

---

1. For a defense of this interpretation and helpful interaction with opposing views, see Andreas J. Köstenberger with David Jones, *God, Marriage, and Family: Rebuilding the Biblical Foundation* (Wheaton, IL: Crossway, 2004), 227–58.

and did not forbid all oath-taking. If this view is correct, then both Jesus and James used hyperbolic language with reference to oaths and should not be understood as prohibiting the use of oaths altogether. Both Jesus and James emphasized the importance of truthfulness in speech. Oaths are criticized because they have become a means by which the truth can be circumvented, so that they have become a facade for lying.

Several arguments support the interpretation proposed here. It is clear elsewhere in Matthew that the Pharisees and scribes used oaths casuistically to avoid telling the truth. They devised a system whereby swearing by the temple was considered to be nothing; therefore, if one swore by the temple, one did not have to fulfill one's oath (23:16). Similarly, they said that swearing by the altar was nonbinding, though if one swore by the gift offered on the altar, then one was obligated to fulfill the oath (23:18–19). Jesus rejected such casuistry, arguing that one should always speak the truth instead of devising subtle schemes to circumvent what one has promised to do (23:20–22). It seems, then, that oath taking itself is not prohibited but rather an abuse of the practice. Jesus spoke hyperbolically to underline the need for truthfulness, since oaths had become a means for evading the truth.

Other evidence in the New Testament confirms the reading proposed here. First, Jesus himself responded to the admonition to take an oath when asked about his identity (Matt. 26:63–64). His submission to such a request seems odd if oaths are categorically rejected. Second, Paul himself appealed to his readers with oath formulas (e.g., Rom. 1:9; 2 Cor. 1:23; Gal. 1:20; Phil. 1:8). Such examples are quite strange if the Jesus tradition was understood to forbid all oaths, particularly since there is good evidence that Paul was familiar with traditions about the historical Jesus.[2] The practice of Paul supports what is being argued here. Jesus did not literally forbid the taking of oaths but emphasized the importance of truth. Third, according to Hebrews 6:13–18, God himself took an oath to underline the certainty of his promises. We have further evidence, then, that early Christians did not understand Jesus to prohibit the use of all oaths. What was proscribed was the frivolous use of oaths, which had become creative ways to dodge telling the truth.

Again, many scholars maintain that Jesus set aside the Old Testament law in saying that instead of practicing an "eye for an eye and a tooth for a tooth" believers should "not resist the one who is evil" but should turn the other cheek if slapped "on the right cheek" (Matt. 5:38–39). However, there are solid reasons for thinking that Jesus responded again to a misinterpretation of the Old Testament law. The expression "an eye for an eye and a tooth for a tooth" enshrines the principle that the punishment should fit the crime.

---

2. Dale Allison, "The Pauline Epistles and the Synoptic Gospels: The Pattern of the Parallels," *NTS* 28 (1982): 1–32; Peter Stuhlmacher, "Jesustradition im Römerbrief: Eine Skizze," *TBei* 14 (1983): 240–50.

As Leviticus 24:19 says, "If anyone injures his neighbor, as he has done it shall be done to him." Offenders of the law should not be punished more severely than is warranted, nor should the penalty be mitigated for one who is rich or famous. Hence, Leviticus 24:22, declares, "You shall have the same rule for the sojourner and for the native, for I am the LORD your God." In the Old Testament "an eye for an eye" is found in civil contexts, where governing authorities are given instructions about the penalties that are fitting for those who have committed crimes (Exod. 21:22–25; Lev. 24:17–22; Deut. 19:21). Hence, "Whoever takes a human life shall surely be put to death" (Lev. 24:17).

Jesus corrected a faulty reading of Old Testament texts which teach that the punishment must fit the crime. Jesus did not dispute the notion that there should be retributive, compensatory penalties for criminal infractions. What he objected to was the notion that this principle could be transferred to the personal sphere. When individuals are insulted by a slap on the right cheek, they are not to respond in kind (Matt. 5:39). A slap on the right cheek is not a physical attack but an insult, for it is given with the back of the hand. Believers are not to return insults with insults. Jesus gives colorful and hyperbolic examples to illustrate his teaching. He does not literally mean that one should hand another his cloak if sued, nor were believers required to volunteer to go the extra mile when Roman soldiers commandeered them to go one mile. Jesus' point was that one should not have a heart of revenge and retaliation when mistreated or abused (Matt. 5:40–41). After all, one could literally volunteer to go the extra mile and give everything one owns to a beggar (vv. 41–42) and still have a heart filled with hatred and revenge. Jesus did not abolish the Old Testament here since the principle that the punishment fits the crime is the heart of justice. What he stood against is personal revenge and retaliation in the lives of believers.

This interpretation is confirmed by Paul. Indeed, the Pauline support for the interpretation defended here is particularly striking, for it occurs in a text in which Paul appealed to Jesus tradition. Like Jesus, Paul commanded believers to "never avenge" themselves (Rom. 12:19). Rather, they should give food and drink to those who are their enemies and "overcome evil with good" (Rom. 12:20–21). And yet in Romans 13:1–7 governing authorities are said to be ordained and instituted by God. They are God's servants who reward good conduct and punish evil. They do not "bear the sword in vain" (v. 4) and are "avenger[s]" and carry out "God's wrath on the wrongdoer." According to Paul, believers are to refrain from taking personal vengeance, and yet governing authorities are to repay evil with justice and to punish criminals in accord with their crime. Remarkably, the Pauline view fits with the interpretation proposed for Matthew 5:38–42, which is even more striking, as noted above, when we realize that Paul drew on Jesus tradition. I conclude, then, that Jesus corrected a misinterpretation of the Old Testament law in which laws that relate to the civil sphere were wrongly applied to the personal sphere.

Finally, Jesus commanded his followers to love their enemies instead of hating them (Matt. 5:43–48). This text strongly supports the notion that Jesus corrected misinterpretations of the Old Testament in Matthew 5:21–48. The Old Testament did not call upon God's people to hate their enemies but just the opposite. They must not hate their brothers (Lev. 19:17–18) and must help the person who hated them (Exod. 23:5). Nor can the call to refrain from hatred be restricted to fellow Israelites only, as Job makes clear (Job 31:29–30). The hatred commended in Psalm 139:21–22 does not violate what Jesus commanded here, for there it represents taking the same stance as God toward his enemies, which does not preclude showing love and kindness to those who hate us. Since the Old Testament does not commend hating enemies, Jesus is most likely responding to a misreading of the Old Testament, reminding his hearers that they must imitate God and shower good on both the evil and the righteous.

SUMMARY

The Old Testament commands in Matthew 5:21–48 were not set aside by Jesus. Rather, he provided the proper interpretation of those commands and applied them in a penetrating way to the lives of his disciples.

REFLECTION QUESTIONS

1. What interpretive standpoint should be adopted in reading Matthew 5:21–48?

2. Is divorce ever legitimate according to Matthew 5:31–32?

3. Should Christians ever take oaths? Why or why not?

4. Given Jesus' teaching in Matthew 5:38–42, may Christians engage in self-defense?

5. Does the Old Testament teach that we should hate our enemies?

Why Do Some Scholars Think Luke–Acts Has a Remarkably Conservative View of the Law?

Some scholars have argued that Luke's view of the law is more conservative than any other writer in the New Testament.[1] I will argue in answering the next question that such a view is mistaken, but I will present here the evidence that leads some scholars to think that Luke did not want his readers to depart from the Old Testament law. The gospel of Luke opens with Zechariah and Elizabeth being commended for "walking blamelessly in all the commandments and statutes of the Lord" (Luke 1:6). The gospel begins by saluting Zechariah and Elizabeth for their law obedience, which could be understood as Luke's imprimatur upon those who abide by the Old Testament law. Luke is also careful to note that Jesus was circumcised on the eighth day (Luke 2:21), just as it was prescribed in the Old Testament law (Lev. 12:3). Furthermore, Joseph and Mary observed what was required in the law for purification (Luke 2:22–24). They consecrated their firstborn, Jesus, to the Lord, just as the law required (Exod. 13:2). And they carried out the purification rite as specified in Leviticus 12, bringing turtledoves and pigeons for a sin offering and burnt offering (Lev. 12:8). Why does Luke take the time to inform us that the law was observed by Jesus' parents? Some argue that he does so because he wanted his readers to abide by the law as well.

---

1. Jacob Jervell, *Luke and the People of God: A New Look at Luke–Acts* (Minneapolis: Augsburg, 1972), 133–51; cf. Donald Juel, *Luke–Acts: The Promise of History* (Atlanta: John Knox, 1983), 103–09.

This case is strengthened by Jesus' traveling to Jerusalem with his parents for Passover (Luke 2:41–52). The Passover required that all males travel to Jerusalem for the feast (Exod. 34:22–23; Deut. 16:1–8); and since Jesus was twelve years old, he was considered an adult and hence obligated to observe Passover. Indeed, Jesus' actions on the Sabbath were not contrary to the law. Jesus defended his healing of the man with the withered hand by declaring that it is "lawful on the Sabbath to do good" (Luke 6:9). His response was similar in the case of the man who had dropsy (Luke 14:1–6), arguing again that his healing was "lawful" and noting that his opponents would set free their sons or animals if they fell into a well on the Sabbath. The inability of the opponents to reply, according to Luke, signifies that Jesus' actions and reasoning were impeccable.

In another account, the synagogue ruler was infuriated that Jesus healed on the Sabbath a woman who was crippled for eighteen years, arguing that the healing should have taken place on another day of the week (Luke 13:10–17). Jesus did not respond by saying he had the right to violate the law. He contended that those opposing him were hypocritical since they took the effort on the Sabbath to untie their animals and lead them to the watering trough.

The disciples' eating grain on the Sabbath was contested by the Pharisees (Luke 6:1–5), presumably because they plucked it and rubbed it with their hands, which the Pharisees interpreted as harvesting. Jesus, however, appealed to the precedent of David, implying that what the disciples did was permissible because of human need. Such a reading of the Sabbath is supported by the Lukan observation that the women "rested" on the Sabbath day "according to the commandment" (Luke 23:56), suggesting that the Sabbath was still required for believers.

When the lawyer asked Jesus what was required for eternal life, Jesus responded by asking the lawyer how he himself read the law (Luke 10:25–26). The lawyer cited Deuteronomy 6:5 and Leviticus 19:18, which mandate that one must love God and one's neighbor (Luke 10:27). Jesus did not contest his interpretation. Instead, he said that he had answered "correctly" and enjoined him to "do this, and . . . live" (Luke 10:28). The law is endorsed as the way to life for the lawyer.

Similarly, when the rich ruler asked Jesus how he could "inherit eternal life" (Luke 18:18), Jesus pointed him to the commandments: "Do not commit adultery, Do not murder, Do not steal, Do not bear false witness, Honor your father and mother" (v. 20). Again, the commandments are recommended as the way of life.

One could argue that the law remains in force only until the coming of John the Baptist, inasmuch as "the Law and the Prophets were until John" and now the kingdom is being proclaimed (Luke 16:16). Those who defend the continuing authority of the law, however, point to the immediately following words in Luke, "But it is easier for heaven and earth to pass away than for one dot of the law to become void" (v. 17). The continuing authority of the law is underscored in the strongest terms.

The ongoing validity of the law also comes to the forefront in Acts. Peter and John were coming to the temple at "the ninth hour" (Acts 3:1), which would be the time of the burnt offering; so presumably they were arriving at that time to participate in the evening burnt offering sacrifice. Stephen's opponents charged that he spoke "blasphemous words against Moses" (6:11), that he spoke against "the law" (6:13), and that he desired to "change the customs that Moses delivered to us" (6:14). But Luke characterizes the men who said these things as "false witnesses" (6:13). Indeed, Stephen turned the tables on his opponents, contending that they were the ones who did not keep the law (7:53).

In addition, Gentiles are instructed to observe regulations that come from the Old Testament law. They were "to abstain from the things polluted by idols, and from sexual immorality, and from what has been strangled, and from blood" (Acts 15:20). The next verse reveals that these regulations were part of the Mosaic law. Indeed, the "for" at the beginning of Acts 15:21 indicates that Luke provides the reason why Gentiles are to observe the prescriptions noted: "For from ancient generations Moses has had in every city those who proclaim him, for he is read every Sabbath in the synagogues." The importance of these commands is underlined since they are reiterated twice more in Acts (15:29; 21:25).

The picture of Paul in Acts is quite striking, for his observance of the Old Testament law is often noted. For instance, Paul circumcised Timothy (Acts 16:3), which is certainly quite astonishing, given Paul's categorical repudiation of circumcision in Galatians (Gal. 2:3–5; 5:2–6). Paul also took a Nazirite vow (Acts 18:18) in accord with the Old Testament law (Num. 6:2, 18). Apparently when Paul returned to Jerusalem, he purified himself in the temple and offered the sacrifices that were required to fulfill a Nazirite vow (Acts 21:26; Num. 6:13–15). Indeed, Paul did not merely offer his own sacrifice, but he also paid the expenses for the sacrifices required for four other men who had taken Nazirite vows (Acts 21:23–24), so that "the days of purification would be fulfilled and the offering presented for each one of them" would be given (v. 26). All of this is designed to prove that the accusations that Paul "teach[es] all the Jews who are among the Gentiles to forsake Moses, telling them not to circumcise their children or walk according to our customs" (v. 21) are false. Thereby they will "all will know that there is nothing in what they have been told about you, but that you yourself also live in observance of the law" (v. 24).

The Paul of Acts, it has often been observed, is a law-abiding Paul. We are not surprised, then, that when Paul commended Ananias to his Jewish hearers that he described him as "a devout man according to the law" (Acts 22:12).

SUMMARY

The evidence that Luke subscribes to a very conservative view of the law is quite impressive, as we have seen in the evidence adduced above. I will argue, however, in the answer to the next question that such a reading of the evidence misreads the Lukan intention.

REFLECTION QUESTIONS

1. What elements in Jesus' birth narrative (Luke 2) point toward careful observance of the law?

2. What elements in the Sabbath accounts point toward Jesus' observance of the law?

3. What role do Old Testament commandments play in Jesus' conversations with others, according to Luke?

4. What evidence in Acts supports the idea that Paul carefully observed the law?

5. Can an interpretation have elements of truth and still be fundamentally flawed?

How Should We Understand the Role of the Law in Luke–Acts?

We saw in the answer to the previous question that some scholars promote the view that Luke had the most conservative view of the law of all the writers of the New Testament. I will argue here that such a judgment misconstrues the Lukan purpose. On the contrary, Luke's view of the law must be assessed from a redemptive-historical standpoint.

The fulfillment of the Old Testament Scriptures plays a major role in Luke-Acts. Those who rightly interpret "Moses and all the prophets" will discern that they are fulfilled in Jesus Christ (Luke 24:27; cf. 4:16–21). Both Jesus' suffering and his resurrection fit with all that is written "in the Law of Moses and the Prophets and the Psalms" (Luke 24:44). What the opponents call a "sect" is actually "the Way," which declares a future resurrection. Paul followed this "Way" because he believed "everything laid down by the law and written in the Prophets" (Acts 24:14; cf. Acts 26:22–23; 28:23). The Old Testament, then, is fulfilled in the gospel proclaimed by Paul, and hence all of Scripture points to Jesus Christ and finds its goal in him. Therefore, the Old Testament, including the Old Testament law, must be interpreted in the light of the coming of Jesus Christ, for he is the climax of all revelation.

Such a perspective explains why Luke testifies that "the Law and the Prophets were until John" (Luke 16:16). Now that Christ had come the kingdom had arrived. But does Luke 16:17 indicate that the law continues to be in force in the same way as in the time before John since not even "one dot of the Law" will "become void"? Such a reading fails to see that Luke is not suggesting a straight-line continuity but emphasizing that Jesus fulfilled everything prophesied in the Old Testament. Jesus stood as the sovereign interpreter of the Old Testament law, explaining that those who divorce and remarry commit adultery (Luke 16:18). In other words, the focus is no longer on the law but on Jesus, who is the fulfillment of the law.

Like the other Synoptics, Luke also includes texts that indicate discontinuity between the law and the new era inaugurated by the Christ (see questions 26–28 for the perspective of Mark and Matthew). Jesus touched the leper and instead of becoming contaminated with uncleanness himself cleansed the leper (5:12–15). Luke also includes the accounts of the woman hemorrhaging blood and Jairus's dead daughter, who are both made well by Jesus (8:40–56). In both instances Jesus was not defiled by touching them, but they were cleansed by his touch. These texts do not directly teach the abolition of the Old Testament law, but they certainly indicate that Jesus had a new and different kind of relationship to the law.

The Sabbath texts are interpreted too simplistically by those who defend the idea that Luke argues for the ongoing validity and continuity of the law. As noted in question 29, the legal validity of what Jesus did on the Sabbath is often emphasized by Luke. It would be reductionistic, however, to see this as the only theme. As we saw in Matthew and Mark, Jesus implied that he is the new David with sovereign authority to allow his disciples to eat on the Sabbath (Luke 6:1–4). Indeed, as the Son of Man he is "Lord of the Sabbath" (Luke 6:5). Again, instead of the Sabbath taking precedence, Jesus takes precedence. Perhaps there is an implication in Luke 13:10–17 that healing on the Sabbath was particularly fitting for one who is the Lord of the Sabbath.

The fulfillment that has dawned in Jesus Christ does not lead to the conclusion that there is no continuity between the law and the new age of redemptive history inaugurated by Jesus Christ. We are not surprised to learn that the commands to love God with all of one's being and to love one's neighbor continue to apply to human beings (Luke 10:25–28). Even in this instance, however, the whole of what Luke says must be considered in order to discern his theology. Jesus did remind the rich ruler of the commands of the law, which were required in order to receive eternal life (Luke 18:18–20). Nevertheless, the rich ruler was deceived about the genuineness of his love for God and neighbor, for such love would be verified only if he followed Jesus in discipleship and surrendered all his riches (vv. 21–23). What is striking here is the centrality of Jesus for obtaining eternal life. The Old Testament commands to love God and neighbor find their goal and criterion in Jesus himself.

Furthermore, Luke does not teach that the law continues to apply in the same way after the death and resurrection of the Christ. We saw in question 29 that the charges raised against Stephen were false (Acts 6:11–14). To say that the charges were false, however, does not mean that the accusations were unrelated to Stephen's preaching. Stephen almost certainly said some things about the temple and the law that were provocative. Some scholars have overemphasized the discontinuity in Stephen's remarks, claiming that he categorically rejected the temple—even during the period of the Old Testament. This latter perspective overstates Stephen's criticisms, and yet there is an element of truth in the analysis. Stephen relativized the significance of the law and the temple in Israel's history. He reminded his hearers that God was with both Abraham and Joseph, even though neither lived in the Land of Promise or enjoyed God's presence in the temple (Acts 7:2–16). Nor should the temple be unduly venerated, for God worked in Israel's history through the tabernacle, and the Old Testament itself acknowledges that the temple cannot fully express or contain the majesty of God (Acts 7:44–50). Stephen did not directly criticize the temple, but he suggested that it must be interpreted in light of the fulfillment of God's saving purposes in Jesus Christ.

The encounter of Cornelius and his friends with Peter confirms that Luke does not merely propound continuity with reference to the law. Peter received a vision of unclean animals while waiting for a meal, and the Lord commanded him to kill and eat the unclean animals (Acts 10:9–16). Peter was taken aback by such a command since it was directly contrary to the Old Testament law, which declared certain foods to be unclean (Lev. 11:1–44; Deut. 14:3–21). Luke unmistakably indicates that the law regarding unclean foods is no longer required when he quotes the heavenly voice, saying, "What God has made clean, do not call common" (Acts 10:15).

The point of the vision in the Lukan narrative is the legitimacy of the mission to the Gentiles. Peter need not worry that Cornelius and the Gentiles were unclean, for he now perceived that no one is "common or unclean" (Acts 10:28). The import of the vision cannot be limited to the Gentile mission, as if the text says only that Gentiles are no longer unclean while still requiring Old Testament food laws. The relationship between food laws and the mission to the Gentiles is inseparable. Gentiles were considered to be unclean because they did not observe purity laws, among other reasons. Hence, Luke clearly teaches that the food laws are now abolished. A new era of redemptive history has arrived, and the gospel is to be disseminated to the Gentiles without the imposition of the Old Testament law. Therefore, when Peter looked back on the Cornelius event in Acts 15, he realized that God "made no distinction" between Jews and Gentiles, "having cleansed their hearts by faith" (v. 9). The "yoke" of the law must not be placed on the Gentiles, for no one among either Jews or Gentiles is able to observe what the law commands (v. 10). Salvation is "through the grace of the Lord Jesus" (v. 11). The law, then, is no longer required to belong to the people of God. Luke emphasizes that the Spirit is received "by faith" (v. 9) and "through grace" (v. 11).

Indeed, Peter's comments in Acts 15 were spoken at the famous apostolic council, where a major meeting was held to determine whether circumcision was required for Gentile converts. Circumcision, of course, was mandated by the Old Testament law (Gen. 17:9–14; Lev. 12:3). The words of Peter, which we just examined (Acts 15:7–11), played a decisive role at the council, and Peter argued that circumcision should not be required since Cornelius and his friends received the Holy Spirit by faith. Therefore, it follows that the Old Testament command to be circumcised was no longer normative. James clearly agreed with the conclusion of Peter, maintaining that the Old Testament prophets as well anticipated the new era that has arrived in Jesus Christ (Acts 15:14–18).

The church drew the conclusion, therefore, that the Gentiles who "turn to God" should not be troubled (Acts 15:19). Those who had stirred up the controversy in Antioch by insisting on circumcision were not carrying out the instructions of the apostles or the church in Jerusalem (Acts 15:24). The only "burden" to be imposed upon the disciples was the apostolic decree (Acts 15:28–29). The decision reached by the apostolic council is absolutely crucial for understanding the Lukan view of the law. Circumcision, which was the entrance rite for admission to the covenant in the Old Testament, was not required for those who desired to enter the church of Jesus Christ. A new era of salvation history had dawned, and the law was no longer obligatory. Luke does not have an extremely conservative view of the law, for he teaches that circumcision as the entrance rite into the covenant had passed away.

It seems curious that other regulations from the Old Testament law were imposed on disciples if circumcision was passé. It has been suggested by some that the apostolic decree and the circumcision of Timothy indicate that the law was still in force for believers in Jesus Christ. The apostolic decree is quite complex and will be examined in question 31, and the question of Timothy's circumcision will be taken up in question 32. Here it should be said only that the apostolic decree and Timothy's circumcision, rightly interpreted, do not teach that the law is still required. They represent theologically legitimate accommodation for pragmatic reasons and therefore should not be adduced as evidence for the continued normativity of the law.

Paul's taking of a vow in which he offered sacrifice in the temple and paid for the sacrifices of others should be interpreted similarly (Acts 18:18; 21:21–26). Paul's vow and his offering of sacrifices do not indicate that he believed the Old Testament law was still normative. Paul had no problems with Jews continuing to observe the law as part of their cultural background. What he objected to was imposing the Old Testament law on the Gentiles for salvation. Hence, Paul did not believe Jewish parents were required to quit circumcising their children or to abandon the Old Testament law (Acts 21:21). Paul himself observed the law when he was with the Jewish people (Acts 21:24; 1 Cor. 9:20). When he was with the Gentiles, however, he did not observe the law (1 Cor. 9:21), so that he could win them to salvation in Christ. The Jews in Jerusalem misinterpreted Paul's flexibility relative to the law when he was with the Gentiles. They believed that he was also demanding that they as Jews cease practicing the law and also thought that Paul himself did not observe the law. But Paul did not advocate that Jews abandon their observance of the law. Indeed, he typically practiced the law as well. But when he attempted to reach Gentiles for the gospel, then he would live like Gentiles (apart from the law) so that he could live in their midst and proclaim to them the good news of Christ.

Other texts that are adduced to support the idea that Luke's view of the law was remarkably conservative have been wrongly interpreted. Jesus' circumcision at eight days old (Luke 2:21) scarcely supports the notion that the law is still mandatory. We have just seen that Acts 15 makes it plain that circumcision was not required for entrance into the people of God. But Jesus was circumcised because he was born into a Jewish family. Indeed, Jesus' circumcision, the observance of purification rituals demanded in the Old Testament (Luke 2:22–24), and the observance of Passover (Luke 2:41–52) must be interpreted in light of where they occur in salvation history (cf. Luke 23:56). Jesus and his family, after all, grew up during the old era of salvation history, at a time when the Old Testament law was still in effect. It does not follow from Jesus' observance of the law as a child that believers who belong to the new covenant inaugurated by Jesus Christ are required to follow the same pattern (Luke 22:20).

Perhaps it was important, according to Luke, to stress that Jesus and his family kept the law in order to show that he was obedient to God's will (cf. Luke 1:6). We have seen that Luke emphasizes elsewhere that the continuing observance of the Old Testament law by Jews—even after the inauguration of the new covenant—is appropriate. But he certainly does not think such observance of the law is required, for he makes it plain that Old Testament food laws and circumcision are not required for Gentiles to be part of the people of God. Justification and forgiveness cannot be obtained through the law of Moses but only through believing in Jesus as the Christ (Acts 13:38–39).

SUMMARY

Luke must be read discerningly in order to grasp his view of the law. On first glance he may seem to be an unabashed supporter of the law; but when he is read more carefully and in light of the story of both Luke and Acts, it becomes clearer that the law should be interpreted in light of salvation history. Now that the new covenant has arrived in Jesus Christ, the law no longer occupies center stage. The law must be interpreted in light of Jesus Christ and his coming. It was the will of God to keep the law during the old era of salvation history, but the law is not required for the salvation of the Gentiles. It is no longer normative now that Christ has come.

REFLECTION QUESTIONS

1. Why is salvation history fundamental for understanding Luke's teaching on the law?

2. How would you explain what Stephen's speech (Acts 7) teaches about the law?

3. Why was Peter's encounter with Cornelius (Acts 10:1–11:18) so important for grasping the Lukan theology of the law?

4. What insight does the Apostolic Council of Acts 15 bring for our understanding of the law in Luke?

5. What is the significance for today of the decision to not require circumcision for salvation?

What Is the Apostolic Decree of Acts 15 and What Does It Contribute to Luke's Theology of Law?

The so-called apostolic decree is described by Luke in Acts 15. The leaders of the churches from Jerusalem and Antioch met in Jerusalem to determine whether circumcision would be mandatory for Gentiles who believed Jesus was the Messiah. As we saw in question 30, they decided that circumcision was not necessary. But James recommended that the Gentiles follow four other prescriptions, and these laws often are called the apostolic decree.

The content of these laws is stated three times. James said that Gentile believers should "abstain from the things polluted by idols, and from sexual immorality, and from what has been strangled, and from blood" (Acts 15:20). The same requirements are recorded in the letter the church of Jerusalem sent to Gentile believers: "Abstain from what has been sacrificed to idols, and from blood, and from what has been strangled, and from sexual immorality" (Acts 15:29). James reminded Paul of the content of the decree when he returned to Jerusalem: "But as for the Gentiles who have believed, we have sent a letter with our judgment that they should abstain from what has been sacrificed to idols, and from blood, and from what has been strangled, and from sexual immorality" (Acts 21:25). Why are these requirements added after the church has agreed that Gentiles are free from the requirement of circumcision? Does the law come in the back door after it has been shut out of the front door? And what do these requirements mean? What precisely is it that the council decided the Gentiles should do?

It should be noted that the issue is actually even more complex, for the correct text of the decree is also in question. A number of Western manuscripts, for instance, leave out the command regarding strangling and add a negative form of the Golden Rule. If this reading is accepted, the decree consists of moral prohibitions. Gentile converts are given instructions as new converts. They must abstain from idolatry, murder ("blood"), from sexual sin, and should do nothing to their neighbors that they would not want their neighbors to do to them.

The advantage of this interpretation is that it removes the main difficulty in the text. If one follows these Western texts, then circumcision is not required for salvation, but this should not be interpreted as if there are no moral requirements for believers. Gentiles would misinterpret freedom from the law if they thought they were free to worship idols, murder their neighbors, commit sexual sin, and mistreat others. Even though the Western text reading nicely answers questions posed by Acts 15, it should be rejected. One of the main rules in textual criticism is that (all other things being equal) the harder reading should be accepted as original. This rule applies well to the apostolic decree. The harder reading includes things strangled, which is eliminated by the Western text. In addition, the best manuscripts also support the inclusion of things strangled and do not contain the negative form of the Golden Rule. In other words, the external evidence of the manuscript tradition also weighs against the Western reading. Both internal and external evidence, then, stand against the Western reading.

Some scholars have argued that the decree stems from the Noahic commands (see Genesis 9), but the text in Genesis says nothing about sexual immorality or things sacrificed to idols, and hence it seems that a reference to the commands given to Noah for Gentiles is not compelling. Witherington intriguingly argues that all the prohibitions relate to worship in pagan temples.[1] But it is difficult to see how the prohibition regarding eating meat with blood in it can be restricted to what took place in pagan temples, and hence it seems that the decree has a wider scope than worship in pagan temples.

Many scholars maintain that the decree draws on Leviticus 17–18. On this view, the decree prohibits eating food that was not slaughtered properly, eating meat with blood in it, marrying within the kinship relationships set forth in Leviticus 18:6–18, and eating food offered to idols. It is quite possible that this reading of the decree is correct, and it shall be evaluated in due course. Richard Bauckham proposes an even more specific interpretation, finding the key in the phrase "in your/their midst" in Leviticus 17:8, 10, 12, 13, and 18:26.[2] According to Bauckham, these commands, which are based on Leviticus 17–18, were required of Gentiles who lived in the midst of Israel. The commands, then, do not represent a pragmatic compromise to facilitate fellowship between Jews

---

1. Ben Witherington III, *The Acts of the Apostles: A Socio-Rhetorical Commentary* (Grand Rapids: Eerdmans, 1998), 460–66.
2. Richard J. Bauckham, "James and the Jerusalem Church," in *The Book of Acts in Its First Century Setting*, vol. 4, *The Book of Acts in Its Palestinian Setting*, ed. Richard J. Bauckham (Grand Rapids: Eerdmans, 1995), 459–80.

and Gentiles according to Bauckham. On the contrary, these commands were required of Gentiles who lived in the midst of Israel.

One of the problems with Bauckham's solution relates to Paul. According to Acts, Paul was at the apostolic council and accepted the apostolic decree. Bauckham thinks that Paul later changed his mind and ended up rejecting the council's decrees. But if Paul disagreed with the other apostles and with Jerusalem on this matter, it seems that he would make his rejection of their position clearer in his argument in 1 Corinthians 8:1–11:1. We would expect Paul in his argument to interact with the case made from Leviticus 17–18, but such interaction is lacking. Perhaps another possibility is preferable if we accept Bauckham's analysis as correct.

Perhaps Paul believed that some Gentiles in certain geographical areas did not live in the midst of Israel. If this latter view is the case, then Paul might have embraced the decree in certain geographical regions. Then as he traveled to different parts of the Roman Empire, the regulations passed in the decree would be inapplicable.

C. K. Barrett, on the other hand, understands the decree mainly in moral terms. He maintains that what is forbidden is idolatry, fornication, murder, and the eating of nonkosher foods.[3] Against Barrett, it seems that the reference to blood does not refer to murder but to the eating of food with blood in it, per Leviticus 17. It might seem strange to have a reference to both blood and the proper drainage of animals, but this may be explained as representing a major concern of Jews. In the same way, it seems unlikely that idolatry in general is proscribed. The context favors a prohibition of eating food offered to idols. It seems to me, then, that a slight adjustment of the majority view best fits the evidence. The word *porneia* refers to sexual sin, but the remainder of the prescriptions deal with issues that were particularly sensitive in fellowship between Jews and Gentiles. The decree, then, speaks to abstaining from eating meat with blood in it, eating meat from which the blood was not drained properly, and eating food sacrificed to idols. The decree adds the restriction about sexual sin since it was a common vice among Gentiles.

If this reading of the decree is correct, why was the decree accepted by the apostolic church in Jerusalem? Did it represent a compromise of the principle of a law-free gospel that was vindicated with the decision that circumcision would not be required?

There is no compromise or contradiction here. The apostolic council determined that the law was not required for salvation. Hence, circumcision must not be imposed on the Gentiles as an initiation rite into the Christian church. The basic principle of a law-free gospel was established at the council, but then James turned to consider the issue of fellowship between Jews and Gentiles. The law was not required for salvation, but the Jerusalem church

---

3. C. K. Barrett, *Acts 15–28*, ICC (Edinburgh: T & T Clark, 1998), 730–36.

recommended observance of some of the laws that were particularly sensitive to Jews. These prescriptions were not mandated for salvation. They were recommended as a means to facilitate fellowship between Jews and Gentiles. This rationale seems to be suggested by James's observation in Acts 15:21: "For from ancient generations Moses has had in every city those who proclaim him, for he is read every Sabbath in the synagogues." James maintained that the Gentiles were aware of Jewish sensibilities since the Mosaic law was read in virtually every city of the Diaspora. Hence, Gentiles would be acquainted with customs that bothered the Jews, and they were asked out of love to refrain from disturbing Jewish brothers and sisters.

This interpretation fits with James's advice to Paul in Acts 21:25. James reminded Paul that Gentiles were not required to observe the law, even though Jews continued to keep it. Instead, the requirements are limited to certain matters that were particularly sensitive for Jewish believers; thus Gentiles were asked to observe some restrictions, not for the sake of salvation, but for the sake of love.

SUMMARY

The role of the apostolic decree in Luke's view of the law is complex and controversial. I have defended the view here that the decree does not contradict the freedom from the Old Testament law that Luke teaches elsewhere. The decree was not required for salvation. The council recommended that Gentiles refrain from certain practices in order to facilitate fellowship between Jews and Gentiles.

REFLECTION QUESTIONS

1. What is the content of the apostolic decree according to the Western text, and why should this reading be rejected?

2. What view of the decree is suggested by those who see the background in Leviticus 17–18?

3. What is Richard Bauckham's understanding of the decree, and how do you evaluate it?

4. What view of the decree do I propose in this chapter?

5. Do the contents of the decree contradict the freedom from the law enunciated in the remainder of Luke–Acts?

Why Did Paul Circumcise Timothy When He Refused to Circumcise Titus?

We are astonished that the circumcision of Timothy was recommended by Paul, especially after the apostolic council had decided that circumcision was not required for believers to become part of the people of God (Acts 15:1–29). All were saved by faith through the grace of the Lord Jesus Christ (vv. 7–11). How, then, do we account for the circumcision of Timothy? Does the circumcision of Timothy constitute a reinstatement of the law? Did Paul sin by circumcising Timothy? Some scholars have even argued that Luke invented the circumcision of Timothy, arguing that Paul never would have circumcised him and that Luke wanted to portray Paul as a good Jew who observed the law.

Indeed, the question becomes even more pressing when we consider the case of Titus in Galatians 2. Some false brothers apparently wanted Titus to be circumcised in accord with the initiation rite for the people of God under the old covenant (cf. Gen. 17:9–14; Lev. 12:3). Paul adamantly contended that Titus must not be circumcised in order to preserve "the truth of the gospel" (Gal. 2:5). If Titus were circumcised, it would send the message that circumcision was necessary for salvation, that one must observe the Old Testament law to be saved. Paul could not tolerate such a state of affairs for even a moment, for it would contradict the truth that salvation is free, that it comes through the grace of Christ and not by observing the law. But then why did Paul circumcise Timothy according to Acts 16? Was he willing, on this occasion, to compromise the truth of the gospel? Did he fall into sin by circumcising Timothy?

There are solid grounds for thinking that Paul did circumcise Timothy and that such an action does not compromise the gospel he preached. Thus, we do not need to adopt the radical conclusion that Luke invented what Paul did here. Indeed, such a view should be rejected because it contradicts the truthfulness of the Scriptures, for the Scriptures are inspired by God and are wholly true (2 Tim. 3:16–17). If Luke included stories of events that did not happen, he would be guilty of deception, and his writings should not be prized as Scripture but rejected as unethical.

Nor should we draw the conclusion that Paul sinned in circumcising Timothy. We must recognize that the case of Timothy was dramatically different from the case of Titus. The circumcision of Timothy captures the principle of 1 Corinthians 9:19–23. In circumcising Timothy, Paul was adapting to the customs of those to whom he ministered, without violating God's norms and will, so that he could win more for the gospel. But was Paul's "adaptation" a violation of the gospel? Did he compromise in order to mollify the Jews when he should have stood fast?

We learn an important fact in Acts 16:1–3 that explains why Paul circumcised Timothy, whereas on another occasion he refused to circumcise Titus. Timothy was the son of a Jewish mother and a Gentile father. Hence, in the eyes of the Jews, Timothy would have been considered Jewish. Anyone who was the son of a Jewish mother was considered to be ethnically Jewish. Paul decided to circumcise Timothy "because of the Jews," which likely means that he circumcised him so that the Jews would not take offense when Timothy came with Paul into synagogues to proclaim the gospel. It would have been difficult for Paul to bring an uncircumcised Timothy into Jewish synagogues for evangelism, since the Jews would have taken offense at a Jewish person (the son of a Jewish mother) who was uncircumcised.

The circumcision of Timothy, therefore, was dramatically different from the circumcision of Titus. Paul refused to circumcise Titus because Titus was a Gentile, and to circumcise him would communicate the truth that Gentiles must be circumcised to belong to the church of Christ. Timothy, on the other hand, was Jewish. Paul agreed to circumcise him because the truth of the gospel was not at stake. Indeed, Paul felt free to circumcise him because the council in Jerusalem had just determined that circumcision was not required for salvation (Acts 15:1–29). Since the apostolic council had just taught that the law was not required to be a Christian, no one would be confused about why Paul circumcised Timothy. No one would think that he was suggesting that circumcision was necessary for salvation. Now that the main principle had been established—the law was not an entrance requirement for the people of God—Paul had freedom to be flexible culturally.

SUMMARY

It is no accident that Paul circumcised Timothy after the council reached the decision that circumcision was unnecessary for salvation. If the gospel was at stake (as in the case of Titus), Paul was completely inflexible and adamant: no circumcision. But if the matter was cultural and circumcision was not required for salvation, then Paul was willing to be perceived as inconsistent. In every instance the highest priority for Paul was the gospel, and he acted to promote its advance. Paul had no animus against circumcision per se. He stood firmly against it only if it was perceived as a requirement for salvation.

REFLECTION QUESTIONS

1. What reason did Paul give for refusing to circumcise Titus (Gal. 2:3–5)?

2. What feature of Timothy's background distinguished him from Titus (Acts 16:1–3)?

3. Was the circumcision of Timothy an unwarranted compromise on Paul's part?

4. What role does 1 Corinthians 9:19–23 play when considering the circumcision of Timothy?

5. What principles can we derive from Scripture as to when we should be flexible on a matter or when we should stand resolutely for the truth?

How Should We Describe the Role of the Law in the Gospel of John?

John does not focus on the law but on Christ, and this is evident from the high Christology of John's gospel. Jesus is the Christ and the Son of God (20:31). He is the Son of Man and the eternal Logos. Indeed, John emphasizes that Jesus is divine (1:1, 18; 20:28) and existed with the Father from the beginning (1:1; 17:5). The law, rightly interpreted, bears witness to Christ, and thus those who do not put their faith in Jesus as the Christ do not rightly interpret the law (5:38–39, 46).

John develops this theme in many ways. The temple in Jerusalem points to Jesus as the true temple (2:19–22). The manna the Lord provided for Israel in the wilderness is fulfilled in Jesus, who is the true bread who has come from heaven and given his flesh for the life of the world (6:25–59). Jesus also fulfills the Feast of Tabernacles (*m. Sukkah* 4:9–10; 5:2–4). The water-pouring rite is fulfilled in Jesus, for one's thirst is satisfied only in him (John 7:37–38). So too, the lighting ritual that was practiced at the feast finds its fulfillment in Jesus as well, for he is "the light of the world" (John 8:12), which is verified by his ability to grant sight to the blind (John 9).

In the Old Testament Yahweh is the shepherd of his people and promises to shepherd them in the future (Ps. 23:1; Ezek. 34:11–16, 23–24), but this promise is realized in the ministry of Jesus as the Good Shepherd who gives his life for the sake of his sheep (John 10:11–18). In the Old Testament the vineyard of the Lord is Israel (Isa. 5:1–7), but Israel failed to produce good fruit; Jesus is the true Vine, the true Israel who always does what pleases the Lord (John 8:29; 15:1). The Lord liberated Israel from bondage at the Exodus, and Israel celebrated the Lord's deliverance at Passover, but Jesus is the true Passover Lamb (John 18:28, 39; 19:14). The brief survey above indicates that the Old Testament finds its meaning and fulfillment in Christ, and hence we would expect the law to function similarly.

The Sabbath, as in the Synoptics, plays a significant role in John's gospel. Jesus healed a man who was an invalid for thirty-eight years (5:1–9). The Jews were indignant because the man carried his bed, for the Jews believed that this constituted work and violated Sabbath regulations (vv. 10–16). What is instructive is that Jesus did not respond casuistically in the first instance. He could have reacted by insisting that carrying one's bed after a healing should not be defined as work. Thereby the charges raised against him could be dismissed as groundless. But Jesus responded in an altogether astonishing way, saying, "My Father is working until now, and I am working" (v. 17).

Jesus' reply is unexpected at two levels. First, he admits that he was working. He avoids technical discussions of work entirely and freely acknowledges that he was working. But if he was working, then was he not violating the Sabbath? This brings us to Jesus' second comment. His work is eminently defensible because, as the Son, he is doing the same thing his Father was doing. His work cannot be criticized since he was imitating God. The Jews were scandalized by Jesus' defense, since it amounted to the claim that he was equal with God (John 5:18). This text is of great significance in tracing out John's theology of the law, for it shows that Jesus is superior to the Sabbath. The Sabbath no longer has the same status now that the Son of God has come. The Sabbath law must be interpreted in light of the coming of Jesus Christ.

Interestingly, Jesus returns to the same healing of the invalid in John 7:19–24, and on this occasion he argues quite differently! Here he offers the kind of legal argument that we might have expected in John 5. Jesus notes that circumcision is performed on the Sabbath without anyone thinking that the law is thereby infringed upon. Hence, his healing of someone on the Sabbath is quite legitimate. So, the argument turns in a different direction, and yet the divine prerogatives of Jesus are not entirely absent from the story. Jesus is like God in that he is able to make a man healthy (John 7:23). Here he imitates God, who can create life where there is death.

One of the most important verses for the Johannine perspective on the law is John 1:17: "For the law was given through Moses; grace and truth came through Jesus Christ." John does not deny that there is grace and truth in the law. Indeed, the preposition *anti* in John 1:16 (translated in the ESV as "grace upon grace") should be translated "instead of" or "in place of," for this preposition is regularly used in terms of replacement and never means "upon." Therefore, the grace in Christ replaces the grace that is in the law. It is acknowledged, then, that there is grace in the law, but the grace found in Christ is superior. Grace and truth exist in the law, but they reach their climax and purest expression in Christ. So, we have another indication that the law points to Jesus Christ.

John does not concentrate on commands that stem from the Old Testament law. Instead, as we would expect from John 1:17, the emphasis lies upon what Jesus instructs his disciples to do. He speaks of "my commandments" (14:15, 21; 15:10) and "my commandment" (15:12), and what "I command you" (15:14, 17), and the "new commandment" that "I give to you" (13:34). The law has reached its fulfillment in Christ, and his commands are authoritative for believers. Obeying the commands of Jesus indicates one's love for him (14:15, 21, 31; 15:10, 14).

John does not focus on the content of the commands. He does zero in, though, on Jesus' command to love one another (15:12, 17). The commandment is new because disciples are to love one another "as I have loved you" (13:34). Jesus' surrender of his life on the cross becomes the paradigm and pattern for the love of disciples. The focus is not on keeping discrete laws, for if disciples follow Jesus, who gave up his life for them, then the purpose of the Old Testament law will be realized in their sacrificial love. In other words, the ethical life the Old Testament demanded has now been expressed in the life of Jesus of Nazareth, for he always did the Father's will (5:19). He did what pleases the Father (8:29) and therefore could not be convicted of sin (8:46). The purpose of the law was always that it would express itself in human lives. Jesus lived to do the Father's will and his life was animated by love, so that he gave his life for the sake of his sheep (10:11). Certainly in John's gospel the cross of Christ becomes the supreme expression of love, and disciples are to follow Christ by showing love like Christ's to others.

SUMMARY

The law does not play a central role in John's gospel, though John does emphasize that the law points to and is fulfilled in Jesus Christ. John particularly stresses Jesus' command to love one another, and Jesus' giving of himself for the salvation of others on the cross becomes the paradigm for such love.

REFLECTION QUESTIONS

1. What is the relationship between the law and Christology in the gospel of John?

2. In what ways does John present Jesus as the replacement of the Old Testament?

3. In what astonishing way does Jesus defend his healing on the Sabbath in John 5?

4. What is the relationship between law under the old covenant and the grace that has come with Jesus, according to John 1:17?

5. What does Jesus emphasize in John when he calls upon believers to keep his commands?

PART 4

The Law in the General Epistles

What Does John Mean by Keeping God's Commands in 1 and 2 John?

Both 1 and 2 John have a similar view of the law as the gospel of John, which is scarcely surprising since they are written by the same author. The evidence that one has come to know God is the keeping of his commandments (1 John 2:3). Those who do not keep his commands are liars, and "the truth" is not in them (1 John 2:4). Although the content of the commands is vague, it is noteworthy that these commands are linked to "truth" and the "word." The "truth" in 1 John is closely associated with the gospel of Christ. Those who do not belong to God fail to "practice the truth" (1:6; cf. 1:8). John addresses readers who already know the truth (2:21; 3:19; 4:6), granting them assurance of their standing with God. The keeping of commandments also is linked in 1 John with doing God's "word" (*logos*, 1 John 2:5). The message John proclaims is characterized as "the word of life" (1:1), and this message centers on the incarnation of Christ (1:1–3), on the truth that the historical Jesus is the Christ (2:22–23; 4:2–3; 5:6), and on Jesus laying down his life as an atonement to secure salvation (2:2; 3:5, 8; 4:9–10). Those who claim to be free from sin do not have this word in them (1:10). It seems, then, that the commands to which John refers are closely tied to the message about Christ that he proclaims. The commands cannot be restricted to Old Testament commands but are identified with the gospel.

The close relationship between the gospel John preaches and God's commands is confirmed by 1 John 2:7–11. John does not write a new command but an "old commandment" that the believers had "from the beginning" (v. 7). The beginning here must refer to the beginning of their Christian lives, and so John underscores that he does not tell them anything new. Still, there is a sense in which the command is new, for it is now being realized in the inauguration of the new age that has arrived in Jesus Christ (v. 8). What is the old command that is new in Christ? John identifies it as "the word that you have heard" (v. 7). I have argued above that this word centers on the gospel of Christ. Hence, the old command, which the context also clarifies is the call to love one another (vv. 9–11), has become a reality through the gospel, which has created a new reality.

The close relationship between the gospel and commands in 1 John is also evident elsewhere. God's command is summarized as believing in Jesus Christ as God's Son and in loving one another (3:23). Again, John forges a close connection between embracing Jesus as the Christ and Son of God and loving one another. Only those who abide in God and enjoy the presence of his Spirit are enabled to keep God's commands (3:24). Indeed, it is those who are "born of God" who know God (4:7). Love is a reality for those who abide in God (4:16) and have been rescued from sin by Christ's atoning sacrifice (4:9–10). Human love is an answering and responsive love, so that love for one another springs from the love of God in Christ, for "we love because he first loved us" (4:19). John rounds out this section by calling attention to the command to love one's brothers (4:21), but the context reveals that this command finds its wellspring in the love of God in Christ, which has created a new love in the hearts of believers.

John circles back to God's commands in 1 John 5:2–3, but he examines the issue from a different angle. Previously, he emphasized that God's commands are kept when believers love one another, but now he says that "we know that we love the children of God, when we love God and obey his commandments" (v. 2). Is John contradicting himself or falling into confusion? Earlier he emphasized that we know we are keeping God's commands when we love one another, and that we know that we love God when we love brothers and sisters. What does it mean, then, to say that our love for brothers and sisters is verified by our love for God and the observance of his commands?

Probably John stresses another dimension of love. Horizontal love for brothers and sisters is not genuine love if it is not animated by love for God. Only those who are "born of God" love the Father and his Son (1 John 5:1). John labors to teach in 1 John 4:7–21 that all human love comes from knowing God's love for us. Hence, true love for fellow believers is a reality only for those who love God. Similarly, no one truly loves brothers and sisters unless he or she keeps God's commands. This seems to imply that love must be defined by moral norms; therefore, love needs to fit within the riverbanks of moral norms to be genuine. Only those who keep God's commands truly love him (1 John 5:3). Love cannot be collapsed into sentimental feelings but also involves the observance of commands. Still, such commands must not be construed fundamentally in terms of obligation and duty. The commands are not a burden since believers have been "born of God" (1 John 5:4). They have a new power that is theirs because of their new life in Christ. They are enabled to do the will of God because they believe that Jesus is the Christ (1 John 5:5). John's instructions on the law do not fall prey to moralism. The obedience of believers is rooted in the gospel, which creates a new reality.

We do not need to linger over the teaching of 2 John, due to its brevity. Still, it is instructive to see that some of the themes present in 1 John appear here as well. The command of the Father is that believers walk in truth (v. 4). Such walking in truth accords with the gospel of Christ, for those who walk in truth confess that Jesus is the Christ in the flesh (v. 7). Believers do not support those who propagate a defective Christology (vv. 10–11). John reiterates that he does not write a new command but the old command—from the time of their conversion—that they should love one another (v. 5). But if 2 John 5 identifies the commandment as loving brothers and sisters, verse 6 reminds us of 1 John 5:2: "And this is love, that we walk according to his commandments; this is the commandment, just as you have heard from the beginning, so that you should walk in it." On the one hand, God's commands are kept if believers love brothers and sisters. On the other hand, love also is defined by the content of the commandments so that love does not devolve into sentimentality. And yet John concludes by using a singular in referring to what God demands: "This is the commandment . . . that you should walk in it" (2 John 6). The commandments of God are viewed as a unity, presumably because commands should not be viewed as separate and discrete entities but as being fulfilled in God's gracious saving work.

SUMMARY

The letters of 1 and 2 John tie closely together the gospel of Jesus Christ and God's commands. One of the central commands that must be embraced is that Jesus is the Christ who has come in the flesh. Those who know God and are born of God practice the commandments, particularly the command to love one another. John does not focus on Old Testament commandments but on the dawning of a new reality in the gospel of Christ.

REFLECTION QUESTIONS

1. What is the relationship between the "word" and commands in 1 John?

2. What does the close link between the gospel and commands in 1 John teach us about Christian obedience?

3. How should we describe the relationship between God's commandments and the injunction to love one another?

4. Why do you think John emphasizes loving one another instead of loving unbelievers?

5. Do we truly know God if we do not love and serve fellow believers?

What Does James Teach Us About Keeping God's Law?

The letter of James is a practical letter that was likely written to Jews who lived outside of Israel (James 1:1). James has a limited purpose and therefore does not address many issues central to the Christian faith. For instance, the death and resurrection of Jesus Christ are not even mentioned. We are not surprised to discover, then, that James does not present us with a comprehensive discussion on the law. Still, what he has to say is of significant interest.

James reminds his readers that partial obedience to the law is not sufficient. The particular sin James mentions is partiality (James 2:1–13), or showing favoritism to the rich over the poor. Those who are partial "are convicted by the law as transgressors" (James 2:9). The law they violate is stated in Leviticus 19:18, where the Lord commanded Israel to love their neighbors as themselves. Perhaps James also is reflecting upon Leviticus 19:15, "You shall do no injustice in court. You shall not be partial to the poor or defer to the great, but in righteousness shall you judge your neighbor." As James reflects on partiality, he comments, "For whoever keeps the whole law but fails in one point has become accountable for all of it" (James 2:10). An illustration follows so that the reader can understand the truth being communicated. No one can claim to be a law keeper if he or she abstains from adultery but commits murder. Compliance with one part of the law while flouting another part is not praiseworthy. Failure to observe any part of the law makes one a lawbreaker instead of a law keeper. So, it seems that James agrees with what we saw in Paul. God demands perfect obedience to his law.

The importance of doing the law is also evident in James 4:11: "Do not speak evil against one another, brothers. The one who speaks against a brother or judges his brother, speaks evil against the law and judges the law. But if you judge the law, you are not a doer of the law but a judge." What James precisely means by this statement is difficult to comprehend. What is clear is that the law must be obeyed rather than assessed and evaluated. Those who slander others have put themselves above the law, and therefore they are implicitly placing themselves above the law as a judge. The humble stance is not to appraise the law but to do it.

If we return to the discussion on partiality, James identifies the law as "the royal law" (James 2:8). Again, the meaning of the phrase is a bit elusive. Perhaps the law is royal because it comes from God as the sovereign Lord and King of all, and hence it is an authoritative and binding word. Such a reading fits with James 2:8–12, where the importance of doing what the law says is underscored. This reading also accords with the message of James as a whole, for James is insistent that the law must be put into practice.

What is the content of the law for James? Are believers still under the Old Testament law? The Jewishness of James is quite evident, and it might lead one to the conclusion that the Mosaic law is still the standard for believers. James clearly draws on the Old Testament significantly. We noted above that his words against partiality seem to come from the indictment against partiality in Leviticus 19:15. Surely, James's concerns for widows and orphans is deeply rooted in Old Testament piety and instruction as well (James 1:27; cf. Exod. 22:22; Deut. 10:18). The concern for edifying speech (James 3:1–12) and for godly wisdom (vv. 13–18) are derived in part from the wisdom literature of the Old Testament. The indictment of the rich who oppress the poor (James 5:1–6) fits with the prophetic denunciations of the rich in the Old Testament (Amos 2:6–8; 4:1–3; cf. Deut. 24:14–15). In addition, James specifically cites two commands from the Decalogue, where both murder and adultery are proscribed (James 2:11; cf. Exod. 20:13–14).

What is striking, however, is what is absent. James never mentions circumcision, Sabbath, or food laws. The ceremonial dimensions of the law are entirely absent, and this fact is more notable when we recall that James was addressed to Jewish Christians (James 1:1). Clearly, James thinks the Old Testament is authoritative, and he even cites certain commands from the law as authoritative. If the churches addressed were Jewish, then it is likely that the Christians in the churches observed Sabbath and food laws and were circumcised. And yet James never mentions such commands, even though other commands from the Old Testament are cited as authoritative. Indeed, James probably alludes to Psalm 19:7 when he speaks of God's law as "the perfect law" (James 1:25).

The key to unlocking James's understanding of the law is to discern what he says about "the word" and "the law of liberty." The law is identified as "the law of liberty" twice in James (1:25; 2:12). Deciphering the significance of the phrase is aided by the context in which the phrase appears, for in each instance James emphasizes the importance of doing God's will

(1:19–25; 2:8–13). The law liberates, then, in that it frees human beings from the shackles of sin so that they are enabled to do God's will. Is James speaking about the Mosaic law here? If so, he seems to contradict Paul who argues that the law produces transgressions (Rom. 5:20; Gal. 3:19) and that it brings death rather than life (2 Cor. 3:6–7; Rom. 7:5–25). However, there are substantial reasons to think that by the law of liberty James refers to the gospel rather than the Mosaic law.

That the "law of liberty" refers to the gospel is confirmed by James's understanding of "the word" (*logos*). We read in James 1:18, "Of his own will he brought us forth by the word of truth." James has in mind the new life that Christians enjoy. The new birth can be traced to "the word of truth," which is another way of describing the gospel. The law that liberates, then, refers to the gospel of Jesus Christ. It is this "implanted word, which is able to save your souls" (James 1:21). The salvation in view here is eschatological salvation that delivers human beings from God's wrath on the Last Day. The means of salvation here is the "implanted word." James draws on the new covenant promise of Jeremiah. The Lord promises, "I will put my law within them, and I will write it on their hearts. And I will be their God, and they shall be my people. And no longer shall each one teach his neighbor and each his brother, saying, 'Know the LORD,' for they shall all know me, from the least of them to the greatest, declares the LORD. For I will forgive their iniquity, and I will remember their sin no more" (Jer. 31:33–34). The word is implanted in that it is now written on the hearts of the people of the Lord.

Both James 1:18 and 1:21 emphasize the grace of God, for it was his powerful word that produced new life and that saves one on the Day of Judgment. The law that liberates, then, is not the Mosaic law, but the word of the gospel, which creates life. So, when James refers to doing the word (1:22–23) or fulfilling "the royal law" (2:8) or of "the law of liberty" (1:25; 2:12), he thinks of a new obedience that is generated by the word of the gospel. It is this gospel that makes people new, and human obedience is a result of God's gracious work. Such a reading is confirmed when we recall that James says nothing about circumcision, food laws, and Sabbath. Believers are no longer under the authority of the Mosaic covenant and its laws. Rather, it is the word of the gospel, which is fulfilled in the new covenant, that has dawned with the coming of the Christ.

SUMMARY

James emphasizes the keeping of the royal and perfect law. We have seen, however, that such observance is traced to the word of the gospel that grants life. James never mentions the ceremonial law and focuses on faith, which leads believers to live a new life.

REFLECTION QUESTIONS

1. What does James mean by the "royal law"?

2. What is the relationship between "the law of liberty" and "the word of truth" in James?

3. What does James allude to when he speaks of "the implanted word" (James 1:21), and why is this significant?

4. Why is it striking that James never mentions the ceremonial law?

5. Does James demand perfect obedience to the law (James 2:10–11)?

What Does the Letter to the Hebrews Teach Us About the Law?

When we consider the New Testament as a whole, it is clear that the canonical writers believed that the Mosaic covenant was temporary and that believers are no longer obligated to fulfill its stipulations.[1] The author of Hebrews engages in a sustained argument against reverting to the Aaronic priesthood and the Levitical sacrificial cultus.[2] He does not claim that the Mosaic covenant was somehow a mistake from its inception. Instead, he hangs his argument on salvation-historical realities.[3] Now that Christ has arrived as the Melchizedekian priest, a return to the Levitical priesthood would constitute a denial of Christ's sacrifice. The Aaronic priests and the Old Testament sacrifices are not rejected wholesale; they are viewed typologically. The Old Testament priesthood and sacrifices pointed to and anticipated the sacrifice of Christ. They are the shadows, but he is the substance. The brute beasts offered in Old Testament sacrifices cannot ultimately forgive, but Christ's sacrifice is atoning since he is a willing and sinless victim. The repetition of Old Testament sacrifices reveals that they do not actually forgive sin, whereas the once-for-all sacrifice of Christ definitively and finally atones for sin.

---

1. The answer here reflects a very slight revision of my section on the law in Thomas R. Schreiner, *New Testament Theology: Magnifying God in Christ* (Grand Rapids: Baker, 2008), 665–68.
2. The letter to the Hebrews is likely directed to believers who were tempted to return to Judaism.
3. For a lucid exposition of the law in Hebrews, see Frank Thielman, *The Law and the New Testament: The Question of Continuity* (New York: Crossroad, 1999), 111–34.

The author of Hebrews maintains that a change of priesthood also constitutes a change of law (Heb. 7:11–12). Indeed, he claims that the law did not bring perfection and was weak and useless (7:18–19).[4] In context, it is clear that his point is that the law does not provide a full and final atonement for sin. Indeed, he proceeds to argue that the promise of a new covenant indicates that the Sinai covenant is now obsolete (Heb. 8:7–13). Once again, the focus is on the failure of the law to provide final forgiveness. A regular feature in Hebrews is the contrast between the stipulations and/or punishments of the Sinai covenant over against what is required now for those belonging to Christ (2:1–4; 9:6–10, 15–24; 10:26–31; 12:25–29; 13:9–12). Indeed, the very first verses of the letter contrast the definitive revelation given in the last days in the Son with the partial, preliminary revelation given under the old covenant (1:1–3). The contrast between Moses and Christ articulated in 3:1–6 is similar in this regard.

It is evident that the author of Hebrews believed that the new covenant has displaced, or perhaps better, "fulfilled," what was promised in the old. Now that the end of the ages has arrived, a return to the old covenant would lead to final destruction. The author is strikingly severe and dogmatic. Those who return to the regulations and sacrifices of the old covenant will be damned, for to do such is to reject the work of Christ on the cross (cf. 6:4–8; 10:26–31; 12:25–29). Hence, he can say that no sacrifice for sins remains for those who turn away from Christ's sacrifice (10:26). This is another way of saying that those who turn back to the Levitical cult have shut themselves off from any possibility of forgiveness. Literal animal sacrifices have passed away, and yet believers offer to God spiritual sacrifices when they praise God's name and when they share financially with those who are in need (Heb. 13:15–16).

The author of Hebrews does not charge the Mosaic covenant with legalism, nor does he find fault with the specific prescriptions in the law per se. Rather, the Mosaic covenant and law had a typological and salvation-historical function. The tabernacle points to the true tabernacle in heaven, where God dwells (cf. 8:1–6; 9:1–10). The Old Testament sacrifices and regulations anticipate the sacrifice of Christ and the era that has dawned in the new covenant (9:11–14, 23–28; 10:1–18). Old Testament sacrifices also point to the need to share with others and to praise God (13:15–16). The promises of land and rest in the Old Testament forecast the heavenly city and the Sabbath rest prepared for the people of God in the age to come (3:7–4:13; 11:9–10, 13–16; 12:22; 13:14).

Is there any continuity between the Old Testament law and the New Testament fulfillment of Christ in Hebrews? The author cites the new covenant promise of Jeremiah 31:31–34 that the law will be written on the heart of

---

4. Attridge says that in Hebrews the law does not produce perfection, whereas in Paul it does not grant life (Harold W. Attridge, *The Epistle to the Hebrews*, Hermeneia [Philadelphia: Fortress, 1989], 204).

believers (Heb. 8:7–13).[5] The author does not work out what the law written on the heart would mean in terms of giving specific prescriptions from the law. He clearly believes there is a place for commands and injunctions, as we learn from the parenesis in chapter 13. What he emphasizes, however, is that the cleansing of sins has been achieved once for all through the death of Christ.

The author of Hebrews writes mainly to forestall his readers from apostasy, and thus he does not concentrate on specific ethical issues. The readers are commended for showing compassion and solidarity with fellow believers in prison (10:34) and are exhorted to continue to show mercy to imprisoned believers (13:3). Hospitality to strangers is encouraged by appealing to the examples of Abraham and Lot, who provided lodging and food to angels without knowing that they were angels (13:2). A number of the exhortations indicate that the church is situated on the margin both socially and financially. This fits with chapter 11, where the heroes of faith were often discriminated against and even persecuted. Hence, believers must visit those who are in prison and provide hospitality to visiting believers. Similarly, they must not be captivated by the love of money but trust that God will provide for their needs (13:5–6). A community under social and financial pressure may crack and fall into disarray and division. Therefore, they are exhorted to live at peace with one another (12:14). They must not let bitterness flourish so that many are polluted (Heb. 12:15). Sexual sin also must be avoided, so that marriage is kept pure and undefiled (13:4). Sexual purity, hospitality, and caring for those who are in need all fit with Old Testament morality.

SUMMARY

Hebrews emphasizes that the new covenant has dawned in Jesus Christ. A new priesthood means that there is a new law, which fulfills what was promised in the old. Now that the new has arrived, believers should not return to the shadows of the old. They live in the age of the fulfillment of what God has promised and have received definitive forgiveness of sins. Going back to the old would be foolish and fatal. Still, believers are called upon to live in a way that pleases God, for God's law is now written on their hearts.

REFLECTION QUESTIONS

1. Does the author of Hebrews indict the law for being legalistic?

---

5. See Barry Joslin, *Hebrews, Christ, and the Law: the Theology of the Mosaic Law in Hebrews 7:1–10:18*, PBM (Carlisle, UK: Paternoster, 2008).

2. Why do Old Testament sacrifices fail to secure forgiveness?

3. Does the author of Hebrews argue only from a vertical perspective, or does he also make his case from salvation history?

4. Is the old covenant still in force according to Hebrews?

5. How should believers now live according to Hebrews?

PART 5

The Law and Contemporary Issues

Is the Sabbath Still Required for Christians?

Believers today continue to dispute whether the Sabbath is required. The Sabbath was given to Israel as a covenant sign, and Israel was commanded to rest on the seventh day. We see elsewhere in the Old Testament that covenants have signs, so that the sign of the Noahic covenant is the rainbow (Gen. 9:8–17) and the sign of the Abrahamic covenant is circumcision (Gen. 17). The paradigm for the Sabbath was God's rest on the seventh day of creation (Gen. 2:1–3). So, too, Israel was called upon to rest from work on the seventh day (Exod. 20:8–11; 31:12–17). What did it mean for Israel not to work on the Sabbath? Figure 5 lists the kinds of activities that were prohibited and permitted.

The Sabbath was certainly a day for social concern, for rest was mandated for all Israelites, including their children, slaves, and even animals (Deut. 5:14). It was also a day to honor and worship the Lord. Special burnt offerings were offered to the Lord on the Sabbath (Num. 28:9–10). Psalm 92 is a Sabbath song that voices praise to God for his steadfast love and faithfulness. Israel was called upon to observe the Sabbath in remembrance of the Lord's work in delivering them as slaves from Egyptian bondage (Deut. 5:15). Thus, the Sabbath is tied to Israel's covenant with the Lord, for it celebrates her liberation from slavery. The Sabbath, then, is the sign of the covenant between the Lord and Israel (Exod. 31:12–17; Ezek. 20:12–17). The Lord promised great blessing to those who observed the Sabbath (Isa. 56:2, 6; 58:13–14). Breaking the Sabbath command was no trivial matter, for the death penalty was inflicted upon those who intentionally violated it (Exod. 31:14–15; 35:2; Num. 15:32–36), though collecting manna on the Sabbath before the Mosaic law was codified did not warrant such a punishment (Exod. 16:22–30). Israel regularly violated the Sabbath—the sign of the covenant—and this is one of the reasons the people were sent into exile (Jer. 17:21–27; Ezek. 20:12–24).

FIGURE 5A: WORK PROHIBITED ON THE SABBATH	
Kindling a fire	Exod. 35:3
Gathering manna	Exod. 16:23–29
Selling goods	Neh. 10:31; 13:15–22
Bearing burdens	Jer. 17:19–27
FIGURE 5B: ACTIVITIES PERMITTED ON THE SABBATH	
Military campaigns	Josh. 6:15; 1 Kings 20:29; 2 Kings 3:9
Marriage feasts	Judg. 14:12–18
Dedication feasts	1 Kings 8:65; 2 Chron. 7:8–9
Visiting a man of God	2 Kings 4:23
Changing temple guards	2 Kings 11:5–9
Preparing showbread and putting it out	1 Chron. 9:32
Offering sacrifices	1 Chron. 23:31; Ezek. 46:4–5
Duties of priests and Levites	2 Kings 11:5–9; 2 Chron. 23:4, 8
Opening the east gate	Ezek. 46:1–3

During the Second Temple period, views of the Sabbath continued to develop. It is not my purpose here to conduct a complete study. Rather, a number of illustrations will be provided to illustrate how seriously Jews took the Sabbath. The Sabbath was a day of feasting and therefore a day when fasting was not appropriate (Jdt. 8:6; 1 Macc. 1:39, 45). Initially, the Hasmoneans refused to fight on the Sabbath, but after they were defeated in battle they changed their minds and began to fight on the Sabbath (1 Macc. 2:32–41; cf. Josephus, *Jewish Antiquities* 12.274, 276–277). The author of Jubilees propounds a rigorous view of the Sabbath (*Jubilees* 50:6–13). He emphasizes that no work should be done, specifying a number of tasks that are prohibited (50:12–13). Fasting is prohibited since the Sabbath is a day for feasting (50:10, 12). Sexual relations with one's wife also are prohibited (50:8), though offering the sacrifices ordained in the law are permitted (50:10). Those who violate the Sabbath prescriptions should die (50:7, 13). The Sabbath is eternal, and even the angels keep it (2:17–24). Indeed, the angels kept the Sabbath in heaven before it was established on earth (2:30). All Jewish authors concur that God commanded Israel to literally rest, though it is not surprising that Philo thinks of it as well in terms of resting in God (*Sobriety*, 1:174) and in terms of having thoughts of God that are fitting (*Special Laws*, 2:260). Philo also explains the number seven symbolically (*Moses*, 2:210).

The Qumran community was quite strict regarding Sabbath observance, maintaining that the right interpretation must be followed (CD 6:18; 10:14–23). Even if an animal falls into a pit it should not be helped on the Sabbath (CD 11:13–14), something Jesus assumes is permissible when talking to the Pharisees (Matt. 12:11). In the Mishnah thirty-nine different types of work are prohibited on the Sabbath (m. *Shabbat* 7:2).

I do not believe the Sabbath is required for believers now that the new covenant has arrived in the person of Jesus Christ. I should say, first of all, that it is not my purpose to reiterate what I wrote about the Sabbath in the Gospels since the Sabbath texts were investigated there. Here it is my purpose to pull the threads together in terms of the validity of the Sabbath for today. Strictly speaking, Jesus does not clearly abolish the Sabbath, nor does he violate its stipulations. Yet the focus on regulations that is evident in Jubilees, Qumran, and in the Mishnah is absent in Jesus' teaching. He reminded his hearers that "the Sabbath was made for man, not man for the Sabbath" (Mark 2:27). Some sectors of Judaism clearly had lost this perspective, so that the Sabbath had lost its humane dimension. They were so consumed with rules that they had forgotten mercy (Matt. 12:7). Jesus was grieved at the hardness of the Pharisees' hearts, for they lacked love for those suffering (Mark 3:5).

Jesus' observance of the Sabbath does not constitute strong evidence for its continuation in the new covenant. His observance of the Sabbath makes excellent sense, for he lived under the Old Testament law. He was "born under the law" as Paul says (Gal. 4:4). On the other hand, a careful reading of the Gospel accounts intimates that the Sabbath will not continue to play a significant role. Jesus proclaims as the Son of Man that he is the "lord even of the Sabbath" (Mark 2:28). The Sabbath does not rule over him, but he rules over the Sabbath. He is the new David, the Messiah, to whom the Sabbath and all the Old Testament Scriptures point (Matt. 12:3–4). Indeed, Jesus even claimed in John 5:17 that he, like his Father, works on the Sabbath. Working on the Sabbath, of course, is what the Old Testament prohibits, but Jesus claimed that he must work on the Sabbath since he is equal with God (John 5:18).

It is interesting to consider here the standpoint of the ruler of the synagogue in Luke 13:10–17. He argued that Jesus should heal on the other six days of the week and not on the Sabbath. On one level this advice seems quite reasonable, especially if the strict views of the Sabbath that were common in Judaism were correct. What is striking is that Jesus deliberately healed on the Sabbath. Healing is what he "ought" (*dei*) to do on the Sabbath day (Luke 13:16). It seems that he did so to demonstrate his superiority to the Sabbath and to hint that it is not in force forever. There may be a suggestion in Luke 4:16–21 that Jesus fulfills the Jubilee of the Old Testament (Lev. 25). The rest and joy anticipated in Jubilee is fulfilled in him, and hence the rest and feasting of the Sabbath find their climax in Jesus.

We would expect the Sabbath to no longer be in force since it was the covenant sign of the Mosaic covenant, and, as I have argued elsewhere in this book, it is clear that believers are no longer under the Sinai covenant. Therefore, they are no longer bound by the sign of the covenant either. The Sabbath, as a covenant sign, celebrated Israel's deliverance from Egypt, but the Exodus points forward, according to New Testament writers, to redemption in Christ. Believers in Christ were not freed from Egypt, and hence the covenant sign of Israel does not apply to them.

It is clear in Paul's letters that the Sabbath is not binding upon believers. In Colossians Paul identifies the Sabbath as a shadow along with requirements regarding foods, festivals, and the new moon (Col. 2:16–17). The Sabbath, in other words, points to Christ and is fulfilled in him. The word for "shadow" (*skia*) that Paul uses to describe the Sabbath is the same term the author of Hebrews used to describe Old Testament sacrifices. The law is only a "shadow (*skia*) of the good things to come instead of the true form of these realities" (Heb. 10:1). The argument is remarkably similar to what we see in Colossians: both contrast elements of the law as a shadow with the "substance" (*sōma*, Col. 2:17) or the "form" (*eikona*, Heb. 10:1) found in Christ. Paul does not denigrate the Sabbath. He salutes its place in salvation history, for, like the Old Testament sacrifices, though not in precisely the same way, it prepared the way for Christ. I know of no one who thinks Old Testament sacrifices should be instituted today; and when we compare what Paul says about the Sabbath with such sacrifices, it seems right to conclude that he thinks the Sabbath is no longer binding.

Some argue, however, that "Sabbath" in Colossians 2:16 does not refer to the weekly Sabbaths but only to sabbatical years. But this is a rather desperate expedient, for the most prominent day in the Jewish calendar was the weekly Sabbath. We know from secular sources that it was the observance of the weekly Sabbath that attracted the attention of Gentiles (Juvenal, *Satires* 14.96–106; Tacitus, *Histories* 5.4). Perhaps sabbatical years are included here, but the weekly Sabbath should not be excluded, for it would naturally come to the mind of both Jewish and Gentile readers. What Paul says here is remarkable, for he lumps the Sabbath together with food laws, festivals like Passover, and new moons. All of these constitute shadows that anticipate the coming of Christ. Very few Christians think we must observe food laws, Passover, and new moons. But if this is the case, then it is difficult to see why the Sabbath should be observed since it is placed together with these other matters.

Another crucial text on the Sabbath is Romans 14:5: "One person esteems one day as better than another, while another esteems all days alike. Each one should be fully convinced in his own mind." In Romans 14:1–15:6

Paul mainly discusses food that some—almost certainly those influenced by Old Testament food laws—think is defiled. Paul clearly teaches, in contrast to Leviticus 11:1–44 and Deuteronomy 14:3–21, that all foods are clean (Rom. 14:14, 20) since a new era of redemptive history has dawned. In other words, Paul sides theologically with the strong in the argument, believing that all foods are clean. He is concerned, however, that the strong avoid injuring and damaging the weak. The strong must respect the opinions of the weak (Rom. 14:1) and avoid arguments with them. Apparently the weak were not insisting that food laws and the observance of days were necessary for salvation, for if that were the case they would be proclaiming another gospel (cf. Gal. 1:8–9; 2:3–5; 4:10; 5:2–6), and Paul would not tolerate their viewpoint. Probably the weak believed that one would be a stronger Christian if one kept food laws and observed days. The danger for the weak was that they would judge the strong (Rom. 14:3–4), and the danger for the strong was that they would despise the weak (Rom. 14:3, 10). In any case, the strong seem to have had the upper hand in the Roman congregations, for Paul was particularly concerned that they not damage the weak.

Nevertheless, a crucial point must not be overlooked. Even though Paul watches out for the consciences of the weak, he holds the viewpoint of the strong on both food laws and days. John Barclay rightly argues that Paul subtly (or not so discreetly!) undermines the theological standpoint of the weak since he argues that what one eats and what days one observes are a matter of no concern.[1] The Old Testament, on the other hand, is clear on the matter. The foods one eats and the days one observes are ordained by God. He has given clear commands on both of these issues. Hence, Paul's argument is that such laws are no longer valid since believers are not under the Mosaic covenant. Indeed, the freedom to believe that all days are alike surely includes the Sabbath, for the Sabbath naturally would spring to the mind of Jewish readers since they kept the Sabbath weekly.

Paul has no quarrel with those who desire to set aside the Sabbath as a special day, as long as they do not require it for salvation or insist that other believers agree with them. Those who esteem the Sabbath as a special day are to be honored for their point of view and should not be despised or ridiculed. Others, however, consider every day to be the same. They do not think that any day is more special than another. Those who think this way are not to be judged as unspiritual. Indeed, there is no doubt that Paul held this opinion, since he was strong in faith instead of being weak. It is crucial to notice what is being said here. If the notion that every day of the week is the same is acceptable, and if it is Paul's opinion as well, then it follows that Sabbath regulations are no longer binding. The strong must not impose their convictions on the

---

1. John M. G. Barclay, "'Do We Undermine the Law?' A Study of Romans 14.1–15.6," in *Paul and the Mosaic Law*, WUNT 89 (Tübingen: Mohr Siebeck, 1996), 287–308.

weak and should be charitable to those who hold a different opinion, but Paul clearly has undermined the authority of the Sabbath in principle, for he does not care whether someone observes one day as special. He leaves it entirely up to one's personal opinion. But if the Sabbath of the Old Testament were still in force, Paul could never say this, for the Old Testament makes incredibly strong statements about those who violate the Sabbath, and the death penalty is even required in some instances. Paul is living under a different dispensation, that is, a different covenant, for now he says it does not matter whether one observes one day out of seven as a Sabbath.

Some argue against what is defended here by appealing to the creation order. As noted above, the Sabbath for Israel is patterned after God's creation of the world in seven days. What is instructive, however, is that the New Testament never appeals to Creation to defend the Sabbath. Jesus appealed to the creation order to support his view that marriage is between one man and one woman for life (Mark 10:2–12). Paul grounded his opposition to women teaching or exercising authority over men in the creation order (1 Tim. 2:12–13), and homosexuality is prohibited because it is contrary to nature (Rom. 1:26–27), in essence, to God's intention when he created men and women. Similarly, those who ban believers from eating certain foods and from marriage are wrong because both food and marriage are rooted in God's good creation (1 Tim. 4:3–5). We see nothing similar with the Sabbath. Never does the New Testament ground it in the created order. Instead, we have very clear verses that say it is a "shadow" and that it does not matter whether believers observe it. So, how do we explain the appeal to creation with reference to the Sabbath? It is probably best to see creation as an *analogy* instead of as a ground. The Sabbath was the sign of the Mosaic covenant, and since the covenant has passed away, so has the covenant sign.

Now it does not follow from this that the Sabbath has no significance for believers. It is a shadow, as Paul said, of the substance that is now ours in Christ. The Sabbath's role as a shadow is best explicated by Hebrews, even if Hebrews does not use the word for "shadow" in terms of the Sabbath. The author of Hebrews sees the Sabbath as foreshadowing the eschatological rest of the people of God (Heb. 4:1–10). A "Sabbath rest" still awaits God's people (v. 9), and it will be fulfilled on the final day when believers rest from earthly labors. The Sabbath, then, points to the final rest of the people of God. But since there is an already-but-not-yet character to what Hebrews says about rest, should believers continue to practice the Sabbath as long as they are in the not-yet?[2] I would answer in the negative, for the evidence we have in the

---

2. So Richard B. Gaffin, Jr., "A Sabbath Rest Still Awaits the People of God," in *Pressing Toward the Mark: Essays Commemorating Fifty Years of the Orthodox Presbyterian Church*, ed. Charles G. Dennison and Richard C. Gamble (Philadelphia: The Committee for the Historian of the Orthodox Presbyterian Church, 1986), 33–51. Gaffin argues that the rest

New Testament points in the contrary direction. We remember that the Sabbath is placed together with food laws and new moons and Passover in Colossians 2:16, but there is no reason to think that we should observe food laws, Passover, and new moons before the consummation. Paul's argument is that believers now belong to the age to come and the requirements of the old covenant are no longer binding.

Does the Lord's Day, that is, Christians worshiping on the first day of the week, constitute a fulfillment of the Sabbath? The references to the Lord's Day in the New Testament are sparse. In Troas believers gathered "on the first day of the week . . . to break bread" and they heard a long message from Paul (Acts 20:7). Paul commands the Corinthians to set aside money for the poor "on the first day of every week" (1 Cor. 16:2). John heard a loud voice speaking to him "on the Lord's day" (Rev. 1:10). These scattered hints suggest that the early Christians at some point began to worship on the first day of the week. The practice probably has its roots in the resurrection of Jesus, for he appeared to his disciples "the first day of the week" (John 20:19). All the Synoptics emphasize that Jesus rose on the first day of the week, i.e., Sunday: "very early on the first day of the week" (Mark 16:2; cf. Matt. 28:1; Luke 24:1). The fact that each of the Gospels stresses that Jesus was raised on the first day of the week is striking. But we have no indication that the Lord's Day functions as a fulfillment of the Sabbath. It is likely that gathering together on the Lord's Day stems from the earliest church, for we see no debate on the issue in church history, which is quite unlikely if the practice originated in Gentile churches outside Israel. By way of contrast, we think of the intense debate in the first few centuries on the date of Easter. No such debate exists regarding the Lord's Day.

The early roots of the Lord's Day are verified by the universal practice of the Lord's Day in Gentile churches in the second century.[3] It is not surprising that many Jewish Christians continued to observe the Sabbath as well. One segment of the Ebionites practiced the Lord's Day and the Sabbath. Their observance of both is instructive, for it shows that the Lord's Day was not viewed as the fulfillment of the Sabbath but as a separate day.

Most of the early church fathers did not practice or defend literal Sabbath observance (cf. *Diognetus* 4:1) but interpreted the Sabbath eschatologically and spiritually. They did not see the Lord's Day as a replacement of the

is only eschatological. I support Andrew Lincoln's view that it is of an already-but-not-yet character (Andrew T. Lincoln, "Sabbath, Rest, and Eschatology in the New Testament," in *From Sabbath to Lord's Day: A Biblical, Historical, and Theological Investigation*, ed. D. A. Carson [Grand Rapids: Zondervan, 1982], 197–220).

3. For a detailed discussion of some of the issues raised here, see R. J. Bauckham, "The Lord's Day," in *From Sabbath to Lord's Day: A Biblical, Historical, and Theological Investigation*, ed. D. A. Carson (Grand Rapids: Zondervan, 1982), 221–50; idem, "Sabbath and Sunday in the Post-Apostolic Church," in *From Sabbath to Lord's Day*, 257–69.

Sabbath but as a unique day. For instance, in the Epistle of Barnabas, the Sab-baths of Israel are contrasted with "the eighth day" (15:8), and the latter is described as "a beginning of another world." Barnabas says that "we keep the eighth day" (which is Sunday), for it is "the day also on which Jesus rose again from the dead" (15:9). The Lord's Day was not viewed as a day in which be-lievers abstained from work, as was the case with the Sabbath. Instead, it was a day in which most believers were required to work, but they took time in the day to meet together in order to worship the Lord.[4] The contrast between the Sabbath and the Lord's Day is clear in Ignatius, when he says, "If, therefore, those who were brought up in the ancient order of things have come to the possession of a new hope, no longer observing the Sabbath, but living in the observance of the Lord's Day, on which also our life has sprung up again by Him and by His death" (*To the Magnesians* 9:1). Ignatius, writing about A.D. 110, specifically contrasts the Sabbath with the Lord's Day, showing that he did not believe the latter replaced the former.[5] Bauckham argues that the idea that the Lord's day replaced the Sabbath is post-Constantinian. Luther saw rest as necessary but did not tie it to Sunday.[6] A stricter interpretation of the Sabbath became more common with the Puritans, along with the Seventh-Day Baptists and later the Seventh-Day Adventists.[7]

SUMMARY

Believers are not obligated to observe the Sabbath. The Sabbath was the sign of the Mosaic covenant. The Mosaic covenant and the Sabbath as the covenant sign are no longer applicable now that the new covenant of Jesus Christ has come. Believers are called upon to honor and respect those who think the Sabbath is still mandatory for believers. But if one argues that the Sabbath is required for salvation, such a teaching is contrary to the gospel and should be resisted forcefully. In any case, Paul makes it clear in both Romans 14:5 and Colossians 2:16–17 that the Sabbath has passed away now that Christ has come. It is wise naturally for believers to rest, and hence one principle that could be derived from the Sabbath is that believers should regularly rest. But the New Testament does not specify when that rest should take place,

---

4. So Bauckham, "Sabbath and Sunday in the Post-Apostolic Church," 274.
5. Cf. the concluding comments of Bauckham, "The Lord's Day," 240.
6. Martin Luther, "How Christians Should Regard Moses," in *Luther's Works*, vol. 35, *Word and Sacrament*, ed. Helmut T. Lehmann (general editor) and E. Theodore Bachman (Phil-adelphia: Muhlenberg Press, 1960), 165.
7. Bauckham's survey of history is immensely valuable. See Bauckham, "Sabbath and Sunday in the Post-Apostolic Church," 251–98; idem, "Sabbath and Sunday in the Medieval Church in the West," in *From Sabbath to Lord's Day*, 299–309; idem, "Sabbath and Sunday in the Protestant Tradition," in *From Sabbath to Lord's Day*, 311–41.

nor does it set forth a period of time when that rest should occur. We must remember that the early Christians were required to work on Sundays. They worshiped the Lord on the Lord's Day, the day of Jesus' resurrection, but the early Christians did not believe the Lord's Day fulfilled or replaced the Sabbath. The Sabbath pointed toward eschatological rest in Christ, which believers enjoy in part now and will enjoy fully on the Last Day.

REFLECTION QUESTIONS

1. What is the strongest argument for continued observance of the Sabbath?

2. What evidence in Paul suggests that the Sabbath is no longer required?

3. How does Hebrews contribute to our theology of the Sabbath?

4. What is the relationship between the Sabbath and the Lord's Day?

5. What is your view on observing the Sabbath today?

Should Christians Tithe?

When thinking about how the Old Testament law applies today, many Christians ask whether tithing is required for believers. In Genesis, before the period of the law, Abraham gave a tenth of the spoils of war to Melchizedek (Gen. 14:20). Hebrews cites this incident to support the superiority of Melchizedek's priesthood to the priesthood of Levi (Heb. 7:4–10). When the Lord affirmed his covenant to Jacob and promised to bless him, Jacob pledged to give God a tenth of all that God granted to him (Gen. 28:22). A tithe meant that a tenth was given to the Lord. In Israel it was required that a tenth of one's seed, or fruit, or flocks be given to the Lord (Lev. 27:30–32; Deut. 14:22–24; cf. 2 Chron. 31:5–6; Neh. 13:5, 12). What Israel tithed was to be given to the Levites to sustain them (Num. 18:21–24; cf. Neh. 10:38; 12:44), and the Levites in turn were to give a tithe of what was tithed to them in order to support the chief priest (Num. 18:25–28). The Lord threatened with a curse those who did not give a full tithe but promised to bless those who fulfilled their obligation to tithe (Mal. 3:8–10).

It is difficult to work out the amount that was actually tithed. Sanders describes two different ways of explaining the Old Testament texts on tithing.[1] According to one view, fourteen tithes were to be given over seven years, while another interpretation sees twelve tithes given over seven years. It is also difficult to know the exact amount that was tithed. In any case, the amount totaled more than ten percent.[2]

There are decisive reasons for concluding that Christians are not obligated to tithe today. Naturally believers are to give generously and sacrificially (2 Cor. 8–9), and for most believers in the Western world such generosity

---

1. E. P. Sanders, *Judaism: Practice and Belief, 63 BCE–66CE* (Philadelphia: Trinity Press International, 1992), 147–49.
2. Ibid., 157–69.

means that they should give more than ten percent. Still, tithing itself is not mandated for the following reasons.

In the Old Testament one of the regular tithes was given to the Levites and to the priests, but the sacrificial system of the Old Testament and the priests and Levites of the old covenant have passed away. All believers are priests (1 Peter 2:9; Rev. 1:6; 5:10; 20:6), and Jesus is the Great High Priest according to Hebrews. The tithe is irretrievably tied to the old covenant, which is no longer in force.

The Old Testament teaches that God's people were to celebrate a tithe every three years in Jerusalem. Such a practice can hardly be normative for the church of Jesus Christ today. It relates to the Jews as a nation, but the Jewish nation is no longer the locus of God's people, although individual Jews are part of the church through faith in Jesus Christ. Furthermore, the earthly Jerusalem is no longer central in God's purposes (Gal. 4:25). Believers are part of the heavenly Jerusalem (Gal. 4:26) and look forward to the city to come (Heb. 11:10)—the new heavens and new earth (Rev. 21:1–22:5).

If tithing were normative today, it is difficult to know what God would require. I have noted above that the amount was not ten percent. Indeed, it is difficult to know what the precise amount was. Most of those who support tithing assume that the amount was ten percent, but Israel clearly paid more than this.

Some support tithing by observing that Jesus commended tithing, even if he placed it in a subordinate position (Matt. 23:23; Luke 11:42). Jesus himself specifically said that tithing should not be neglected. On first glance this argument seems persuasive, but if we look more closely it is evident that this argument does not hold up. Jesus also commended offering sacrifices in the temple (Matt. 5:23–24), but no one today thinks such would be advisable if the temple were rebuilt. His positive words about tithing are explicable when we consider that Jesus ministered before the Cross and Resurrection. Jesus himself obeyed the law, for he was "born under the law" (Gal. 4:4). His positive words about tithing were directed to Pharisees who lived under the old covenant. But we can no more take his words as a commendation for tithing today than we can his words about offering sacrifices.

Others point to the example of Abraham paying a tithe to Melchizedek or Jacob giving God a tenth of all that he received. Such examples, however, hardly mandate tithing for today. Abraham's gift to Melchizedek was a one-time event. There is no evidence that Abraham regularly gave to the Lord a tenth of what he received. Jacob's giving of a tenth was a sign of his gratefulness to God for promising to be with him and to protect him. His gratefulness and generosity still speak to us today, but a historical description of what Jacob gave at one point in his life does not support the idea that all believers must give God a tenth of their income. Abraham was commanded by God to sacrifice Isaac, but we hardly derive from that fact that we should offer our own sons up as sacrifices.

What is remarkable is that nowhere in the rest of the New Testament is tithing ever mandated. Some of the principles with reference to tithing may apply to believers, but the practice itself is not required. For instance, when believers in the New Testament hear about the poor, they are not commanded to give "the poor tithe." Instead, they are exhorted to be exceedingly generous in helping those who are in need (Acts 2:43–47; 4:32–37; 11:27–30; Gal. 2:10; 1 Cor. 16:1–4; 2 Cor. 8:1–9:15).

SUMMARY

Even though tithing is not mandated, there is no call in the New Testament to hoard one's possessions or to live selfishly. Believers are commanded to support those who proclaim the gospel (Matt. 10:10; Luke 10:7; 1 Cor. 9:6–14; 1 Tim. 5:17–18). Those who are blessed with wealth are to enjoy the good things God has given them, but they are also to be generous to those in need (1 Tim. 6:17–19). The New Testament clearly teaches that wealth is dangerous because it can seduce us so that we stray from the Lord. God is to be our treasure, and hence believers are to give generously and freely. For most believers in the West, that means giving more than a tithe. Still, the tithe itself is not mandated by Scripture, and Scripture is our rule and authority rather than a tradition that requires believers to tithe.

REFLECTION QUESTIONS

1. Why would it be difficult to practice the Old Testament tithe even if we desired to do so?

2. Should we tithe since Jesus commended the practice?

3. What New Testament evidence suggests that tithing is not required for believers?

4. Should we tithe since Abraham and Jacob tithed?

5. If you are convinced that tithing is not required, then should we spend more money on ourselves?

What Is Theonomy, or Christian Reconstructionism, and How Should It Be Evaluated?

Let me say right up front that in a book of this nature I do not intend to describe or critique theonomy in any detail. Much has been written in defense and in criticism of the movement, and it would carry me far beyond the parameters of this book to handle these matters in detail.[1] Theonomy, or what is sometimes called Christian reconstructionism, is a movement that argues that nations or states should be ruled by the standards of Old Testament civil law. The name *theonomy* fits with such a viewpoint, for *theonomy* means "God's law." The theonomy movement was birthed in Presbyterian circles, though it is by no means limited to Presbyterians. Indeed, some charismatic churches have espoused theonomy as well. A number of scholars and authors have defended theonomy. Perhaps the most prominent is Rousas Rushdoony (1916–2001), who was the author of many books, including the massive *Institutes of Biblical Law*.[2] Probably the most scholarly defense of theonomy comes from Greg Bahnsen (1948–1995).[3]

Most Presbyterians have divided the law into three categories: moral, civil, and ceremonial, arguing that the civil and ceremonial law have passed away, while the moral law remains in force (for my analysis of this tripartite division, see question 14). Theonomists differ from this interpretation, for they argue that only the ceremonial law has passed away, whereas the civil and moral law

---

1. For a helpful critique, see William S. Barker and W. Robert Godfrey, *Theonomy: A Reformed Critique* (Grand Rapids: Zondervan, 1990).
2. Rousas John Rushdoony, *Institutes of Biblical Law* (Phillipsburg, NJ: Presbyterian & Reformed, 1980).
3. Greg L. Bahnsen, *Theonomy in Christian Ethics*, 3rd ed. (Nacogdoches, TX: Covenant Media Press, 2002).

are still binding. The theonomist argues that all of life belongs to God. There is no realm where he does not reign as Lord. Therefore, God's standards and norms should be authoritative for states and nations. They reject categorically the idea that human laws should function as the norm for nations and states, maintaining that there is no justification for the notion that secular states are independent of God's rules. They point to texts like Matthew 5:17–20, which teach that Jesus did not come to abolish the law but to fulfill it, and thus argue that even the tiniest part of the law continues to function as an authority.

The theonomist movement has appealed in particular to Christians in the United States, especially as the United States has become more secular and drifted further from biblical norms. The theonomy movement also solves the problem of what the norms should be for governments. If God's law does not function as the norm, then on what basis are laws established for nations? Are the laws of the state an arbitrary imposition of the will of human beings? Theonomists have clear and definite answers to such questions, pointing to God's law as the standard for nations.

The theonomist movement, if we may quote Luke, has caused no little controversy, especially in Presbyterian circles. Scholars have debated the meaning of the Westminster Confession, and whether the Westminster Standards support theonomy. Naturally, they have disagreed on the interpretation of biblical texts as well. It is not my purpose here to enter into a debate on the meaning of the Westminster Confession, though it seems to me that the anti-theonomy interpretation is more probable.[4]

What matters to me is what the Scriptures teach on the subject, and anyone who has read the rest of this book already knows how I estimate the theonomy movement. I would argue that it is clear from Romans 10:4, 2 Corinthians 3:4–18, Galatians 3:15–4:7, and other texts as well that believers are no longer under the Mosaic covenant and law. The entire law has ceased to be an authority for believers. Hence, the notion that the civil laws for Israel should continue to function as the rules for nation-states today represents a fundamental misreading of the Scriptures. Believers are no longer under the law, for the law was given to Israel, which functioned as both a political and an ecclesiastical community. No nation today occupies the place of Israel, for no nation can claim to be God's chosen nation. Sometimes believers (though not all theonomists) in the United States will identify their country as God's chosen nation, but such a statement is a theological misstep, for it appropriates to a modern nation-state what was true only of Israel. The people of God now hail from every tribe, tongue, people, and nation and cannot be restricted to or linked with any particular nation. Indeed, the New Testament gives no

---

4. For a critique of the theonomist reading of the Westminster confession, see Ligon Duncan, "*The Westminster Confession of Faith:* A Theonomic Document?" http://www.providencepca.com/essays/theonomy.html (accessed May 15, 2009).

indication that nations themselves would ever become Christian. There may be many individual Christians, or even a majority of Christians, in a nation, but nations themselves are not Christian.

All of this is not to say that the Old Testament law should be ignored in modern nation-states. The moral norms of the law—those laws that reflect the character of God—naturally play a role in determining the laws of a nation. The vital question here, however, is whether believers are under the Old Testament law. If they are, then adulterers and homosexuals (Lev. 20:10, 13), Sabbath breakers (Exod. 31:14; Num. 15:32–36), and rebellious children (Deut. 21:18–21) should be put to death by governing authorities, for that is what the Old Testament law commanded Israel to do. But if the Scriptures teach that the Mosaic covenant and Mosaic law have passed away and thus do not function as the standard of ethics for believers today, then there is no necessary mandate to follow the Old Testament when it teaches that adulterers and homosexuals should be put to death.

Indeed, we can probably discern the reason why such a penalty was inflicted in the Old Testament. Israel was to be a holy people to the Lord. Such blatant sins were not to characterize the people of God, who were specially consecrated to him and were to serve as a kingdom of priests in the world. But no nation today fills the role of Israel. No nation is specially holy to the Lord. Indeed, in most nations today the majority of the citizens are unbelievers, and so we are not astonished if blatant sins are committed in such countries. The modern state is not necessarily called upon to appropriate the penalties contained in the Old Testament law, for there is the recognition that the state is not holy to the Lord. The people of God, the church of Jesus Christ, is to be holy—not the nation-state. Now what I have written could be misunderstood. I am not suggesting that it is God's preceptive will that nations do evil! I am saying only that there is no indication that nation-states today are to pattern themselves after Israel. Such a move is to turn the clock back regarding salvation-history and to live in the old covenant era.

If dispensationalists tend to read the new covenant in light of the old when it comes to eschatology, some Presbyterians are prone to reading the new covenant in light of the old in terms of ecclesiology and on the question of the law. Again, this is not to say that the Old Testament law teaches us nothing about what laws and penalties should apply today. For instance, I think there are solid grounds for saying that premeditated murder deserves the death penalty (cf. Gen. 9:6; Rom. 13:4).[5] However, what sins deserve criminal status is a difficult question that cannot be answered simply by appealing to the law for Old Testament Israel. The standards required for believers should not necessarily be imposed on citizens in nation-states. It is instructive, as noted earlier, that in one case Paul replaced the death penalty of the Old Testament

---

5.   It should be noted that Genesis 9:6 occurs before the inauguration of the Mosaic covenant.

with excommunication from the church (1 Cor. 5:13). There seems to be an implicit recognition here that the death penalty does not apply in the same way that it applied under the old covenant (e.g., to adulterers and those who committed same-sex acts).

Let me say again that this does not mean that the Old Testament law is excluded from the process when a nation passes laws and enacts penalties. Of course, many nations are almost completely non-Christian and will not pay any heed to the Old Testament at all. But if a nation has a number of influential believers involved in the political process, the norms of Scripture will naturally play an important role in determining laws and penalties for breaking such laws. In many instances the laws given to Israel are illustrative of justice and function as a pattern for nations today. As I argued earlier in question 28, the Old Testament mandate that the punishment should fit the crime is the principle of all justice. Indeed, the notion that some crimes deserve physical punishment whereas others demand financial compensation, which we find in the Old Testament, is still reflected in our justice system today. Nevertheless, the laws and penalties of an ancient agricultural society, where the church and state were one, should not necessarily be ours today. How we apply the moral norms of Scripture to political life is a matter of wisdom and prudence and cannot be resolved simply by pointing to Old Testament Israel.

SUMMARY

The theonomist movement, though its motivations are laudable and its devotion to the Old Testament law praiseworthy, is fundamentally off the mark. It fails to see that the Mosaic covenant and law have passed away. Furthermore, it does not perceive the differences between Israel and the church and thus tries to make modern nation-states into theocratic entities.

REFLECTION QUESTIONS

1. How would you define *theonomy*?

2. What, exegetically, is the fundamental problem with theonomy?

3. If theonomy is rejected, should believers even consider the Old Testament law when formulating laws for a nation?

4. Is the United States a Christian nation?

5. What is your own view of the theonomist movement?

What Role Does the Law Have in Preaching?

This is a fitting question for the conclusion of this book, and it should be evident by now that we must answer this question at several different levels. First, we must always preach in light of the story line of the entire Bible. One of the crucial questions we always must ask in investigating any text is where the text lands in terms of the whole flow of redemptive history. The laws of the Mosaic covenant represent a period of time and a covenant that is no longer in force. Therefore, we cannot simply find some law from Exodus or Leviticus and preach it as binding on Christians today, unless we justify such a claim from the whole canon of Scripture. I have argued in this book that some of the laws in the Old Testament are part of the law of Christ and hence are still authoritative commands for believers today. The New Testament reaffirms, for instance, that the prohibitions against idolatry, adultery, murder, and stealing are God's permanent will for his people. We discern this from reading the whole counsel of God, by relating the old covenant to the new, and by seeing how the New Testament applies God's law to the lives of those redeemed by Christ. The law of Christ, then, functions as God's standard for his people today. In other words, we can determine which moral norms to preach as applicable today only when we read the Old Testament from the standpoint of the New Testament. We understand the whole story of Scripture truly when we see it in light of the fulfillment Christ brings.

Second, there is always the danger that a focus on moral norms will crowd out the gospel. The gospel can easily be turned into a self-help program so that radical forgiveness of sins is replaced by ethics, as if our goodness qualifies us to obtain eternal life. The moral norms required for the people of God are a result of the grace of God that has saved us in Jesus Christ. They are the fruit of new life in Christ, not the basis of our new life in Christ. They reflect whether we belong to the people of God; they are not the means by which we become part of the people of God. Biblical preaching emphasizes the importance of good works and godly living, but it always puts the accent on the good news of justification, so that our good works are viewed as a response to the grace of God. Good works are necessary to receive an eternal reward, but faithful preaching is careful to point out that such works are never the basis of our relationship with God. We are called to a godly life of virtue, but virtue must be explicated in light of the gospel, or the call to live in a new way actually may undermine the gospel we proclaim. Any obedience that is ours is a result of the Spirit's work in our lives (Rom. 8:4). It is as we walk in the Spirit (Gal. 5:16) and yield to the Spirit (Gal. 5:18) that the "fruit of the Spirit" (Gal. 5:22–23) becomes ours. Hence, our new life is not autonomous. It is not the product of our own strength or moral willpower. We do not become changed people because we are working hard on being gentle, kind, or loving. The new life is supernatural. It is the consequence of being crucified with Christ (Gal. 2:20) and experiencing his powerful love for us.

Third, the moral norms of the law have a convicting function. They remind us that we are all sinners (Rom. 1:18–3:20) and that we fall short of God's glory (Rom. 3:23). Some are deeply conscious of their sins, so the message that God loves them and desires them to be saved (1 Tim. 2:4) is liberating. None of us, however, fully grasps the extent of our sinfulness in this life. God uses the moral norms of the law to remind us what it means to love him and to love others. The law of Christ calls upon us to be perfect (Matt. 5:48), but we all fall short of perfection. The law convicts us of our sins and drives us to Christ (Gal. 3:21–25). God intended that the law would enclose all things under sin, so that human beings would understand through the law that they are slaves of sin. The law, then, puts us to death so that we find life in Christ. Faithful preaching reminds us of what is required of us, and the law functions as a hammer (as Luther taught) that breaks us to pieces so that we seek solace and salvation in Christ alone. When it is rightly preached and rightly understood, the law removes the illusion that we can be right with God through our works. It exposes the wickedness of our hearts so that we put our trust in Christ alone for salvation. As a result, we magnify God in Christ for what he has done to save us. We don't just *say* that we trust in Christ for salvation. We *feel* a sense of our utter lostness apart from Christ. We rejoice that Christ has saved us from our own perversity and wickedness. Evil is no longer merely used to describe others, such as Osama bin Laden. We confess and acknowledge our own sin. Such an acknowledgment does not leave us in misery, for we rejoice in the love of God in Jesus Christ that has rescued us as sinners. We do not need to hide our sins from God or anyone else, for we know what it is to be a forgiven sinner. True preaching brings gravity over our sin and gladness over our great salvation.

Finally, we are reminded by Psalms 19 and 119 and the law of Christ that the Lord uses moral norms in our lives as Christians. Those who are filled with the Spirit (Eph. 5:18) also are filled with the word (Col. 3:16). It is clear from the New Testament epistles that the instruction given to the churches also included moral exhortation. It is evident that the New Testament letters are filled with what is technically called parenesis (exhortations), which trace out what it means to be followers of Christ (cf. Rom. 12:9–21; Eph. 4:17–6:9; Col. 2:20–4:1; etc.). Apparently, biblical writers did not believe that moral norms necessarily quenched life in the Spirit. They were convinced that moral exhortations could be used by the Spirit to inspire believers to trust in God and to live lives that are pleasing to him. Moral exhortations do not necessarily lead to legalism or works-righteousness, even if there is a danger that they can lead in such a direction. Certainly the apostle Paul, whose letters are filled with moral exhortations, believed that such exhortations are helpful in one's spiritual life and can drive believers to trust in the power of the Spirit and to live in a way that is pleasing to God. Some who understand grace overreact and rule out the "shoulds" and the "oughts" of the New Testament. They become more "biblical" than the Bible! But grace and demand are not necessarily opposed to one another. God's grace also gives us the ability to live in a way that pleases God, even if we never reach perfection. Paul thought it was helpful to Christians to say that divorce is wrong (1 Cor. 7:10–11), that Christians should marry only fellow believers (1 Cor. 7:39), and that sexual immorality should be forsaken (1 Cor. 6:12–20; 1 Thess. 4:3–8). He did not believe that such commands would lead Christians to become legalists; otherwise, he would not have included these commands.

It is important in preaching, then, to follow the lead of the New Testament. The exhortations in the New Testament must be proclaimed in light of God's saving work in Christ; but God uses such exhortations to conform us to Christ, and hence we should follow the pattern of New Testament writings in admonishing believers to live in a way that pleases the Lord.

SUMMARY

What role does the law have in preaching? We must consider where a command is in the story line of the Bible and in terms of the redemptive-historical scheme we see in Scripture. The moral norms of the Bible cannot be preached apart from the canonical context and apart from the whole counsel of God. In addition, when we preach God's commands, we must always preach them in light of the gospel of Jesus Christ. God saves us by his mercy, and then he gives us commands by which we respond to his grace. It is incredibly easy to turn things around so that law precedes grace, and thereby the moral norms of the law become for us a ladder by which we try to be right with God or to impress him with our works. Obeying God is always a response to his grace; it is never a means by which we become right with God.

We also should preach the law to drive people to Christ. The law exposes our sin and puts us to death, so that we realize that salvation can never be found in ourselves but gained only through the atoning sacrifice of Jesus Christ.

Finally, good preaching includes moral exhortation. Such exhortations are part of what the Holy Spirit uses to help us trust in Christ so that we are conformed more and more to his likeness. The "should's" and "ought's" of the Bible can be used legalistically, but we must beware of becoming unbalanced. When we preach, we need to proclaim God's great act of salvation (Eph. 1–3), and our response to his grace (Eph. 4–6).

REFLECTION QUESTIONS

1. How do we know if a command from the Bible is still for today?

2. How can we preach in such a way that we do not produce legalists in our churches?

3. Do you think we should preach the law in order to bring people to conviction of sin?

4. What is the role of moral exhortation in our preaching?

5. How, practically, can we fulfill our responsibility to preach the whole counsel of God?

Annotated Bibliography

Avemarie, Friedrich. *Tora und Leben: Untersuchungen zur Heilsbedeutung der Tora in der frühen rabbinischen Literatur.* TSAJ 56. Tübingen: Mohr Siebeck, 1996. This book is obviously for experts and requires knowledge of German. Avemarie argues that we find a tension in rabbinic literature between God's electing grace and the need to do good works. Therefore, one cannot say that works are always subordinated to election. Hence, we have evidence in some sayings of a legalistic orientation.

_____. "Erwählung und Vergeltung: Zur optionalen Struktur rabbinischer Soteriologie." *NTS* 45 (1999): 108–26. Here the thesis of the book just described above is summarized in a journal article.

Bahnsen, Greg L. *Theonomy in Christian Ethics.* 3rd ed. Nacogdoches, TX: Covenant Media Press, 2002. Bahnsen's work is the most sophisticated and articulate defense of theonomy, or what is sometimes called Christian reconstructionism.

Barker, William S., and W. Robert Godfrey. *Theonomy: A Reformed Critique.* Grand Rapids: Zondervan, 1990. A useful critique of the theonomy movement.

Carson, D. A., ed. *From Sabbath to Lord's Day: A Biblical, Historical, and Theological Investigation.* Grand Rapids: Zondervan, 1982. An insightful study of the Sabbath exegetically, theologically, and historically.

Carson, D. A., Peter T. O'Brien, and Mark A. Seifrid, eds. *Justification and Variegated Nomism.* 2 vols. Grand Rapids: Baker, 2001, 2004. The first volume contains a collection of essays that examine Jewish literature that is roughly contemporaneous with the New Testament. The essays show that Sanders's view that the Judaism of the Second Temple period was characterized by covenantal nomism is overly simplistic. The second volume examines the New Testament and offers a rigorous critique of the New Perspective from an exegetical standpoint. Almost all of the essays deserve a careful reading.

Das, A. Andrew. *Paul, the Law, and the Covenant.* Peabody, MA: Hendrickson, 2001. In this important book, Das demonstrates that the demand for perfect obedience (contrary to the New Perspective) was actually quite prominent in Second Temple Judaism, and in some streams of Jewish literature there is a final vindication according to works. The book also contains fresh and penetrating exegesis of Paul relative to the law.

Deidun, Thomas J. *New Covenant Morality in Paul.* Rome: Biblical Institute Press, 1981. Deidun considers Paul's ethics in light of the new covenant in this careful study.

Dunn, James D. G. *The New Perspective on Paul.* Grand Rapids: Eerdmans, 2008. This volume contains the substance of Dunn's defense of the New Perspective on Paul. It is must reading for those who desire to understand the New Perspective.

Elliott, Mark A. *The Survivors of Israel: A Reconsideration of the Theology of Pre-Christian Judaism.* Grand Rapids: Eerdmans, 2000. Elliott emphasizes that only a remnant who obeyed God's law would receive God's salvation. Hence, he calls into question Sanders's view that most Jews would enjoy eschatological blessing. Instead, such blessing was contingent upon obedience.

Fuller, Daniel P. *Gospel and Law: Contrast or Continuum?* Grand Rapids: Eerdmans, 1980. Fuller argues that scholars have wrongly emphasized a contrast between the old covenant and the new. He sees instead a continuum. In my judgment Fuller fails to see the newness of what has been introduced by Christ.

Gathercole, Simon J. *Where Is Boasting? Early Jewish Soteriology and Paul's Response in Romans 1–5.* Grand Rapids: Eerdmans, 2003. Gathercole criticizes the New Perspective, maintaining that a final vindication according to works is present in Second Temple Jewish literature. His exegesis of key Pauline texts also calls into question views defended by the New Perspective.

Gundry, Stanley N., ed. *Five Views on Law and Gospel.* Grand Rapids: Zondervan, 1993. This volume is a helpful resource for those who want a map of some of the positions in evangelicalism on the role of the law in the Christian life. Greg Bahnsen defends theonomy, Walter Kaiser the continued normativity of the Old Testament law, Douglas Moo what is often called the new covenant view, Wayne Strickland the dispensational view, and Willem VanGemeren a typical Reformed view. One of the helpful features of the book is the evaluation of each position by the other four contributors.

Horton, Michael. *God of Promise: Introducing Covenant Theology.* Grand Rapids: Baker, 2006. A helpful introduction to covenant theology.

Hübner, Hans. *Law in Paul's Thought.* Edinburgh: T & T Clark, 1984. Hübner argues that Paul's thought developed from Galatians to Romans so that in Romans he qualifies and revises some of what he said in Galatians. I explain in my book on Paul's theology of the law why this thesis is unpersuasive.

Kim, Seyoon. *Paul and the New Perspective: Second Thoughts on the Origin of Paul's Gospel.* Grand Rapids: Eerdmans, 2002. An exegetically vigorous and convincing critique of the New Perspective.

Moo, Douglas J. "'Law,' 'Works of the Law,' and Legalism in Paul." *WTJ* 45 (1983): 73–100; "Jesus and the Authority of the Mosaic Law." *JSNT* 20 (1984): 3–49; *Romans.* NICNT. Grand Rapids: Eerdmans, 1996. Doug Moo's writings on the law are among the most helpful. His 1983 article on the law is helpful in sorting out definitions and other key issues. The 1984 article on Jesus' view of the law is technical but deserves careful reading. He works out his view on the law in his careful exposition of Romans. For a summary of Moo's perspective, see his chapter in the book titled *Five Views on Law and Gospel* above.

Piper, John. *Counted Righteous in Christ: Should We Abandon the Imputation of Christ's Righteousness?* Wheaton, IL: Crossway. 2002. An exegetically careful defense of the imputation of Christ's righteousness.

_____. *The Future of Justification: A Response to N. T. Wright.* Wheaton, IL: Crossway, 2007. Piper subjects Wright's understanding of justification to analysis and finds it to be wanting.

Poythress, Vern S. *The Shadow of Christ in the Law of Moses.* Phillipsburg, NJ: Presbyterian & Reformed, 1995. An exposition that focuses on the fulfillment of the Old Testament law in Christ.

Rainbow, Paul A. *The Way of Salvation: The Role of Christian Obedience in Justification.* Waynesboro, GA: Paternoster, 2005. Rainbow rightly emphasizes the importance of obedience for final salvation, but he does not always integrate his view well with the biblical view of justification.

Räisänen, Heikki. *Paul and the Law.* Philadelphia: Fortress, 1983. Räisänen argues that Paul's view of the law is contradictory. I point out the weaknesses of this view in my book on Paul's theology of the law.

Sanders, E. P. *Paul and Palestinian Judaism: A Comparison of Patterns of Religion.* Philadelphia: Fortress, 1977. This volume represents Sanders's groundbreaking and massive work in which he challenges the idea that the Judaism of Paul's day was legalistic. Sanders argues that it was characterized by covenantal nomism.

_____. *Paul, the Law, and the Jewish People.* Philadelphia: Fortress, 1983. Sanders here develops his view of the law and applies it to the Pauline literature. Unfortunately, he maintains that Paul's view of the law is incoherent.

_____. *Jesus and Judaism.* Philadelphia: Fortress, 1985. Sanders's project continues with his exposition of Jesus' relationship to Judaism. He continues to argue that the Judaism of Jesus' day was not legalistic.

Saucy, Robert L. *The Case for Progressive Dispensationalism: The Interface Between Dispensational and Non-Dispensational Theology.* Grand Rapids: Zondervan, 1993. Dispensationalism is changing today. Here we find a helpful defense of what is called progressive dispensationalism.

Schreiner, Thomas R. *The Law and Its Fulfillment: A Pauline Theology of Law.* Grand Rapids: Baker, 1993. The book especially focuses on the Pauline view of the law and critiques the New Perspective. The contribution of other New Testament authors relative to the law is also discussed.

Seifrid, Mark A. *Christ, Our Righteousness: Paul's Theology of Justification.* Downers Grove, IL: InterVarsity, 2000. A helpful contribution on Paul's view of justification that includes a critique of the New Perspective.

Stendahl, Krister. *Paul Among Jews and Gentiles and Other Essays.* Philadelphia: Fortress, 1976. Stendahl's work often is considered to be the starting point for the New Perspective.

Stuhlmacher, Peter. *Reconciliation, Law, and Righteousness: Essays in Biblical Theology.* Philadelphia: Fortress, 1986. Stuhlmacher's work in biblical theology is well known, and here we find a number of helpful essays on the law.

_____ and Hagner, Donald A. *Revisiting Paul's Doctrine of Justification: A Challenge to the New Perspective.* Downers Grove, IL: InterVarsity, 2001. A compact and helpful critique of the New Perspective by two well-known New Testament scholars.

Thielman, Frank. *Paul and the Law: A Contextual Approach.* Downers Grove, IL: InterVarsity, 1994. Thielman investigates Paul's theology of the law in all of his letters and provides a helpful critique of the New Perspective.

_____. *The Law and the New Testament: The Question of Continuity.* New York: Crossroad, 1999. This relatively brief work provides a very helpful exposition of the law in New Testament writings.

Westerholm, Stephen. *Israel's Law and the Church's Faith: Paul and His Recent Interpreters.* Grand Rapids: Eerdmans, 1988. Westerholm elegantly defends the Reformers' reading of the law in this important work.

_____. *Perspectives Old and New on Paul: The "Lutheran" Paul and His Critics.* Grand Rapids: Eerdmans, 2004. Westerholm updates his view in this volume, which is clearly the best single work on the New Perspective. Westerholm provides a history of scholarship, including all the key contributors. He also defends exegetically the view that the Reformation reading of Paul was substantially correct.

Wright, N. T. *The Climax of the Covenant: Christ and the Law in Pauline Theology.* Minneapolis: Fortress, 1992. Wright is one of the most prominent proponents of the New Perspective. Here we find some more technical essays on Pauline theology.

_____. *What Saint Paul Really Said: Was Paul of Tarsus the Real Founder of Christianity?* Grand Rapids: Eerdmans, 1997. This is a popular exposition of Wright's reading of Paul, which will be worked out in his major work on Paul that is due out in the future.

_____. *Justification: God's Plan and Paul's Vision.* Downers Grove, IL: InterVarsity, 2009. Wright defends his view of justification in response to Piper's critique.

Yinger, Kent L. *Paul, Judaism, and Judgment According to Deeds.* SNTSMS 105. Cambridge: Cambridge University Press, 1999. Yinger surveys well the theme of judgment according to works in Judaism and Paul, though his own resolution of the issue is unsatisfying.

List of Figures

Scripture Index

Ancient Sources Index